Information Security Management Metrics

A Definitive Guide to Effective
Security Monitoring and Measurement

Information
Security
Management
Metrics

A Definitive Guide to Effective
Security Monitoring and Measurement

W. Krag Brotby, CISM

CRC Press
Taylor & Francis Group
Boca Raton   London   New York

CRC Press is an imprint of the
Taylor & Francis Group, an **Informa** business

Auerbach Publications
Taylor & Francis Group
6000 Broken Sound Parkway NW, Suite 300
Boca Raton, FL 33487-2742

© 2009 by Taylor & Francis Group, LLC
Auerbach is an imprint of Taylor & Francis Group, an Informa business

No claim to original U.S. Government works
Printed in the United States of America on acid-free paper
10 9 8 7 6 5 4 3 2 1

International Standard Book Number-13: 978-1-4200-5285-5 (Hardcover)

Library of Congress Cataloging-in-Publication Data

Brotby, W. Krag.
    Information security management metrics : a definitive guide to effective security monitoring and measurement / W. Krag Brotby.
        p. cm.
    Includes bibliographical references and index.
    ISBN 978-1-4200-5285-5 (hardcover : alk. paper)
    1. Information technology--Security measures. 2. Computer security.
3. Business enterprises--Computer networks--Security measures. 4. Data protection. I. Title.

    HD30.2.B78 2009
    658.4'78--dc22
                                                                    2009000669

Visit the Taylor & Francis Web site at
http://www.taylorandfrancis.com

and the Auerbach Web site at
http://www.auerbach-publications.com

Contents

Acknowledgments xi
Introduction xiii

Chapter 1
Security Metrics Overview 1
    1.1   Metrics and Objectives 4
    1.2   Information Security 7
    1.3   IT Security 8
          1.3.1   Why the IT Metric Focus 8
    1.4   Other Assurance Functions 8
    1.5   Stakeholders 10
    Endnotes 10

Chapter 2
Security Metrics 13
    2.1   Security Program Effectiveness 14
    2.2   Types of Metrics 15
    2.3   Information Assurance / Security Metrics Classification 17
    2.4   Monitoring vs. Metrics 18
    Endnotes 18

Chapter 3
Current State of Security Metrics 21
    3.1   Quantitative Measures and Metrics 21
          3.1.1   Performance Metrics 22
          3.1.2   Discussion 25
    3.2   Financial Metrics 25
          3.2.1   Return on Investment (ROI) 26
                  3.2.1.1   Payback Method 26
                  3.2.1.2   ROI Calculation 27

3.2.1.3 NPV 29
3.2.1.4 IRR 29
3.2.2 Return on Security Investment (ROSI) 30
3.2.2.1 SLE and ALE 30
3.2.2.2 ROSI 31
3.2.2.3 A New ROSI Model 31
3.2.2.4 A More Complex Security ROI 32
3.2.3 Security Attribute Evaluation Method
(SAEM)...35
3.2.4 Cost-Effectiveness Analysis...35
3.2.4.1 Cost-Benefit Analysis...36
3.2.5 Fault Tree Analysis 36
3.2.6 Value at Risk (VAR) 37
3.2.7 ALE/SLE 37
3.3 Qualitative Security Metrics...38
3.3.1 Cultural Metrics...39
3.3.2 Risk Management through Cultural
Theory 39
3.3.3 The Competing Values Framework..................................... 40
3.3.4 Organizational Structure... 42
3.4 Hybrid Approaches..43
3.4.1 Systemic Security Management 43
3.4.2 Balanced Scorecard.. 44
3.4.3 The SABSA Business Attributes
Approach 46
3.5 Quality Metrics 48
3.5.1 Six Sigma..48
3.5.2 ISO 9000 49
3.5.3 Maturity Level..49
3.5.4 Benchmarking...50
3.5.5 Standards...50
3.5.6 OCTAVE 51
Endnotes..51

Chapter 4
Metrics Developments..53
4.1 Statistical Modeling...54
4.2 Systemic Security Management 55
4.3 Value at Risk Analysis..56
4.4 Factor Analysis of Information Risk
(FAIR) 57
4.5 Risk Factor Analysis 58
4.6 Probabilistic Risk Assessment (PRA) 58
Endnotes..61

Chapter 5

Relevance...**63**
    5.1   Problem Inertia.. 64
    5.2   Correlating Metrics to Consequences 64

Chapter 6

The Metrics Imperative **67**
    6.1   Study of ROSI of Security Measures...............................68
    6.2   Resource Allocation 69
    6.3   Managing without Metrics 70
    Endnotes..71

Chapter 7

Attributes of Good Metrics **73**
    7.1   Metrics Objectives 75
    7.2   Measurement Categories...75
    7.3   Effective Metrics.. 77
        7.3.1   What Is Being Measured?...............................79
        7.3.2   Why Is It Measured?......................................80
        7.3.3   Who Are the Recipients? 81
        7.3.4   What Does It Mean? 81
        7.3.5   What Action Is Required? 81

Chapter 8

Information Security Governance...**83**
    8.1   Security Governance Outcomes 84
    8.2   Defining Security Objectives...85
        8.2.1   Sherwood Applied Business Security Architecture
                (SABSA) 86
        8.2.2   CobiT 86
        8.2.3   ISO 27001 89
        8.2.4   Capability Maturity Model 90
    8.3   Current State 91
    8.4   Information Security Strategy 91
    Endnotes..92

Chapter 9

Metrics Development—A Different Approach **93**
    9.1   The Information Security Manager 94
    9.2   Activities Requiring Metrics 96
        9.2.1   Criticality and Sensitivity 97
        9.2.2   Degree of Risk or Potential Impact................97
        9.2.3   Risk over Time 97
        9.2.4   Options and Cost-Effectiveness 97

9.3 Ranking Metrics and Monitoring Requirements 98
  9.3.1 Monitoring, Measures, or Metrics? 98

Chapter 10
Information Security Governance Metrics 101
10.1 Strategic Security Governance Decisions 101
  10.1.1 Strategic Security Governance Decision Metrics 102
10.2 Security Governance Management Decisions 103
  10.2.1 Strategic Direction 103
  10.2.2 Ensuring Objectives Are Achieved 104
  10.2.3 Managing Risks Appropriately 104
  10.2.4 Using Resources Responsibly 105
10.3 Security Governance Operational Decisions 105

Chapter 11
Information Security Risk Management 107
11.1 Information Security Risk Management Decisions 108
11.2 Management Requirements for Information Security Risk 109
  11.2.1 Criticality of Assets 109
  11.2.2 Sensitivity of Assets 110
  11.2.3 The Nature and Magnitude of Impacts 110
  11.2.4 Vulnerabilities 110
  11.2.5 Threats 111
  11.2.6 Probability of Compromise 111
  11.2.7 Strategic Initiatives and Plans 111
  11.2.8 Acceptable Levels of Risk and Impact 112
11.3 Information Security Operational Risk Metrics 112

Chapter 12
Information Security Program Development Metrics 115
12.1 Program Development Management Metrics 116
12.2 Program Development Operational Metrics 117

Chapter 13
Information Security Management Metrics 119
13.1 Security Management Decision Support Metrics 120
13.2 Security Management Decisions 122
  13.2.1 Strategic Alignment 123
  13.2.2 Risk Management 125
    13.2.2.1 Metrics for Risk Management 126
  13.2.3 Assurance Process Integration 132
  13.2.4 Value Delivery 134
  13.2.5 Resource Management 136
  13.2.6 Performance Measurement 136

13.3 Information Security Management Operational Decision
   Support Metrics 137
   13.3.1 IT and Information Security Management 137
   13.3.2 Compliance Metrics 138
Endnotes 147

Chapter 14
Incident Management and Response **149**
14.1 Incident Management Decision Support Metrics 150
   14.1.1 Is It Actually an Incident? 150
   14.1.2 What Kind of Incident Is It? 151
   14.1.3 Is It a Security Incident? 151
   14.1.4 What Is the Severity Level? 151
   14.1.5 Are There Multiple Events and/or Impacts? 152
   14.1.6 Will an Incident Need Triage? 152
   14.1.7 What Is the Most Effective Response? 152
   14.1.8 What Immediate Actions Must be Taken? 153
   14.1.9 Which Incident Response Teams and Other Personnel
      Must be Mobilized? 153
   14.1.10 Who Must be Notified? 153
   14.1.11 Who Is in Charge? 153
   14.1.12 Is It Becoming a Disaster? 153

Chapter 15
Conclusions **155**
15.1 Predictive Metrics 155

Acronyms 157

Appendix A
Metrics Classifications **165**
A.1 IA Program Developmental Metrics 165
   A.1.1 Policy Management Metrics 165
   A.1.2 Process Maturity Metrics 165
A.2 Support Metrics 166
   A.2.1 Personnel Support Metrics 166
   A.2.2 Resource Support Metrics 166
A.3 Operational Metrics 166
   A.3.1 Operational Readiness Metrics 166
      A.3.1.1 Management Readiness Metrics 167
      A.3.1.2 Technical Readiness Metrics 167
   A.3.2 Operational Practice Metrics 167
   A.3.3 Operational Environment Metrics 167
A.4 Effectiveness Metrics 168

A.4.1 Metrics for Technical Target of Assessment (TTOA) 168
    A.4.1.1 Metrics for Strength Assessment.......................168
    A.4.1.2 Metrics for Weakness Assessment 169
Acknowledgments 170
Endnotes...170
References..170

Appendix B
Cultural Worldviews **171**
Endnotes...173

Appendix C
The Competing Values Framework **175**
C.1 Cultural Dimensions 175
    C.1.1 Horizontal: In/Out...175
    C.1.2 Vertical: Stability/Flexibility...................................175
C.2 The Competing Values Map 175
    C.2.1 Hierarchy...176
    C.2.2 Market..176
    C.2.3 Clan..176
    C.2.4 Adhocracy 177

Appendix D
The Organization Culture Assessment Instrument (OCAI) **179**

Appendix E
SABSA Business Attribute Metrics..**181**
Endnotes... 200

Appendix F
Capability Maturity Model..**201**
Level 1—Initial 201
Level 2—Repeatable...201
Level 3—Defined..202
Level 4—Managed 202
Level 5—Optimizing 202

Appendix G
Probabilistic Risk Assessment **205**
DR. MICHAEL STAMATELATOS
G.1 What Is Probabilistic Risk Assessment? 205
G.2 What Are the Benefits of PRA? 207

Index **211**

Acknowledgments

Venturing into the murky waters of information security management metrics has been a challenge that I would not have willingly undertaken without the support, urging, and assistance of others. Special thanks go to Ray Kaplan, for his many contributions, suggestions, and review, and to my wife Melody, for graciously accepting my often obsessive work at strange hours of the night.

A debt of gratitude is also acknowledged to others who have supported this effort giving their time to advising, reviewing, and commenting on this exposition, including ISACA associates of notable competence, Bruce Wilkins, Gary Barnes, and Ron Hale, and other professionals, including Charles Neal, formerly of the FBI, and Adam Hunt, currently with Inland Revenue in New Zealand. Thanks is also due John Sherwood and David Lynas, from the United Kingdom, for their assistance and support with the SABSA architectural material in this work.

And finally, appreciation is also due my unusually helpful and cooperative publisher and staff in bringing this hopefully illuminating work to light.

Introduction

The failures of information security during the past decade are nothing short of spectacular. The inability of organizations to prevent increasingly dramatic compromises has led to huge financial losses, produced a great deal of embarrassment, and put every sector of the global economy at risk. Despite increasingly draconian legal, commercial, and regulatory activity, the losses continue to mount, national interests are still at risk, and "information crimes" proliferate unabated.

Few will argue that it isn't a problem and, despite greatly increased security efforts, a growing one. The true cost from all security failures globally is impossible to determine with any certainty but, by most credible estimates, ranges well into the hundreds of billions of dollars. One study by Ponemon Institute LLC in 2007 determined that security breaches resulting in the loss of customer records cost U.S. organizations an average of $182 per record lost. With more than 100 million *reported* records compromised that year, losses from this source alone could approximate more than $18 billion. It should be noted that evidence suggests breaches are underreported by nearly two-thirds as a result of companies fearing adverse publicity and actual losses may be much higher. Regardless of the precise numbers, the situation is in dire need of some answers—and some solutions.

The first requirement for developing an answer is clearly framing the problem. An extensive review of the literature and numerous studies and surveys provides indications of the underlying causes and the scope of risks. They also point to an obvious solution consistent with the answer to virtually all organizational maladies—*management.*

If, indeed, management is the problem, what are the underlying issues that result in inadequate or ineffective security management? Studies show many contributory factors but a few stand out—one of them is the lack of meaningful security management metrics providing the essential feedback necessary to effectively manage information security risk. It's axiomatic that what isn't measured won't be managed. When coupled with inadequate or nonexistent security governance structures, organizational cultures not conducive to good security, and a lack of understanding and support from the "C" suite, the arguably deplorable state of information security is not altogether surprising.

Occasioned by growing awareness of the deficiencies in the ability to measure security and possibly dire necessity, a number of works have been written on IT security metrics in the past few years, yet there have been few if any efforts to address the issue of effective metrics for information security management. This work is an endeavor to address this urgent need. The intent is to provide an approach and methodology to devise metrics that support strategic, management, and operational decisions needed to develop and manage a successful information security program.

The project has proven more arduous and complex than anticipated when it started more than three years ago, and there is no illusion that it will be the last word on the subject. Information security management is an emerging area and likely to see many improvements in the coming years as organizations and governments face mounting pressures for more effective security and greater efficiency. But the discipline is in the early stages of being defined, and the boundaries of scope and responsibility are vague at best. Although this work has been reviewed by seasoned information security experts and practitioners and subject to numerous additions and rewrites, there are undoubtedly incomplete areas and aspects that will be the subject of considerable debate.

This book is generally not technical but assumes some familiarity with information security. The scope and depth of coverage are designed to provide those charged with strategic oversight as well as those that manage, operate, or advise on information security with the information needed to understand, design, and implement effective security management measures, metrics, and monitoring. There are four major areas covered:

1. An overview of the current state of information security, governance, and the metrics imperative
2. A summary of many of the current diverse options for measures, metrics, and monitoring
3. An exploration of the attributes of and criteria for good metrics; what can be measured and how
4. Processes and methods for developing effective security management metrics; a detailed, practical approach to meet strategic, management, and operational metrics requirements

Overview

For most contemporary organizations, information is their single most valuable asset. Indeed, it is generally the one critical asset of the business. Events have demonstrated that companies can survive the loss of virtually all other assets including people, facilities, and equipment, but very few can continue with the loss of their information and the knowledge based on it (e.g., accounting data, operations and process knowledge and information, customer data). With this realization more than a decade ago, well-known management consultant Peter Drucker wrote, "Knowledge is fast becoming the sole factor of productivity, sidelining both capital and labor."[1] During the intervening years, the technology systems that handle critical information have become pervasive and dependence on them has arguably become absolute.

Concurrently, we have witnessed ever more spectacular failures of security to deal with the dramatic rise in cyber attacks and growth of "information" crimes. Coupled with security's seeming inability to stem mounting losses from information system interruptions and data theft, senior management often reluctantly but increasingly understands its organization's dependence on information and the systems that process it. In addition, governments have become aware of the perils to national critical infrastructures that failure of these systems poses and have responded with a raft of restrictive legislation and regulatory requirements. The payments card industry has banded together to require a standard of security for all credit card transactions in an effort to stem the tide of fraud, identity theft, and protected information compromises.

As a result, security has gained visibility in boardrooms, organizations have significantly increased security spending, and security positions are being elevated in organizational structures, as evidenced by the chief information security officer (CISO) becoming commonplace during the past decade:

> Some 40 percent of this year's respondents report their companies employ a chief information security officer (CISO) or chief security officer (CSO), up from 31 percent in 2004.[2]

Although these efforts have served to improve security significantly, they have generally been insufficient to counter the growth of cybercrime or reduce total losses. One reason is that responses to security-related crises are invariably reactive. That is, improvements in security have been a reaction either to financial losses or credit card industry mandates or to governmental interdiction through law and regulation. In either instance, security is behind the power curve, always trying to catch up, and, more often than not, in a firefighting, crisis mode.

Another factor is that security is often seen by management as a bottomless pit of costs—at best, a necessary evil. It is generally perceived as a constraint to business, and despite the best efforts of the security industry, it is not commonly viewed as an "enabler."

In addition, chief information officers are usually oriented toward technology and charged with overseeing IT systems in addition to often overseeing security. Yet there is typically as much, or more, information that is not resident in technology systems but exists in some physical form or in someone's head. CIOs do not generally consider these other forms of information within their purview, notwithstanding that critical or sensitive information retains those characteristics regardless of how it is stored, processed, or transported.

Governance

As security costs and complexity have escalated, the result has been increased attention to the area of *security governance*. Although still not the norm, it has become evident that for security to become more effective, it must be addressed as a part of overall corporate governance. It cannot be a stand-alone add-on function but must be an integral part of doing business. In addition, it will become evident that information security management metrics are not possible absent the basic elements of governance.

As efforts to develop security governance frameworks and management methodologies are taking place, it is becoming clear that there are difficult questions regarding how to measure something as nebulous and poorly defined as security outside the process and performance measures applied to IT systems. From a management perspective, improvements in information technology metrics are still incapable of providing answers to the following questions:

- How secure is the organization?
- How much security is enough?
- How do we know when we have achieved security?
- What are the most cost-effective solutions?
- How do we determine the degree of risk?
- How well can risk be predicted?
- Is the security program going in the right direction?

Attempts to provide meaningful answers to these questions and others can ultimately be addressed only by developing relevant measures—metrics that specifically address the requirements of management to make appropriate decisions about the organization's safety. It should be noted that the term *metrics* describes a broad range of tools used to evaluate data in many parts of an organization. Basically, a metric is a measurement compared to one or more reference points to produce a meaningful result.

Although technical security metrics have improved significantly in recent times, they typically do not provide information useful or relevant to management beyond technical IT security. For example, knowing that there are a particular number of open vulnerabilities in the network is generally meaningless to senior management. By itself, this information says nothing about the likelihood of exploitation, viable threats, potential impacts, or costs to remedy. This state of affairs is reflected in a recent case study,[3] where, when questioned about the value of security reports they received, most executives answered, "Not much."

To change this situation, security metrics aligned with, and shown to support, the strategic organizational goals in a manner that is meaningful to executives are required. For instance, in the U.S. federal government, measurement and reporting of security metrics must reflect legislative and CIO-articulated requirements, as well as the missions of the various agencies.[4]

Metrics Overview

It is axiomatic that you can't manage what you can't measure. This holds as true for security as it does for any other field of endeavor, be it manufacturing widgets, promoting sales, flying airplanes, or managing supply chains. Historically, progress in effective management has invariably been accompanied by the ability to increasingly measure processes and results with greater accuracy.

Security, unlike many other activities, poses particular problems. One is the lack of a clear, consistent definition of *security*. With dozens of definitions available on the Web and in the literature—ranging from a thing such as that offered as collateral to secure a loan, to various forms of action or activities related to safety—it may be an unfortunate choice of terms, and *information assurance* (IA) may be a better alternative.

This confusion is compounded by a lack of consensus or clarity about exactly what it (security) should accomplish and when it has, in fact, accomplished it. Certainly, there is general agreement that security should address risks to information resources. But this is a rather imprecise statement and difficult to measure. In contrast, these are not problems when flying airplanes or managing supply chains, where both process and outcomes are precisely definable.

As previously mentioned, the ability to measure many specific technical aspects of IT security has improved substantially, but these measurements are incapable of telling us much about the state of overall information security, or safety, of the enterprise. They can't address what corporate secrets are walking out the door or innocently divulged in elevators, or what liabilities are being created by unvetted information on a Web site or by misguided e-mails. They cannot provide much guidance for managing an enterprise-wide information security program or assurance that it is in alignment with and supports the organization's strategic objectives.

As Michael Rasmussen of Forrester Research is purported to have said:

> What gets measured gets done. The world of security, however, has fallen far from this mark. Historically, information security has been tactical and reactive as opposed to managed and measured. Information security in many organizations can be characterized as a "fly by night operation"—operating in the dark.

Defining Security

The first problem is the definition of information security (Infosec). It is generally described as the process of ensuring the confidentiality, integrity, and availability of information resources. Some efforts include adding accountability and nonrepudiation as well. This shopworn definition, however, speaks to the practice of security, not to what it is. It speaks to processes, not objectives, and not to standards of measurement. It provides little guidance as to scope or range of responsibilities. Although availability can be measured in ways not necessarily relevant to security, there is no defined measure of confidentiality or integrity. It can be argued that a measure of percentage uptime or downtime is a consistent, numerical measure of availability. However, the security definition of *availability* is that resources are available as and when needed. If downtime occurs when a critical resource is needed, the requirements of security have not been met regardless of percentage uptime.

The lack of a concise scope and definition of *security* renders the problem of creating standardized meaningful metrics difficult. To some extent, this has resulted in the practice of security painting itself into a corner. Practitioners can't tell management what it is or how to measure it, how much of it they need, or when they have too much.

In addition, the term *security* means very different things to different people. To a VP of sales, it might mean whatever is necessary to preclude negative effects on sales. To a CFO, the measure might be minimizing financial uncertainty, costs, and losses while maximizing revenues. To senior management, the security bottom line might be measured in overall impacts of adverse events, including such nebulous quantities as reputational damage, impact on share value, and so on. The point is that security as viewed from individual perspectives generally means desirable outcomes and an absence of significant impediments to those outcomes—in other words, *safety from adverse outcomes*. Of course, what one part of an organization may consider adverse, another may think is of little consequence, and the perception of safety will vary widely across the enterprise as well.

Is There a Solution?

It is fair to say that among security product vendors, technical practitioners, and legions of "official" pundits, technical security has taken on a life of its own—a life that all too often diverges from the needs of business management. Given that business functions as an end-to-end process, errors or failures anywhere in the entire process are a security, or organizational safety, problem. However, the ever-increasing number of specialists, whether security, audit, risk, or disaster recovery, increasingly segment what is in fact a continuous process; they talk different languages, don't communicate effectively if at all, and tend to create separate fiefdoms or silos. There is nothing systemic to organizations that works to fix that.

Another issue is that security in the commercial world has always been the unwanted stepchild and has grown of dire necessity into the thing it is today. It may be time to reexamine the entire field of security, safety, and assurance from the improved perspective of hindsight. The solution may be to go back to basics and consider what it is we are trying to accomplish with the practice of security. It may serve to consider what it will take to integrate the many diverse assurance functions into a holistic whole that deals with the entire issue of organizational *preservation*. This will, in turn, help clarify what constitutes relevant metrics and what we might consider effective, useful monitoring. It is the intent of this book to endeavor to shed light on the security, or assurance, landscape by considering what can and should be measured, and, more importantly, why and for whom. For the balance of this book, the term *security* will be used in the broad sense to mean "assurance of safety or the absence of danger" and incorporate the notion of safety and preservation of the organization. How those safety-related activities are subdivided within any particular organization is not critical, but clarity about roles and responsibilities is. The fundamental function of all measures is to provide the information needed to make appropriate decisions, and that, in turn, is a function of roles and responsibilities.

Endnotes

1. Drucker, Peter, *Management Challenges for the 21st Century,* HarperBusiness, 1999.
2. "Best Practices in Security Governance," Aberdeen Group, USA, 2005.
3. Schwartz, Mathew, 5/2/2006 Case Study, Enterprise Systems.
4. NIST Special Publication 800-65, Integrating IT Security into the Capital Planning and Investment Process. National Institute of Standards and Technology, Information Technology Laboratory, Computer Security Division, Computer Security, Security Resource Center. http://csrc.nist.gov/publications/PubsSPs.html

Chapter 1

Security Metrics Overview

Metrics is a term used to denote a measure based on a reference and involves at least two points, the measure and the reference. Security in its most basic meaning is the protection from or absence of danger. Literally, security metrics should tell us about the state or degree of safety relative to a reference point and what to do to avoid danger. Contemporary security metrics by and large fail to do so. They tell us little about the actual degree of "safety" of our systems or processes, much less about the organization as a whole. They say little about the appropriate course of action, and they are typically not specific to the needs of the recipient.

Clearly, there are designs and architectures as well as modes of operation and practices that generally result in safer operations than others. But unlike the Insurance Institute's crash rating tests for automobiles capable of predicting the outcomes of accidents in terms of injuries, there is nothing comparable for designing security systems or programs.

As with all other aspects of organizational activity, defining objectives for security is critical to determining an approach to getting there. It is also a requirement for developing meaningful metrics from both an operational standpoint and a strategic one. Without specific objectives to guide the direction for information security and to provide a reference point from which to measure, management will remain inconsistent, haphazard, and reactive. Providing those objectives and the "rules of engagement" is the function of information security governance.

The issue of security metrics has seen considerable activity in recent times, and there are numerous approaches to monitoring and measuring "security" available. However, the majority of these efforts generally apply to subsections of technical, or IT, security with a few notable exceptions. While these technical metrics are in many cases very effective at the specific task for which they were designed (e.g., Tripwire and others from intrusion detection systems), they say little about the overall security, or safety, of the organization and provide little guidance for effective management. Measuring the state of "safety" of an organization is vastly broader than knowing how many packets a firewall dropped and is typically well beyond the scope of IT, or for that matter, information security.

If, in fact, the goal is to achieve meaningful "security metrics," then the approach to monitoring and measuring must strive to broaden its base to increasingly aggregate measurements from all the assurance functions an organization depends on to remain "safe." It would also be useful to develop a standardized set of metrics that could be generally applied using the same yardstick. Such a standardized set of security metric would have a set of required attributes such as being meaningful, actionable, consistent, and repeatable. However, even if a measure is well defined, the critical element is to track the measure across industries over time to determine what "31 inches of security" actually means in terms of probable costs, losses, and so on. As an example, the life insurance industry knows that an individual who smokes two packs of cigarettes a day, has high blood pressure, and lives in Los Angeles has a probable life expectancy that can be determined with a degree of accuracy at least on a statistical basis. No such correlations exist for security metrics. Some instances of proprietary solutions in particular situations do exist where to a limited extent such correlations exist, but these correlations lack the depth and breadth for general application. Work continues on these tools by the private sector and governments. For example, SecurCompass® is a proprietary security assessment tool that compares individual organizations to the averages for various industries using 500 metrics that are mapped against the security goals of executive management.[1] The limitations of this approach are much the same as an audit. While perhaps more useful in some respects, it is still a snapshot in time as opposed to an ongoing real-time measure of organizational safety capable of capturing changes as they occur. It isn't a compass that can tell us to turn left or right. Other similar approaches exist but suffer the same limitations.

One promising effort that is publicly available is the Metrics Center™, which is being developed and managed by PlexLogic in conjunction with SecurityMetrics.org.[2]

An effort to define objectives for technical security metrics suitable for management could, for example, be a dashboard that would show the results of an integrated system that monitored internal and external threats, system and process vulnerabilities, asset criticality and sensitivity, and the ongoing state of an organization's incident response capabilities simultaneously, and then present management with a real-time indicator of financial exposure. This hypothetical gauge would have a redline set at acceptable risk limits and a risk never to exceed (RNE, to coin a new acronym) mark that would be consistent with levels that would cause major harm to the organization. Obviously, the state of metrics is far from this objective, but it may nevertheless be useful to chart a direction for there to be any hope of achieving the goal.

Full audits and comprehensive risk assessments are typically the only activity organizations undertake that provides this breadth of perspective. While important and necessary, from a security management point of view, these provide only history or a snapshot, not what is needed in day-to-day security management. The 20-20 hindsight provided by audits also suffers from the assumption that a prudent path to the future can be paved with experiences of the past. In the dynamic world of security, with its ever-changing threat landscape, this is often not a safe assumption.

For some time, vendors have made efforts to integrate a variety of technical security indicators and to provide a "security dashboard." Significant progress has been made. For example, besides offerings from Computer Associates (CA Unicenter®), and IBM (IBM Tivoli), many others such as Intellitactics™ SAM are being offered. A number of primarily technical data can be "rolled up" to present a real-time picture of *technical* security performance. Although still not yet widely deployed, these systems can be useful in managing the operations of IT security and can be combined with monitoring tools such as event correlation and tracking and SIM, to some extent useful for security program management as well. Many current solutions such as ClearPoint Metrics go to lengths to present metrics in forms such as scorecards, and on a schedule that matches what a financial executive would expect.

All of this security metrics and compliance dashboard activity is a subset of the flurry of activity that is taking place in the measurement and reporting of organizational performance. In a discussion of the rise of compliance dashboards, Susan Jendrey quotes Michael Rasmussen, Vice President of Enterprise Risk and Compliance Management at Forrester Research:

> The dashboard provides a portal view into the state of compliance. Ultimately, the purpose of the compliance dashboard is to gather metrics and show measurement of compliance. It is a detection and reporting tool for things that can or have gone wrong.
>
> If you ask any IT vendor if they have a compliance dashboard, the vast majority of them will step up and state that they do," muses Rasmussen. Early corporate adopters must be savvy in selecting a viable solution, since there is no single standard for information display, data integration support, and system architecture standards.
>
> For example, CXO Systems' dashboard focuses on key IT risk indicators, which include compliance. There are a number of vendors building specific IT risk and compliance management dashboards, such as Archer Technologies, BindView, Hewlett-Packard, ITM Software, and Brabeion. There are specific SOX solution dashboards from vendors such as Certus and HandySoft. Then there are vendors such as Axentis, Paisley, Qumas, Open Pages, and IBM that provide broader enterprise risk and compliance dashboards, Rasmussen explains.[3]

It is important to note that most of the work on dashboards has been rolling low-level metrics into higher level views. This does not necessarily result in something that executive management can use. As pointed out subsequently, this might be perfectly acceptable as long as the metrics are used to support business cases rather than as ends unto themselves.

Given the demonstrable benefits these systems can provide, the lack of greater penetration into enterprise information systems can be attributed to a lack of awareness, complexity, cost, and overhead. It is also likely that a persuasive business case has not been prepared nor a basis for computing return on investment developed. And it can be a significant job since dashboard agents must be deployed to all monitored systems and the data collected must be massaged and normalized in a way that allows meaningful integration. In addition, these efforts generally start from the wrong perspective in that they measure what they can, not necessarily what various recipients need.

As the importance of information security has become more apparent to senior management, the inability of current approaches to provide suitable "feedback" to effectively manage the plethora of required assurance functions has become increasingly clear. There is a growing consensus that security management technologies available today are insufficient for the needs of either executive or enterprise security managers. In part, the problem was recently stated by Shmuel Klinger, vice president of architecture and applied research in the CTO office at EMC, when speaking about security management:

> I think in general we are on the completely wrong trajectory in management. Things are more complex, there are more moving parts, and management as an industry are chasing the wrong trends. These trends will have us falling on our face. *We are increasing the amount of management data that we collect to a level of detail that no one cares about, which poses a nightmare for integration.*[4]

Another issue that must be considered is that in many organizations, the only way that security, or safety, issues are aggregated is by risk management and audit. But, the focus of risk management is not on performance or strategic alignment of security with business objectives; it is on identifying all sorts of risk and developing the controls or countermeasures to mitigate or manage it. Risk management is obviously important, but it is functionally different from both *operational* and *strategic* security management at the CISO or VP level. Audit is essential as well, but it provides only history, and it is hard to navigate with only a rearview mirror.

1.1 Metrics and Objectives

Metrics require objectives. Without defined objectives for an information security program it is not possible to develop useful metrics. It will not be possible to determine whether progress is being made or whether the program is headed in the right direction. Since we measure to manage, we must know what objectives we are managing to. In fact, most or all elements of information security governance must be implemented as a prerequisite for developing effective metrics. Without the underpinnings of governance—that is, the structure, rules, and processes to operate a security program toward defined objectives—it will be difficult to know what information is needed or, indeed, its relevance. Without clarity as to the destination, directional information, even if available, will be of little use.

Considerable high-level guidance for information security governance has been developed by the Information Security and Control Association (ISACA), which proposes six outcomes of information security governance and management:

1. Strategic Alignment—Strategic alignment of information security in support of business objectives
2. Risk Management—Executing appropriate measures to mitigate risks and reduce potential impacts on information resources to an acceptable level
3. Business Process Assurance—Integration of all relevant assurance functions to maximize the effectiveness and efficiency of security activities
4. Value Delivery—Optimizing security investments in support of business objectives to achieve the best return on security investments
5. Resource Management—Using information security knowledge and infrastructure efficiently and effectively
6. Performance Measurement—Monitoring and reporting on information security processes to ensure objectives are achieved

While few security practitioners would argue that these six objectives are important for IT and information security, the majority of organizations globally have made no effort nor are planning to implement metrics to track and manage achieving them. This is dramatically highlighted by the recent *IT Governance Global Status Report*[5] study of more than 7000 organizations. Table 1.1, from the global survey of IT and information security executives, shows the results of governance and metrics implementation for five of the aforementioned objectives and the utilization of ROI for IT.

The conclusion that must be drawn is that most senior management has yet to understand that like every other aspect of business, optimal and cost-effective security, or IT operations generally, cannot be attained without appropriate feedback mechanisms to gauge direction and performance. Surprising as these numbers are, it is nevertheless likely that as the cost of IT and security continues to increase and regulations become increasingly restrictive in the face of mounting losses from cybercrime, they will improve in the coming years.

Another ongoing issue is that while numerous studies over the years have shown the majority of losses (and therefore risk) to organizations comes from insiders, most security systems and their metrics still deal with external threats and establishing a secure "perimeter" after decades of advice from security practitioners to the contrary.

Table 1.1   Results of Governance and Metrics Implementation

	Have Implemented	*Implementing Now*	*Considering Implementing*	*Not Considering*
IT strategy alignment with business strategy	16%	12%	21%	51%
Resource management	18%	12%	20%	50%
Value delivery	9%	9%	21%	61%
Risk management	9%	9%	16%	66%
Performance of IT	10%	10%	14%	66%
ROI management of IT	7%	8%	13%	72%

Source: IT Governance Global Status Report, IT Governance Institute 2006.

In a 2003 survey conducted by Harris Interactive Service Bureau and compiled by Vontu, a provider of software security solutions, noted the following key findings:

- 62 percent of survey respondents reported that incidents at work could put customer data at risk for identity theft.
- 66 percent said their coworkers, not hackers, pose the greatest risk to consumer privacy.
- 70 percent said that government regulations play a role in raising awareness at their workplace about identity theft and database security.
- Nearly 50 percent said that government still has not done enough to help thwart identity theft.
- 46 percent said it would be "easy" to "extremely easy" for workers to remove sensitive data from a corporate database.

If the results of this and other surveys are credible, greater emphasis must be placed on monitoring and metrics of internal activities. These results also indicate that controls and metrics other than technical ones will require more attention.

1.2 Information Security

To help gain clarity around the topic of security management metrics, the term *information security* needs a reasonably precise working definition. The word *information* has a meaning different from *data* and *knowledge,* although in common speech they are often used interchangeably. *Information* can be defined as "data with meaning and purpose."[6] *Knowledge* can be defined as actionable information. Knowledge, in turn, is stored and disseminated as organized information.

We have already discussed that fundamentally, security is the assurance of safety. As a result we could define *information security* to include the assurance of the safety of data that has meaning and purpose and conclude that any other data is probably useless and a liability that needlessly consumes resources.

The purview of information security includes all aspects of information whether spoken, written, printed, electronic, or relegated to any other medium regardless of whether it is being created, modified, viewed, transported, stored, or destroyed. This is contrasted with IT security, which is concerned with security of information within the boundaries of the technology domain. Typically, confidential information disclosed in an elevator conversation or sent via regular mail would be outside the scope of IT security. However, from an information security perspective, the nature and type of compromise is not important, just the fact that security has been breached.

The IT Governance Institute defines the role of information security as

> the protection of information assets against the risk of loss, operational discontinuity, misuse, unauthorized disclosure, inaccessibility, or damage. It is also concerned with the increasing potential for civil or legal liability that organizations face as a result of information inaccuracy and loss, or the absence of due care in its protection.[7]

In the broader context of the organization, this definition constitutes a rather inclusive mandate typically beyond the scope of a typical security officer, and even a CISO. However, given the fact that according to a recent study by the Brookings Institution, intangible assets (i.e., knowledge, information, data, goodwill, patents, IP, etc.) constitute 80 percent of the value to the typical organization today, the only surprise is the lack of integrated, concerted efforts to protect these assets consistent with a reasonable level of due care.

If "security" equates to the assurance of safety, the activities of security departments typically deal with only a subset of what makes an organization "safe." Other aspects of "safety" fall to a host of the other "assurance" providers and managers. For example, environmental safety may be the purview of facilities management, whereas product safety may be the responsibility of quality assurance. From a "security," or safety, standpoint, these activities, among many others, are highly relevant. In fact, when all organizational activities concerned with the assurance of safety are considered, they constitute a substantial component of all organizational activities and operational costs. A point of interest from an organizational structure perspective is that these assurance providers are generally not structured and governed by their strategic relevance or objectives but typically, by the operational processes they serve. The obvious example is that for most organizations, security is governed by IT, not by risk management.

1.3 IT Security

By definition, information technology security revolves around the machinery that processes, stores, and transports information. While IT security is concerned with the security of information within its boundaries, the focus is on technology. Yet, people and physical processes are inevitably interjected into technical processes at numerous points and typically represent the greatest risk of information compromise through accident, carelessness, ignorance, or intention. Technical controls and metrics certainly play an increasing part in catching mistakes, unauthorized access, and other threats to information security but can do little about social engineering, industrial espionage, carelessness, or fraudulent inputs.

1.3.1 Why the IT Metric Focus

This raises the question why IT security seems to get most of the attention while other assurance functions highly relevant to security do not. In part, it is due to the rapid evolution and recently realized level of dependence organizations have on IT systems in the face of ever more spectacular failures. Another factor is that other assurance functions have a longer history and more established and tested controls. Quality assurance, for example, has its modern roots in Deming's "zero defect" work over 50 years ago.

Another reason for the focus on IT security metrics is because they are relatively easy and can be automated. IT is machinery and lends itself to oil pressure and temperature gauges. The number of corporate secrets compromised at the local pub is far harder to get a handle on. Information security beyond the borders of technology is far more difficult to control and has been an issue since the birth of civilization, with encryption nearly as ancient. Roman couriers were concerned with it, and the famous World War II poster, "Loose lips sink ships" also deals with the subject.

1.4 Other Assurance Functions

The typical organization has a number of activities, or departments, that in some manner deal with safety, security, or risk management as contrasted with those that produce something. They often include

- Legal
- Audit
- Accounting
- Information Security
- IT Security
- Physical Security
- Business Continuity/Disaster Recovery
- Human Resources
- Quality Assurance
- Risk Management
- Change Management
- Project Office
- Privacy Office
- Insurance Office
- Compliance
- Facilities Management

Admittedly, some of these devote only a portion of their efforts directly to safety, or security. Nevertheless, collectively these activities all have a role in "security," and are certainly relevant to organizational safety and risk management. From a management perspective, integrated reporting on a common basis from all these activities insofar as risk and security are concerned would be very desirable in providing a comprehensive picture of the overall "safety" of the organization.

> In the past, management of the risk inherent in a business was a function embedded within the individual roles of the "C Suite." The traditional approach was to treat individual risks separately and assign responsibility to an individual or small team. Managing a singular kind of risk became a distinct job, and performing that job well meant focusing exclusively on that one particular area. The problem with this stovepiped approach is that it not only ignores the interdependence of many business risks but also suboptimizes the financing of total risk for an enterprise.
>
> Breaking stovepipes and addressing the suboptimizing of investments requires a new way of thinking about the problem. This new thinking brings together the various stakeholders in the problem set to work closely together...[8]

There are probably better terms than *security* to denote the functions typically assigned to the department with that name. Arguably, it is one of many assurance functions that collectively look after the organization's safety and minimize its exposure to danger. Collectively, these functions are charged with *preservation* of the organization.

The relevance is that typical "security" metrics cannot of themselves, no matter how well conceived, provide much assurance of organizational safety. They are typically narrowly focused on the operational performance of specific technologies and generally serve only technical managers. These metrics fail to provide comfort to senior management that fraud will be prevented, that theft will be detected in a timely manner, and that someone won't physically steal technically "secure" servers.

The conclusion that can be drawn is that to measure and to report on the "security" of an organization and to provide the information needed for prudent strategic and management decision making, metrics must draw on a far broader set of data than is the current practice.

1.5 Stakeholders

Any discussion of metrics must first and foremost consider the constituency. That is, who will be the recipients of metrics and monitoring feedback and reports; who will monitor, maintain, and calibrate the metrics; and so on? What information is needed by whom? The issue can be summed up by the question, "Who needs to know what when?"

A fundamental division exists between *technical* metrics necessary to operate and maintain the security machinery and *management* metrics needed to effectively and efficiently manage security and related activities. In some cases, metrics will clearly fall into one or the other category. In others, it is not as clear, and the metric might serve both, or as is frequently the case, neither.

Management metrics will be further subdivided depending on whether they are used to manage a security program or they are used to report an overview of the state of security to higher levels of management for strategic purposes. To reiterate, the critical component of metrics will be to determine who are the recipients and what information they require to discharge their responsibilities.

Endnotes

1. SecurCompass®, Solutionary. Security ROI Metrics. http://solutionary.com/solutions_ services/scm_sroim.html and http://solutionary.com/pdfs/SecurCompass_Overview.pdf
2. The Metrics Center. https://www.metricscenter.org/. According to the Web site, "The Metrics Center is an open, electronic forum dedicated to enhancing the effective and efficient use of metrics to measure, analyze, and improve corporate governance, risk management, and compliance. A community mailing list is maintained and managed by SecurityMetrics.org at http://www.securitymetrics.org. The Metrics Center offers two initial services: Metrics Catalog and YouAreHere™ Benchmarks. The Metrics Catalog is a tool for the security metrics community to organize and to share metric definitions. YouAreHere™ Benchmarks allow companies to compare their performance in selected areas with peers by submitting answers to short, simple surveys."

3. Jendrey, Susan. "Looking Agents: The Rise of Compliance Dashboards." Retrieved July 24, 2008 from http://itcinstitute.com/display.aspx?id=532

4. Dubie, Denise. Network World. September 21, 2006. Emphasis added.

5. *IT Governance Global Status Report*, IT Governance Institute 2006.

6. Drucker, Peter. "Management Challenges for the 21st Century," *Harpers Business*, 1993.

7. Brotby, Krag. "Information Security Governance, Guidance for Security Managers," ITGI 2008.

8. Booz, Allen Hamilton. "Convergence of Enterprise Security Organizations," November 8, 2005.

Chapter 2

Security Metrics

Security metrics are not well developed outside of a narrow range of IT-centric measures. While these measures may be useful for managing specific technologies such as patch management or server hardening, they are of little use in "managing" overall security. That is, there is not much available to determine the overall effectiveness of the aggregate assurance processes much less the parts identified as security. There is little to guide the direction of a security program or provide the basis for making good decisions.

Indeed, Andrew Jaquith of the Yankee Group expressed it well at the Metricon 1 metrics conference in 2006 during a keynote speech:

> Security is one of the few areas of management that does not possess a well-understood canon of techniques for measurement. In logistics, for example, metrics like "freight cost per mile" and "inventory warehouse turns" help operators understand how efficiently trucking fleets and warehouses run. In finance, "value at risk" techniques calculate the amount of money a firm could lose on a given day based on historical pricing volatilities. By contrast, in security ... there is exactly nothing. No consensus on key indicators for security exists.[1]

Although some would consider this somewhat overstated, it does illustrate the point. There is a degree of consensus among security practitioners as to some meaningful management metrics. However, from a management standpoint, the most meaningful metrics are historical rather than real-time or predictive. Trends in impacts, for example, are meaningful in terms of the effectiveness of security activities. Unfortunately, we have to suffer the consequences before we obtain the measurement, not unlike finding out the brakes are defective because the car crashed.

2.1 Security Program Effectiveness

Some would argue that a security program is effective if there have been no significant security incidents that impacted the organization. This might serve as a practical guide in some respects, but it is similar to stating that not having crashed an automobile while driving blind in the dark is an indication that one is traveling in the right direction. While this might constitute an outcome acceptable to the organization, this is a useless metric insofar as the result might be equally indicative of excessive security, merely good luck, or that impacts simply haven't been detected. In other words, it cannot serve to guide the security program direction or focus. This concept was well illustrated by the authors of the 2005 book on the Sherwood Applied Business Security Architecture (SABSA) when they pointed out that

Security Is a Complex System

To understand the concepts of security measurement, the two words, security and measurement must be defined. The security of an organization involves much more than specific technical controls like policy, firewalls, passwords, intrusion detection, and disaster recovery plans. Security is certainly comprised of technical controls, but also includes processes that surround technical controls and people issues. These three characteristics of security make it a complex system and when combined together it can be called a security program.

For any complex system, applying basic system engineering concepts will improve the performance of the system. The concepts of design, planned implementation, and scheduled maintenance and management can significantly increase the effectiveness and performance of a security program. One of the fundamental precepts of systems engineering is the ability to measure and quantify. Measurement enables design, accurate implementation to specifications, and management activities including goal setting, tracking progress, benchmarking, and prioritizing. In essence, measurement is a fundamental requirement for security program success. An effective security program involves design and planning, implementation, and ongoing management of process, people, and technology that impact all aspects of security across an entire organization.[2]

2.2 Types of Metrics

There exists a bewildering array of taxonomies, frameworks, and types of security and security-related metrics. This proliferation testifies to the inadequacy of any particular approach to adequately satisfy all, or perhaps any, requirements. To some extent, this is due to the problems identified earlier in determining what exactly security is, what it should do beyond providing relative safety or mandated compliance, and defining clear objectives and knowing when they have been achieved.

No attempt will be made here to categorize every possible metric that is available for information security. Instead, an overview of the broad categories and currently popular choices are provided to aid in selection of approaches. Although their practical application has yet to be demonstrated in general practice, some of the more esoteric approaches that may hold promise are also reviewed here.

Many of these approaches can effectively be used together to gain different perspectives. For example, ITIL is about service delivery whereas CobiT is about control points. These, and others, can be complementary and help round out the picture.

Security metrics can be categorized by *what* they measure. This can include

- Process
- Performance
- Outcomes
- Quality
- Trends
- Conformance to standards
- Probabilities

How these things are measured can be further categorized by the *methods* used to measure them. Methods can include

- Maturity
- Multidimensional scorecards
- Value
- Benchmarking
- Modeling
- Statistical analysis

Some approaches may incorporate several types and combinations in an effort to be more comprehensive. Not all things measured can use all methods described. For example, probabilities would not be measured using maturity levels. In addition, the foregoing are not in the same classes and, as there is not a generally accepted comprehensive taxonomy of security-related metrics, some elements in the first group may, in fact, be measured by other elements in the first group. For example, processes may be measured in terms of quality; outcomes can be measured in terms of conformance to standards.

Development of a taxonomy of security metrics is still a work in progress, but some efforts have been made in this direction. A complete system has been developed for use in Common Criteria for evaluating component security primarily for government use but is of little use in security operations or management. A substantial amount of work on the subject has been done by Anne and Lynn Wheeler in a document titled "Security Taxonomy and Glossary,"[3] and other efforts are under way.

Some useful work has also been performed under a U.S. government grant resulting in a paper titled "Information Assurance Measures and Metrics—State of Practice and Proposed Taxonomy"[4] prepared at Mississippi State University's Center for Computer Security Research. It sets forth an initial effort at a metrics taxonomy and metrics classification methodology. This document represents one of the more useful compilations in the literature and is included in its entirety in Appendix A.

The basic requirements for a taxonomy include the requirement that categories are mutually exclusive and collectively encompassing. Also, note the use of the term *Information Assurance* (*IA*) instead of *information security*.

The proposed taxonomy defines 10 fundamental characteristics of metrics, including the following categories:

- Objective/Subjective: Objective IA metrics (e.g., mean annual downtime for a system) are more desirable than subjective IA metrics (e.g., amount of training a user needs to securely use the system). Since subjectivity is inherent in information assurance, subjective IA metrics are more readily available.
- Quantitative/Qualitative: Quantitative IA metrics (e.g., number of failed login attempts) are more preferable than qualitative IA metrics (e.g., Federal Information Technology Security Assessment Framework [FITSAF] self-assessment levels) because they are discrete, objective values.
- Static/Dynamic: Dynamic IA metrics evolve with time; static IA metrics do not. An example of a static IA metric can be the percentage of staff that received an annual security training refresher. This metric can degrade in value if the content of the course does not change over time. A dynamic IA metric can be the percentage of staff who received training on the use of a current version of the software package. Most metrics used in penetration testing are dynamic. Dynamic IA metrics are more useful than static IA metrics because best practices change over time with technology.
- Absolute/Relative: Absolute metrics do not depend on other measures and either exist or not. An example might be the number of SANS-certified security engineers in an organization. Relative metrics are only meaningful in context (e.g., the number of vulnerabilities in a system cannot provide a complete assessment of the system security posture). The type and strength of

countermeasures is also important in this context for making any decision about the system's IA posture.

■ Direct/Indirect: Direct IA metrics are generated from observing the property that they measure (e.g., the number of invalid packets rejected for a firewall). Indirect IA metrics are derived by evaluation and assessment (e.g., ISO Standard 15408). It is normally preferred to measure behavior directly, but when that is not feasible, indirect measures are used to postulate the assurance posture. IA is a triad of cooperation between the technology that provides assurance, the processes that leverage that technology, and the people who make the technology work in operational use in the real world.

2.3 Information Assurance / Security Metrics Classification

The "Information Assurance Measures and Metrics—State of Practice and Proposed Taxonomy"[5] white paper prepared at Mississippi State University's Center for Computer Security Research, goes on to classify IA metrics for organizational security into four categories based on what they measure:

1. Program developmental metrics
2. Support metrics
3. Operational metrics
4. Effectiveness metrics

An overview of the taxonomy and detailed descriptions of each are included in Appendix A.

Executive security program management will be most interested in using the program developmental metrics classification of this scheme. This classification includes policy management metrics, process maturity metrics, and some aspects of the effectiveness metrics classification. For instance, the effectiveness metrics classification includes measures of policy compliance such as the number of intrusion attempts.

IT security management and system administration will be most interested in operational metrics. However, effectiveness metrics will be of interest for risk management and controls selection.

Security metrics may also be classified according to how they are measured. For example,

■ Quality
■ Maturity
■ Throughput
■ Frequency
■ Magnitude

The practical considerations for security metric measurement include

1. What is being measured?
2. Why is it being measured?
3. How it is being measured?
4. When was it measured?
5. Where was it measured?
6. Who is it being measured for?
7. What does it mean?
8. To whom?

In the following chapters we will endeavor to identify the current approaches to various security metrics. Then, we subsequently propose another perspective that will hopefully be more useful for security management.

2.4 Monitoring vs. Metrics

Monitoring and metrics are often spoken in the same breath but are obviously quite different. From a management perspective, both can serve the same purpose of providing information to guide an information security program. *Monitoring* can also mean simply paying attention to the information supplied by metrics, but usage in this book assumes that metrics are being observed, and *monitoring* herein refers to the process of observation of security-related processes by some means as opposed to measuring it. Here, we are considering non-measurement-related monitoring such as would be the case with CCTV cameras, direct or indirect observation or oversight of procedures, log reviews, and so on.

For some activities it may be necessary to have metrics and some form of monitoring. This may be a result of a high level of criticality requiring fail-safe controls or it may be because the metrics are unreliable or inaccurate. Some activities require monitoring because there are no available metrics.

Better metrics may require less monitoring and vice versa. Given an option, metrics are likely to be the better option in that they will provide more readily quantifiable scalar information and are likely to be more cost-effective. In any event, the focus is on obtaining the feedback necessary to manage effectively.

Endnotes

1. SecurityMetrics.org—http:://www.securitymetrics.org
2. Sherwood, John, Andy Clark, and David Lynas. *Enterprise Security Architecture—A Business Driven Approach.* CMP Books, 2005.
3. Wheeler, Anne, and Lynn Wheeler. www.garlic.com /~lynn

4. Vaughn, Rayford B., Jr., Associate Professor, Department of Computer Science, Mississippi State University; Ambareen Siraj, Department of Computer Science, Mississippi State University; and Ronda Henning, Harris Corporation, Government Communications, Systems Division, Department of Computer Science, *Information Assurance Measures and Metrics—State of Practice and Proposed Taxonomy.* See the end of *Appendix A* for a complete reference to this work.

5. Vaughn, Rayford B., Jr., Associate Professor, Department of Computer Science, Mississippi State University; Ambareen Siraj, Department of Computer Science, Mississippi State University; and Ronda Henning, Harris Corporation, Government Communications, Systems Division, Department of Computer Science, *Information Assurance Measures and Metrics—State of Practice and Proposed Taxonomy.* See the end of *Appendix A* for a complete reference to this work.

Chapter 3

Current State of Security Metrics

An examination of the security metrics landscape reveals a tremendous diversity of approaches and methods employed to achieve some degree of feedback. This includes quantitative, qualitative, and a variety of hybrid approaches. While most of the discernible approaches to security metrics are represented here, there are undoubtedly security managers who have devised unique metrics solutions suitable for their specific situations that are not represented.

This exposition is of necessity in summary form as most of the methods described will by themselves fill a book. However, the depth of coverage of the various methods should be adequate for practitioners to determine whether any particular metric, measure, or monitoring approach is suitable for their particular situation. If an approach appears to meet a particular requirement, it would be advisable to seek additional material for greater depth and implementation guidance.

The fact that no definitive, markedly superior approach to security metrics has surfaced demonstrates that the entire field is still in a state of flux. Nevertheless, some of the following approaches may provide information that is reasonably adequate for security management, provided the criteria proposed in the following chapters are adopted.

The broadest classification of metrics will be quantitative, qualitative, and combinations or hybrids.

3.1 Quantitative Measures and Metrics

Most quantitative metrics will be technical and derived from IT systems. Typically they will relate to vulnerabilities or to performance. Technical metrics are the most common because of several factors. One is that in most organizations, rather than a strategic organizational activity, it is still largely a function of IT under the auspices of a CIO, although it is no longer the case in the majority of financial institutions as a result of regulatory requirements.

Another reason is that in most organizations, it is not clear what should be measured and what can safely be ignored, and the result is typically what can be easily measured is. This turns out to typically be a deluge of technical metrics that are virtually useless from a strategic management perspective. Some practitioners suggest that by correlating this data and information combined with suitable manipulation, a level of meaningful abstraction suitable for management purposes is possible. This argument is suspect in that operational measures can provide little information related to strategic direction just as the automobile fuel gauge provides no indication of location.

In part, there is also the issue of the suppliers of technology and the economic realities of what is profitable. Many nontechnical, potentially useful metrics offer no economic benefit to technology purveyors and therefore lack impetus. These nontechnical approaches are typically developed and promoted by nonprofit educational or governmental entities lacking the financial and marketing clout of the technology manufacturing and service sector.

Another possible underlying cause is the fact that since IT has had such immense impact on virtually all organizations and is highly complex and pervasive, it has resulted in the upside down situation where the *process often drives the objectives* rather than the other way around. It seems what is done is what's technically feasible as opposed to the objectives being determined and the processes evolved to accomplish them. The focus is more about how well the machinery is performing than whether objectives are being achieved.

There is nevertheless a ray of hope in this menagerie of metrics confusion. It is clear from research, and perhaps altogether obvious, that better security and more effective controls result in fewer losses and better survivability. A 2005 Aberdeen Group study of several dozen companies concluded that

> Firms operating at best-in-class levels are lowering financial losses to less than one percent of revenue whereas other organizations are experiencing loss rates that exceed five percent.[1]

Other studies also show a strong correlation between security expenditures, level of controls, governance orientation and culture, and cyber-related losses. While this makes intuitive sense, it is not clear that any of these indicators are markedly better or more predictive than any other.

3.1.1 Performance Metrics

For security management, performance metrics and measures are most effectively used to monitor important or critical processes against some reference point. The requirement is to determine the specific point in critical processes where the earliest indication of probable or actual failure will be indicated as well as the kind of failure it will lead to.

A physical example is the oil pressure gauge in an automobile. While it actually only measures the pressure of oil, it is (mostly) well known that a precipitous drop in pressure signals eminent engine failure and corrective action must be taken quickly. From a security management perspective, there are certain process metrics that can serve the same purpose if (1) the process is critical to important operations, and (2) the relationship between the metric and relevant consequences is understood.

While this seems obvious, it is not borne out in practice insofar as numerous detailed technical metrics are collected without understanding the aforementioned conditions. For example, consider the number of port scans launched against a network. This is neither relevant to critical operations nor indicative of any particular consequences. It provides no indication of what action should be taken.

Typical performance metrics and possible meanings can include such items as

- Packets dropped by a firewall—Could be an indication of impending attack
- Processor or bandwidth utilization—A potential threat to availability or indication of virus proliferation
- Remaining storage capacity—Can signal a threat to integrity or data loss
- Changes in file sizes—May indicate virus infection
- Additional files on servers—Could be malware
- Failed logon attempts—Could signal unauthorized access attempts
- Viruses detected in user files—Indication of ineffective, nonexistent, or not-updated virus software
- Unauthorized Web site access—Possible threat to confidentiality and integrity
- Admin violations—Inadequate training or compliance failure
- Intrusion successes—Insufficient or failed access controls

Measurements or monitoring of these possible threats might be of interest but are typically not useful for security management because the only action clearly indicated is further investigation.

Many other technical measures and metrics are even less useful for managing security. Examples include measures such as

- 74 percent of available patches applied
- 22 viruses detected and isolated
- 64 failed logon attempts
- 891 port scans
- 19 intrusions detected
- 81 percent user accounts in compliance
- 93 percent audit items closed

Of course, depending on the context, most of these will be of interest to someone. For instance, the chief engineer who is tasked with keeping the "security machinery" oiled and running properly will likely be able to make use of them. However, none of them are particularly relevant to an executive security manager. Indeed, none of them may be of use to an information security manager.

From a security management perspective, what would having this data mean and how would it be useful?

- Without knowing whether the patches applied are the critical ones as compared to the ones that aren't, not much is known.
- The question that logically arises regarding the number of viruses detected is, how many weren't?
- Trends provide the only point of reference that gives some meaning to password resets and still begs the question of its relevance to organizational safety.
- What relevance to management is the number of port scans? What action should be taken?
- How many intrusions weren't detected?
- How important are the user accounts not in compliance?
- Are the open audit items critical?

The obvious conclusion is that none of these measurements provides guidance for management. They are not actionable for the management of a security program. They only indicate the possible need for further investigation. This is borne out by the results of a recent survey of security managers who stated that they use metrics and measures almost totally to support budget requests and expenditures, not to manage the program.

Improvements in these measurements will probably increase security of an organization. However, it cannot be determined if

- They will be inadequate, just enough, or too much
- These are the areas of greatest potential impact, or they will be addressed proportionately
- Resources are being allocated according to need and benefit
- Improvements will align optimally with, and support, organizational objectives

Perhaps most significantly, these measures provide little or no information on the greatest risk, the failure of adequate procedures, or procedural compliance.

There are numerous other metrics available for both technical and nontechnical performance measurement. Technical performance metrics might include

- System utilization
- Downtime
- Conformance to SLAs
- SPAM filtering effectiveness
- Number of attacks prevented, contained
- Incident response times
- Vulnerability discovery to remediation times
- Incident recovery times
- Disaster recovery test results

Performance metrics of nontechnical controls might include

- Failure rates of controls
- Effectiveness of controls
- Operational cost of controls
- Maintenance costs of controls
- Business impacts of controls
- Return on investment (ROI)
- Return on security investment (ROSI)
- Internal rate of return (IRR)
- Value at risk (VAR)
- Net present value (NPV)
- Key performance indicators (KPIs)
- Key goal indicators (KGIs)

3.1.2 Discussion

From a security management perspective, process or performance metrics are most effectively used to monitor processes critical or important to systems operations or when they are indicative of an impending threat or problem. They are more useful as "warning lights" than as management tools. They provide operational feedback but little, if any, strategic or management information.

These metrics operate on the premise that if the processes are understood and controlled, outcomes will be known. The problem with the approach conceptually is that a great deal of detail must be known and many of the processes must be measured to have reasonable assurance of desired results. For example, vulnerability scans are standard practice in most organizations. While knowing which vulnerabilities exist is useful for patch management or perhaps designing compensatory controls, it is of little use in attempting to manage a security department since little can be determined about risk or potential impacts or alignment with business objectives. Without knowing whether viable threats exist to exploit the vulnerabilities, risk cannot be determined and therefore cannot be "managed." Unless risk is ascertained and the value of potentially affected resources known, likelihood and impact cannot be calculated either.

As a general rule, process security metrics have been primarily developed for and are relevant to technical, or IT, security operations with possible exceptions for particularly critical processes or controls. Physical security metrics normally don't directly monitor processes but focus on performance or outcomes.

3.2 Financial Metrics

Organizations are generally run by numbers and increasingly security program management will be as well. Financial information is a type of "performance" metric that management is usually very interested in. In general, the more sophisticated an organization is, the more various financial metrics are being used to primarily determine the return on investment for various security projects or mechanisms. In these cases, financial metrics are used to develop business cases that justify program expenditures. Considerable research to develop better financial metrics continues. While financial metrics still suffer from a significant degree of speculation, they are an important approach for practitioners to consider.

In a compendium of classic papers on measuring corporate performance, respected management consultant Peter Drucker explains that, historically, financial performance metrics have been used to record the past. Computers have long since changed not only what a business is, but how financial and other information of all types is used by management.[2] Accordingly, we focus on the use of financial metrics and discuss their use in security program management.

Considerable research to develop better financial metrics for security management continues. The important thing to note as we proceed in this exploration is that current performance metrics still suffer from a significant degree of speculation. However, they are an important approach for practitioners to consider. In the following sections, we summarize some of the contemporary approaches to performance metrics.

3.2.1 Return on Investment (ROI)

Return on investment (ROI) is a classic measure of profitability. It is widely touted as a modern management technique and is generally used to compare alternative investment strategies. The basic notion of ROI is that the investment of capital is entitled to a return. As Allen Sweeny states in his 1979 classic *ROI—Basics for Nonfinancial Executives*, ROI is a classic tenet of money management that dates to ancient Greece and Biblical times.[3] ROI answers the question of which alternative investment will have the greatest return. That is, it measures the benefit or the loss that will result from an expenditure of resources. The goal can be to determine if an investment is justified by the savings, the earnings, or the intangible benefits that accrue to it.

The 2007 CSI Computer Crime and Security Survey points out that the use of ROI in information security management loosely refers to the time that it takes to recoup an investment—not the above conventional definition used in financial management.[4,5]

3.2.1.1 Payback Method

Perhaps the simplest metric for comparing investments is the payback method. It evaluates the future cash flow from an investment. It answers the question, "How long will it take to recoup the investment?" It is calculated by this formula:

$$\text{Payback Period} = \text{Investment} / \text{Cash Flow per Year}$$

If the payback period is less than or equal to the life of the project, then the investment *may* be warranted, all other things considered. In other words, it might be worthy of further investigation. If the payback period is greater than the life of the project, then the investment is quite likely not justified.

In *Financial Intelligence*, Berman and Knight point out that this method does not account for how much the investment will return over the life of the project:[6]

Strengths

■ Simple to use and explain
■ Is a simple and quick reality check

Weaknesses

■ Doesn't tell us much
■ Does not consider cash flow beyond break-even
■ Does not consider the time value of money
■ Compares two dissimilar factors: cash outlay today and projected cash flows tomorrow

As Berman and Knight phrase it, the payback method is only a rough rule of thumb.

3.2.1.2 ROI Calculation

The most basic ROI calculation is:

$$ROI = \text{Net Income} / \text{Net Investment}$$

More completely, here is how the ROI calculation nets out the income side:

$$ROI = \text{Expected Returns} - \text{Cost of Investment} / \text{Cost of Investment}$$

You can see how this can be useful in security management when the ROI calculation is expanded to take into consideration the accountant's view:

$$ROI = \text{Net Savings (Earnings) after Depreciation and Tax} / \text{Net Investment}$$

That is, the net income can be a savings.

There are several different ways to calculate ROI. This one is what nonfinancial people usually refer to as *ROI*. For completeness, it is important to note that in financial management, it is called the *accounting method* of ROI calculation. Some of the other methods of calculating ROI were mentioned earlier in the list of nontechnical controls. They include net present value (NPV), internal rate of return (IRR), and return on security investment (ROSI). The practitioner should be familiar with all of these methods since they are used to manage the business and they are useful in security program management.

Table 3.1 Information Security Management's Use of Business Judgment[21]

	ROI	NPV	IRR
2004	55%	25%	28%
2005	38%	18%	19%
2006	42%	19%	21%
2007	39%	21%	17%

The importance of this familiarity is illustrated by the annual CSI Computer Crime and Security Survey's results.[7] Information security practitioners are using ROI, NPV, and IRR. The CSI survey calls the use of these financial metrics *business judgment*. Starting in 2004, a question was added to the survey to find out how popular ROI, NPV, and IRR are.[8] Table 3.1 shows the CSI survey's findings from 2004 to 2007. In 2007, 5000 surveys were sent out, 494 were returned, and 314 people responded to the question about what form of business judgments were being used. Surveys were sent to information security practitioners in U.S. corporations, government agencies, financial institutions, medical institutions, and universities.

Allen Sweeny lists the strengths and weaknesses for the accounting method of calculating ROI:

Strengths

- Emphasizes the accounting for profit or loss
- Easy to calculate

Weaknesses

- Does not recognize the time value of money
- Assumes that the investment itself and its benefits will last for the depreciable life of the asset
- Does not give weight to the timing of cash flows

As you can see, the discussion of the methods of calculating ROI is a necessarily detailed business, one that is the stuff of financial managers and accountants. Accordingly, here we will briefly mention NPV and IRR, and spend more time on ROSI, a new ROSI, both derivatives of ROI.

Further exploration of these financial metrics can begin with Allen Sweeny's book and should continue with discussions with the organization's financial management and accounting professionals, hopefully resulting in the adoption of methods that match the way that organizations regularly use financial metrics. Indeed, for security managers a Master's in Business Administration (MBA) is becoming desirable.

3.2.1.3 NPV

Net present value (NPV) is a method of ROI calculation that acknowledges the fact that money has a "time value." That is, throughout recent history, the use of money has usually been rewarded with interest. The familiar savings account serves as an example of this. If you deposit $1.00 in a bank account that pays 10 percent compound interest year over year, you will have $1.61 at the end of 5 years. That $1.61 is the future value of the dollar that you are investing today.

Of more interest to us is today's value of a promised future value given an interest rate. That is, what is the present value of some money that we will receive in the future? Money has a time value because it is better to receive money today than it is to receive it tomorrow. If we have to wait to receive it, it is worth less to us. In other words, if we can get a 10 percent return (interest), what is the present value of the dollar we expect to receive in the future?

Present value is calculated like this:

$$\text{Present Value} = \text{Value Today} / \text{Future Value}$$

Again using our example of 10 percent interest (cost of money), the present value of $1 received in the future is .909. Again using the above example, we'd need to do the same calculation for years 2 through 5.

While useful, Sweeny points out that present value methods have strengths and weaknesses as well:

Strengths

- Measures the time value of money
- Concentrates on cash—both timing and the amounts of cash flows
- Facilitates ranking and comparison

Weaknesses

- More difficult to understand and calculate
- Does not readily relate to accounting for profit and loss
- Assumes cash flows can be invested at the same rate of return to discount the project

3.2.1.4 IRR

Internal rate of return (IRR) is a method of ROI calculation also called the *discounted cash flow* (DFC). Allen Sweeny explains IRR/DCF as seeking to find out whether the present value of cash earnings (savings), which equals the investment at a present value factor—rate of return—is acceptable. If that present value is equal to or greater than what is expected, then the investment is acceptable.

The details of present value methods such as NPV are the stuff of financial management and accountants. Security practitioners need a basic understanding of these methods beyond what we can present here. However, their primary responsibility is to consult with their organization's financial management and accountants to find out what methods are in use, and then to employ these in their analysis work and their proposals.

ROI, IRR, and NPV are well discussed in more detail in the financial management literature.

3.2.2 Return on Security Investment (ROSI)

The obvious weakness of using ROI for information security management is that it does not explicitly factor risk into the calculation.

In security management it is also necessary to account for risk mitigation. Moreover, since there is no such thing as solutions that deliver 100 percent security, it is important to take into consideration how much a particular solution mitigates risks.

3.2.2.1 SLE and ALE

The time-honored way of representing risk is to express it as the amount of the loss that will be experienced with a Single Loss Expectancy (SLE).

SLE can be defined as the monetary value that is expected from the manifestation of a threat that results in an impact:

$$\text{Single Loss Expectancy (SLE)} = \text{Asset Value} \times \text{Exposure Factor}$$

where the exposure factor is the percentage of asset lost in an incident. As an example, if the value of the asset is reduced by two-thirds, the exposure factor value is .66. If the asset is completely lost, the exposure factor is 1.0. The result is a monetary value that is in the same units in which the asset value is expressed (Euros, dollars, yen, etc.).

The well-known single loss expectancy (SLE) and annual loss expectancy (ALE) approach has been subject to a great deal of criticism and has fallen out of favor as it has become abundantly evident that finding any substantive basis for determining the "expectancy" has not been found.

$$\text{Annual Loss Expectancy (ALE)} = \text{SLE} \times \text{Annual Rate of Occurrence (ARO)}$$

The annual rate of occurrence (ARO) is the estimated number of times a threat on a single asset is estimated to occur. The higher the risk associated with the threat, the higher the ARO. For example, if insurance data suggests that a serious fire is likely to occur once in 25 years, then the ARO is 1/25 = 0.04.

3.2.2.2 ROSI

Return on security investment (ROSI) was introduced in 2002. It is a derivative of ROI. ROSI deals with balancing risk and the cost of a mitigating (risk-reducing) solution for that risk. ROSI uses single loss expectancy (SLE) to calculate *risk exposure*, or annual loss expectancy (ALE).

As discussed, SLE is the cost of a single loss. It is expressed as the value of an asset value and an exposure factor for that asset. ALE is the SLE multiplied by the frequency of occurrence, typically the number of such losses over the course of one year.

This risk exposure is then multiplied by the percentage of the risk that is mitigated (or reduced) by the solution under consideration. Then, the solution cost is subtracted to produce a numerator. Finally, this derived value is divided by the solution cost to yield the ROSI.

For comparison, here are the ROI and ROSI calculations:

ROI = Expected Returns − Cost of Investment / Cost of Investment

ROSI = (Risk Exposure * %Risk Mitigated) − Solution Cost / Solution Cost

The weakness of the ROSI approach is the high degree of guesswork involved in determining the risk exposure, as well as the extent to which a particular solution will reduce either the frequency of occurrence or the magnitude of the impact of a loss.

3.2.2.3 A New ROSI Model

In 2004, Lockstep Consulting proposed an improved ROSI model for the Australian government. This new ROSI combines the annualized loss expectancy method and the Australian Standard Threat & Risk Assessment (TRA) framework. It adds likelihood and severity estimates to provide greater granularity and increased accuracy. This report explains the improved ROSI as follows:

A hybrid ROSI model, combining Annualised Loss Expectancy and Australian-standard Threat and Risk Assessment (TRA), is proposed, and recommended for four reasons:

1. The proposed model is financially quantitative,
2. It separates out the contributions made to the overall cost-benefit by different security countermeasures,
3. It makes use of a widely familiar security tool, making it easy to grasp with minimal new training, and

4. The model is readily extendible to provide statistical modeling of the spread of security costs given the variable nature of likelihood and impact of real life security threats.

The proposed ROSI model augments the TRA table with quantified likelihood and severity estimates, to produce a "bottom up" calculation of expected annual losses with and without treatment by security countermeasures.[9]

The basic ROSI tool augments the standard TRA table as follows:

- For each threat, the tool incorporates the corresponding annual frequency and the per-incident cost.
- For each threat, the tool calculates the expected annual untreated cost (being simply the product of the annual frequency and the per-incident cost).
- For each proposed countermeasure, the user enters the anticipated upfront cost of implementation, the annual cost of maintaining the countermeasure, and the amortization period (number of years) over which the upfront cost is to be spread when calculating return.
- For each countermeasure—or collected set of countermeasures—the user enters the residual likelihood and severity anticipated after treatment.
- Finally, for each threat, the tool calculates the expected annual treated cost.

The following figures illustrate the basic tool in action. It is based on an extract from an actual government Threat & Risk Assessment. Parts of the tables shaded grey are taken from the original TRA (Figures 3.1 and 3.2).

3.2.2.4 A More Complex Security ROI

In practice, the calculation of ROI is a bit more complicated than the foregoing calculation in Section 3.2.1.2. Complicating matters include the fact that different industries and sectors of the economy calculate ROI differently. As Debra Herman points out, ROI can alternatively mean other things besides profit[10]:

- Increased operational efficiency
- Cost avoidance
- Cost savings
- Loss prevention

Herman points out that costs can be direct, indirect, or a combination of both. Moreover, she illustrates that ROI calculations on security expenditures is complex. In her extensive treatment of security ROI calculation, Herman presents a *Taxonomy of Security ROI Parameters* that includes

No.	Asset	Potential Incident (Threat to the Asset)	Likelihood	Severity	Estimated Risk	Annual rate of occurrence	Direct Cost per incident	Opportunity Cost per incident	Total UNTREATED Annual Cost
A8	Availability of D-XYZ internet connection	Destruction of key infrastructure e.g. routers, PIX, switches)	Negligible	Serious	Nil	0.05	$ 1,000,000		$ 50,000
A9		Failure of Cooling System	Medium	Significant	Medium	2	$ 10,000		$ 20,000
A10		Mis-configuration of key infrastructure e.g. routers, PIX, switches)	Low	Serious	High	1	$ 1,000,000		$ 1,000,000
A11		Hardware failure of key infrastructure e.g. routers, PIX, switches)	Very Low	Damaging	Low	0.5	$ 100,000		$ 50,000
A12		Incorrect building patching	Low	Significant	Medium	1	$ 10,000		$ 10,000
A13		Denial of service attack on carrier or provider network infrastructure	Very Low	Significant	Low	0.5	$ 10,000		$ 5,000
A14		DNS hardware failure	Negligible	Damaging	Nil	0.05	$ 100,000		$ 5,000
A15	Availability of D-XYZ internet email	Denial of service attack on email system	High	Damaging	High	12	$ 100,000		$ 1,200,000

Figure 3.1   TRA with calculated annual cost of incidents, untreated.

No.	Counter Measures	Upfront Cost per Counter-measure	Recurring Cost per Counter-measure	Residual likelihood	Residual severity	Total TREATED Annual Cost	Saving Per Threat	Notes on mitigations
A8	Business Continuity Plan (1)	$ 50,000	$ 20,000					
	Spare parts (4)	$ 50,000	$ 10,000					
	Service level agreements (5)	$ 0	$ 0					
	Physical security (access control procedures and controls for computer room) (6)	$ 10,000	$ 10,000	Negligible	Minor	$ 50	$ 49,950	Harm reduced to Minor by BCP; Likelihood to Very Low by Environ controls
A9	Environmental controls for computer room (2)	$ 30,000	$ 5,000		Minor			
	Business Continuity Plan (1)	Counted	Counted					
	Service level agreements (5)	Counted	Counted	Very low		$ 500	$ 19,500	Likelihood reduced to Negligible by Config Mgt
A10	Configuration management system (8)	$ 70,000	$ 10,000					
	Change control procedures (15)	$ 30,000	$ 5,000	Negligible	Serious	$ 50,000	$ 950,000	
A11	Business Continuity Plan (1)	Counted	Counted					Won't affect the likelihood of an event, but reduces harm by better recovery
	Spare parts (4)	Counted	Counted					
	Service level agreements (5)	Counted	Counted	Very low	Minor	$ 500	$ 49,500	
A12	Standards for cabling including labelling and coding (9)	$ 10,000	$ 0					
	Physical security (6)	Counted	Counted	Very low	Significant	$ 5,000	$ 5,000	
A13	Large capacity network connection (10)	$ 10,000	$ 10,000	Very low	Minor	$ 500	$ 4,500	Redundancy means minor effect on failover
A14	Redundant Internet connection (7)	$ 10,000	$ 0					
	Replication of DNS server (11)	$ 10,000	$ 20,000	Negligible	Minor	$ 50	$ 4,950	No amelioration of degree of harm
A15	Network based Intrusion Detection System (NIDS) (12)	$ 70,000						
	Use DSD evaluated products (13)	$ 20,000	$ 5,000					
	Deny all unless explicitly allowed firewall rules (14)	$ 0	$ 0	Low	Significant	$ 10,000	$ 1,190,000	

Figure 3.2 TRA with calculated annual cost of incidents, treated.

- Problem identification and characterization
- Total cost of security feature, function, or control
- Depreciation period
- Tangible benefits—worst case, best case
- Intangible benefits—worst case, best case
- Payback period
- Comparative analysis of costs
- Assumptions

In any case, risk is factored into the calculation. However, all but the most narrowly scoped ROI calculations suffer from one shortcoming: They all depend on considerable guesswork.

3.2.3 Security Attribute Evaluation Method (SAEM)

A PhD thesis at Carnegie Mellon University on an approach titled the Security Attribute Evaluation Method[11] addresses the issue of cost-benefit analysis of security attributes in different architectures providing a basis for design decisions. The process requires a multiattribute risk assessment to create a prioritized list of risks that are then evaluated by security specialists to estimate controls benefits of mitigation options. Multiattribute analysis, traditionally used in the Decision Sciences, is used to systematically evaluate decision alternatives when the decision outcomes are uncertain. Multiattribute methods used in risk assessments result in a *threat index* for each risk based on estimations of threat frequencies and expected outcomes. An outcome can have several consequences. For example, an attack could result in lost revenue, public embarrassment, and regulatory penalties. These consequences are called *attributes* in multiattribute analysis. As a result, an outcome is a vector of attributes where the value of the attribute is the level of damage.

3.2.4 Cost-Effectiveness Analysis

Cost-effectiveness analysis (CEA) is a form of economic analysis that compares the relative expenditure (costs) and outcomes (effects) of two or more courses of action. Cost-effectiveness analysis is often used where a full cost-benefit analysis is inappropriate; e.g., the problem is to determine how best to comply with a legal requirement.

CEA is a technique for comparing the relative value of various strategies. In its most common form, a new strategy is compared with current practice (the "low-cost alternative") in the calculation of the cost-effectiveness ratio:

$$\text{CE ratio} \frac{\text{cost}_{\text{new strategy}} - \text{cost}_{\text{current practice}}}{\text{effect}_{\text{new strategy}} - \text{effect}_{\text{current practice}}}$$

The result might be considered to be the "price" of the additional outcome purchased by switching from current practice to the new strategy.

3.2.4.1 Cost-Benefit Analysis

Closely related formal techniques include cost-benefit analysis and benefit-effectiveness analysis. Cost benefit is typically used to determine the financial feasibility of a particular course of action and may be used to compare options as well. At the most basic level it consists of totaling all relevant costs compared to all benefits reduced to financial terms. In some cases both intangible costs and benefits may be difficult to quantify, as in the case of the possible benefit of improved public perception of an organization. The intangible costs from a breach, such as reputation damage, can also be difficult to reduce to purely financial terms.

3.2.5 Fault Tree Analysis

Fault tree analysis is explained in the following extract from *The Fault Tree Handbook* prepared by NASA:

> While not traditionally a cost-benefit tool, Fault Tree Analysis (FTA) and its spin-off methods such as Failure Modes Effects [and Criticality] Analysis (FMEA and FMECA) seem to have promise for studying the root causes of security breaches and the mitigating effects of countermeasures. A Fault Tree is a graphical tool which attempts to trace all failure modes of a complex system back to logical combinations—simply AND and OR relationships—of component failures. If good data is available on the failure rates of all critical components, then FTA can generate the expected failure rate of the overall system.
>
> To apply this technique to IT security, we might produce a tree that portrays the cause-and-effect relationships between attack vectors and system failure. The application of countermeasures would be expected to prune branches of the tree, so that the overall effect with and without treatment could be compared.
>
> Importantly, orthodox FTA is based on the twin assumptions that (1) components fail randomly according to well characterised statistics, and (2) at the lowest level of the tree, component failures are independent of one another. Yet in software and therefore in IT security, failures are not random, but rather are due to systematic design error. Further, it is in the nature of most software that the failure of one line of code can indeed affect other parts of the program. Therefore we believe caution is needed in applying FTA and related reliability engineering techniques to IT security. It was beyond the scope of the present study to explore these issues in more depth. The fact that IT security incidents are often

the result of deliberate actions rather than bottom up component failures is another complication worthy of further study.[12]

3.2.6 Value at Risk (VAR)

Value at risk (VAR) is a mathematical analysis of the probability of the extent to which losses to assets will occur during a certain period of time with typically a confidence factor of 95 or 99 percent. While widely used in financial institutions to determine the amount of reserves they should maintain, it is a general concept that research indicates may be a suitable approach for information security management.

> Value at Risk (VAR), a new methodology for Information Security Risk Assessment. VAR summarizes the worst loss due to a security breach over a target horizon, with a given level of confidence. More formally, VAR describes the quantile of the projected distribution of losses over a given time period. Most of the tools that are used for ISEC risk assessment are qualitative in nature and are not grounded in theory. VAR is a useful tool in the hands of an ISEC expert as it provides a theoretically based, quantitative measure of information security risk. Using this measure of risk, the best possible balance between risk and cost of providing security can be achieved. Most organizations, especially those heavily invested in eBusiness, already have determined the acceptable level of risk. The dollar amount of this risk is then computed. When the total VAR of an organization exceeds this amount, the organization is alerted to the fact that an increased security investment is required.[13]

3.2.7 ALE/SLE

The well-known single loss expectancy (SLE) and annual loss expectancy (ALE) approach has been subject to a great deal of criticism and has fallen out of favor as it has become abundantly evident that finding any substantive basis for determining expectancy has not been found.

Single loss expectancy can be defined as the monetary value expected from the manifestation of a threat resulting in an impact, which is mathematically expressed as:

Single Loss Expectancy (SLE) = Asset Value × Exposure Factor

where the exposure factor is represented as the percentage of asset lost. As an example, if the value of the asset is reduced by two thirds, the exposure factor value is .66. If the asset is completely lost, the exposure factor is 1.0. The result is a monetary value in the same unit as the single loss expectancy is expressed (Euros, dollars, yen, etc.).

The Annual Loss Expectancy (ALE) = SLE × Annualize Rate of Occurrence (ARO)

The annual rate of occurrence (ARO) is the estimated number of times a threat on a single asset is estimated to occur. The higher the risk associated with the threat, the higher the ARO. For example, if insurance data suggests that a serious fire is likely to occur once in 25 years, then the annualized rate of occurrence is 1/25 = 0.04.

3.3 Qualitative Security Metrics

The range of qualitative metrics is equally diverse. Often less favored as being generally imprecise and relatively subjective, they can be provided by a variety of methods generally providing indicators for such things as process quality, operational maturity, or multiple dimensions provided by a balanced scorecard approach. For many or most management activities, qualitative metrics are likely to be more useful than available quantitative measures for managing a security program. While most available metrics regarding information systems is "hard" numerical data, interpreting the data into meaningful management information is usually imprecise and speculative. As previously mentioned, the typical type of available data includes such things as the number of viruses detected, which only invites the more meaningful question, "How many viruses weren't detected?"

This will change in time since organizations are managed primarily by numbers and for several decades there have been efforts to quantify financially the aspects of risk to manage security activities. These efforts include the often questionable computations of annual loss expectancy (ALE) and single loss expectancy (SLE) in an effort to quantify risk in financial terms and provide guidance to protection efforts. Significant efforts have been expended on other financial metrics such as value at risk (VAR), return on security investment (ROSI), net present value (NPV), return on investment (ROI), internal rate of return (IRR), and others. These metrics, while quantitative in their outputs, are highly qualitative as far as their inputs.

This is not to suggest that they are without merit; they may be useful in many situations. It is just to make it clear that these are really qualitative metrics in the guise of quantitative ones. If used in the qualitative sense with consistent and standardized methodologies, they will provide *relative* values that can be useful for allocating resources and prioritizing protection efforts.

There is also a class of quasimetrics or soft-metrics identified as *indicators*. These include key performance indicators (KPIs), key goal indicators (KGIs), and key success factors (KSFs). Sometimes included in this group are critical success factors (CSFs). For some activities the KGIs can be relatively precise, as can the KPIs.

Key goal indicators can to some extent serve the requirement for setting objectives as previously discussed. Once objectives are reasonably defined, key performance indicators can be developed as metrics of progress against the goal. KPIs will usually be most effective if agreed upon by all stakeholders. This will provide some assurance that the information will be meaningful.

3.3.1 Cultural Metrics

Corporate culture may, in the final analysis, be the single most significant determinant of security in an organization. Auditors recognize the impact of culture by opining as to the "tone at top," essentially an understanding that without support from senior management resulting in a culture conducive to good security, it will be difficult, if not impossible, to achieve.

> The contemporary definition of organizational culture (OC) includes what is valued, the dominant leadership style, the language and symbols, the procedures and routines, and the definitions of success that characterize an organization. OC represents the values, underlying assumptions, expectations, collective memories, and definitions present in an organization.[14]

Studies in a branch of psychology called *behavioral economics* dealing with, among other things, departure from rational choice have exposed many of the cultural factors that can undermine efforts at achieving good security. Some of these include selective recall and biased assimilation. Selective recall is the normal inclination of individuals to remember only those facts that support their current position. Biased assimilation is the mechanism by which individuals conform their beliefs about risk to their cultural evaluation of the activities being assessed. In other words, their cultural worldviews determine the interpretation and significance of facts. Worldviews can be assessed in several ways, but one standard approach will place individuals somewhere on a chart with hierarchists and individualists on opposite ends of one dimension, and egalitarians and communitarians on opposite ends of the other dimension.

Studies show that determining these worldviews is highly predictive of widely varying individual response to the same set of facts regarding, among other things, risk. It is a safe assumption that corporate managers considering risks to the organization are subject to the same mechanisms and will tend to respond in a similar manner.

The implications for information security and risk management are significant.

3.3.2 Risk Management through Cultural Theory

Applying aspects of culture to risk management, a recent article titled, "Formulating Information Systems Risk Management Strategies through Cultural Theory,"[15] made a compelling case for a cultural metric. The two dimensions provide a framework of four types of "ways of life" or worldviews, namely, hierarchy and egalitarianism, fatalism and individualism (Figure 3.3).

Hierachists are characterized by their adherence to structure and established classifications such as race, gender, and age. They are primarily concerned with things that disrupt the social order and typically place a great deal of faith in experts.

Those with an egalitarian worldview believe that merit and charisma are the requirements of leadership, and authority is not granted by virtue of position.

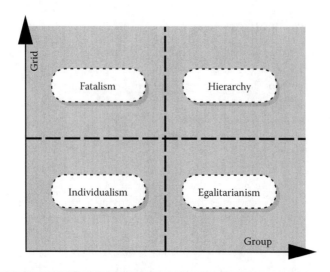

Figure 3.3 Ways of life.

Characterized by a strong sense of equality, they are concerned with situations or events that might increase inequalities among individuals. They are typically skeptical of experts and suspicious of their authority and prefer to make their own decisions based on copious information.

Individualists do not feel bound by roles and believe boundaries are subject to negotiation. Social norms are usually of little concern, and they are typically worried about events or situations that might limit their freedom. They may be reluctant to follow procedures and abide by rules insofar as they might limit their autonomy.

Fatalists generally see themselves as outsiders with little control or impact on their environment. They typically follow the rules and often believe social classification should be based on ancestry. They generally prefer routine jobs and would rather be unaware of risks since they consider them unavoidable and not within their power to deal with.

These generalizations may be relevant to consider although the extent to which any individual will fit the stereotype will differ considerably. Nevertheless, the risks to the organization posed by personnel with different worldviews are quite different in degree and type and have identifiable characteristics, some of which have been identified above. Depending on the criticality of security activities, these are issues that may be of relevance to security managers.

3.3.3 The Competing Values Framework

The competing values framework is based on a series of empirical studies of organizational effectiveness.[16] The results were the discovery of two dimensions of effectiveness. The first is related to organizational focus, the polarities being an internal focus on the people in the organization to an external focus of the organization itself. The second dimension represents the contrast between stability and control and flexibility and change.

The competing values framework received its name because the criteria within the four models seem at first to carry conflicting messages. Organizations should be on the one hand adaptable and flexible and on the other stable and controlled.

The University of Twente in the Netherlands published the following article describing the framework. Appendix D has the complete assessment process, called the *Organization Culture Assessment Instrument (OCAI)*.

Core Assumptions and Statements

The framework has four quadrants as shown in Figure 3.4.

1. Internal Process Model: Based on hierarchy, emphasis on measurement, documentation and information management. These processes bring stability and control. Hierarchies seem to function best when the task to be done is well understood and when time is not an important factor.
2. Open Systems Model: Based on an organic system, emphasis on adaptability, readiness, growth, resource acquisition and external support. These processes bring innovation and creativity. People are not controlled but inspired.
3. Rational Goal Model: Based on profit, emphasis on rational action. It assumes that planning and goal setting results into productivity and efficiency. Tasks are clarified; objectives are set and action is taken.

	Flexibility and discretion		
Internal	**Clan**	**Adhocracy**	External
focus and integration	**Hierarchy**	**Market**	focus and differentiation
	Stability and control		

Figure 3.4 Competing values map.

4. Human Relations Model: Based on cohesion and morale with emphasis on human resource and training. People are seen not as isolated individuals, but as cooperating members of a common social system with a common stake in what happens.

While the models seem to be four entirely different perspectives or domains, they can be viewed as closely related and interwoven. They are four subdomains of a larger construct: organizational and managerial effectiveness. The four models in the framework represent the unseen values by which people, programs, policies, and organizations live and die.

3.3.4 Organizational Structure

Organizational structure is arguably one of the manifestations of organizational culture. If that is accurate, it can be assumed that it is also the major factor in the implementation of information security. The problem then is to determine how an organization is functionally structured, which is invariably different from what is represented by the organizational charts. A more accurate approach to the inner workings of an organization can be represented by a sociogram or sociomap. The field of sociometry has developed several approaches to determine the centers of influence in an organization by mapping the number and strength of linkages between various members of the organizations. Two methods are described in Wikipedia:

WIND

These types of Sociomaps are used in political and marketing research (STORM stands for Subject To Object Relation Mapping). Data used for these types of maps are rectangular matrices, where each respondent rates preference of selected objects, such as political parties, brands, products, and so on. In order to create a Sociomap, for each object a position in the map is calculated, and all respondents (becoming a kind of granule) are placed on the map according to their preferences—the distance of the granule to objects is proportional to respondent's preferences of the objects. On the places in the map where more respondents gather, hills start to form, so the final Sociomap depicts typical configurations of preferences by hills formed under or between the objects (in this sense a STORM Sociomap is a data mining approach based on visual pattern recognition). In the following step, undecided voters or customers (the hills between the objects) can be visualized and analyzed. This type of analysis therefore enables one to visualize preferences and target specific groups of respondents with similar preferences or attitudes.

While it may not be entirely evident to what extent structure is directly relevant to security, certainly it is helpful to know the centers of influence to more efficiently target the case for security or efforts to modify culture. It will also be helpful to know if the centers of influence are the centers of resistance to security:

The Informal Organization

We now know that work doesn't really get done through the formal boxes on the org chart, and neither does security. If you were to map the flow of influence in your organization (a "sociogram"), you would find that real influence flows through multiple "hubs" that have very little relationship to the formal org chart. A hub is often a person with high levels of influence and information in the system. These persons are shown to have multiple linkages that connect them widely throughout the organization. Their many connections often exist because of informal power, credibility, influence, and expertise, qualities that the old-style organizational charts never see and therefore never portray.[17]

3.4 Hybrid Approaches

Efforts to provide more comprehensive "holistic" measures of security have been or are in the process of being developed. The concept is to widen the scope of data collected to provide a more realistic and hopefully more useful picture of the multidimensional aspects of security.

3.4.1 Systemic Security Management

Issues that have begun to be considered by emerging security models such as the systemic security management approach adds, in addition to the usual elements of people, processes and technology, the relevance of culture and organizational structure to the practice of security as shown in Figure 3.5.

To sum up the ICIIP Model and its rationale, we intend to show that security issues have been studied too simplistically, as a somewhat static and two-dimensional collection of three independent issues. To do it justice, security needs to study not only a three-dimensional concept (with the added issue of organizational design), but also requires an appreciation and understanding of how people, process, technology, and organizational design all interact among themselves to create that complex mix of elements and issues that the question of security really is.[18]

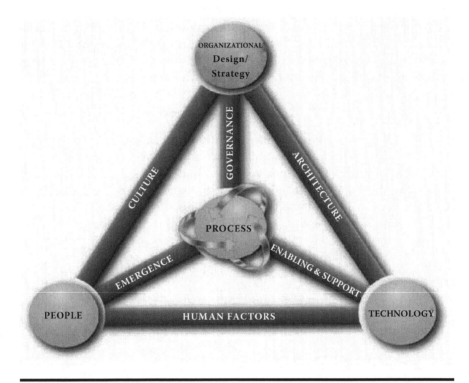

Figure 3.5   Balanced scorecard.

3.4.2 Balanced Scorecard

The balanced scorecard (BSC) has many adherents in part because it is one of the few existing measurement methods useful for supporting strategic and management decisions. The multidimensional approach combining a quantitative financial measure with a set of qualitative measures can serve to translate an organization's strategic objectives into a coherent set of performance measures.

> Balanced scorecard (BSC) is a tool that translates an organization's mission and strategy into a comprehensive set of performance measures that provides the framework for a strategic measurement and management system.[19]

There are four perspectives for the measurements:

1. The Financial Perspective—Covering the traditional measurements of cost per unit, revenue growth, profitability, gearing, etc.
2. The Customer Perspective—Covering both subjective measurements (such as customer satisfaction surveys) and objective measurements (such as customer acquisition rates, customer retention rates, etc.).

3. The Internal Process Perspective—Focusing on efficiency measures such as how long it takes to answer a customer query, fulfill a customer order, open a new customer account, etc.
4. The Innovation and Learning Perspective—Addressing the need to change and adapt constantly through measurements of investment in training, innovation processes, etc.

Balancing these four perspectives in terms of goals with matching measurements provides a more holistic and useful view of what the organization needs to be achieved (Figure 3.6).

The Balanced Scorecard Collaborative Web site states the benefits of using BSC:

- Clarify the vision throughout the organization;
- Gain consensus and ownership by the executive team;
- Provide a framework to align the organization;
- Provide structure for multiple initiatives;
- Drive the capital and resource allocation process;
- Integrate the strategic management process across the organization;
- Focus teams and individuals on strategic priorities.

The Collaborative goes on to state:

The Balanced Scorecard is a powerful framework to help organizations rapidly implement strategy by translating the vision and strategy into a set of operational objectives that can drive behavior, and therefore, performance. Strategy-driven performance measures provide the essential

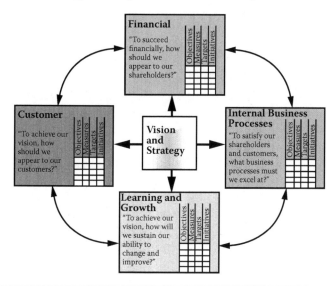

Figure 3.6   Balanced business scorecard.

feedback mechanism required to dynamically adjust and refine the organization's strategy over time. The Balanced Scorecard concept is built upon the premise that what is measured is what motivates organizational stakeholders to act. Ultimately all of the organization's activities, resources, and initiatives should be aligned to the strategy. The Balanced Scorecard achieves this goal by explicitly defining the cause and effect relationships between objectives, measures, and initiatives across each perspective and down through all levels of the organization. Developing a Balanced Scorecard is the first step in creating a Strategy-Focused Organization.[20]

Creating a Strategy-Focused Organization is based on five principles:

1. Translate strategy into operational terms and performance objectives;
2. Align the organization to the strategy;
3. Motivate the people by making strategy everyone's job;
4. Adapt to make strategy a continual process of change;
5. Mobilize the resources for ongoing change through executive leadership.

The five principles of the Strategy-Focused Organization illustrate how Balanced Scorecard adopters have taken their groundbreaking tool to the next level. These organizations have used the Scorecard to create an entirely new performance management framework that puts strategy at the centre of key management processes and systems. In general, situations where there is a lack of focus or direction, a new strategy, or a need to achieve organizational alignment to a common vision, are conducive to the Balanced Scorecard approach.

3.4.3 The SABSA Business Attributes Approach

The SABSA (Sherwood Applied Business Security Architecture) approach views business risk as something that is a threat to a "business virtue," which is something of value requiring protection. These "virtues" are labeled *business attributes* and experience of the authors has identified 85, which are shown in Figure 3.7 and classified under seven specific headings.

The attributes are derived from "business drivers," which are the needs of the business in terms of security, such as availability, access control, and integrity. Each of the identified business security drivers is mapped to one or more attributes.

Regardless of the organization or sector, the business drivers are much the same, and experience shows that this taxonomy of business attributes is universal.

Appendix C provides detailed definitions for each business attribute in the diagram.

The business attributes have been arranged in seven major classes:

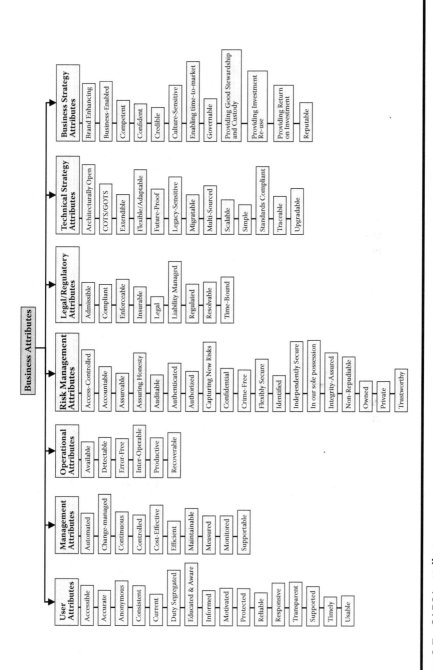

Figure 3.7   **SABSA attributes.**

- User Attributes—Relating to the users' experience of security in the system
- Management Attributes—The security requirements for managing the system
- Operational Attributes—Concerned with security that protects day-to-day operations
- Risk Management Attributes—Comprising the usual extended set of "security" requirements to identify and manage business risks
- Legal and Regulatory Attributes—Covering compliance issues
- Technical Strategy Attributes—Addressing the strategic aspects of technical architecture
- Business Strategy Attributes—What the senior managers and the board want to see

From a metrics perspective, each of the attributes addressed by an architecture requires measurement in some manner. The table in Appendix C describes a possible metric, measure, or means to monitor each of the attributes identified in Figure 3.6.

3.5 Quality Metrics

Quality can be a useful measure of some security-related activities but is more likely to be a meaningful characteristic of metrics themselves. The quality of security processes in terms of the number of errors per million operations (Six Sigma metric) can be used, but where there is an option it is not going to be as meaningful as measuring directly the outcome of the activity itself. As an example, the quality of a speedometer, including its accuracy, is useful for selecting the instrument and the degree to which you can trust its readings but is not indicative of how fast you are traveling. So, while higher quality of processes may result in better outcomes, correlating quality of process to its effectiveness is not possible to any significant degree. In other words, doubling the quality of a security activity won't typically cut the risk in half.

Nevertheless, there are some activities where direct results cannot be measured or feedback will be delayed, rendering it ineffective as management information. An example could be the handling of PII (personally identifiable information) or other protected or classified material. Under these circumstances, the quality of the handling process is the only assurance measure available other than the negative feedback that might result from a significant breach. The quality of a process will provide only a measure of assurance provided the process has been shown to be correct and that proper execution leads to the desired results.

Good quality of bad processes is not likely to produce the desired results.

3.5.1 Six Sigma

Six Sigma is a popular methodology used to manage process variations that cause defects, or errors, defined as unacceptable deviation from the mean or target. The objective is to systematically develop processes to manage variations that cause defects to less than 3.4 per million events.

There is some debate as to the origins, with conflicting claims about who actually developed the methodologies, but Six Sigma is nevertheless a well-developed approach to statistical quality control that has seen application in a variety of fields in a number of organizations. The tools used by and for Six Sigma are actually a subset of the quality engineering discipline and can be considered to be a part of the ASQ Certified Quality Engineer body of knowledge.

The Six Sigma methodology focuses on process improvement by reducing variances using a measurement strategy. Two methodologies are employed: DMAIC, the acronym for define, measure, analyze, improve, and control, which targets existing processes that do not meet defined targets; and DMADV (define, measure, analyze, design, and verify), which is an process improvement system for new processes and products.

3.5.2 ISO 9000

ISO 9000 is a group of international quality management standards originally designated 9001, 9002, and 9003. These have been integrated in the new ISO 9001:2000 and are supported by standards bodies in more than 120 countries. Certification of quality systems by external agencies is available for the standard. This standard has not seen significant use in information security but can be an effective approach to managing security services delivery.

The approach is based on eight fundamental principles:

1. Focus on your customers
2. Provide leadership
3. Involve your people
4. Use a process approach
5. Take a systems approach
6. Encourage continual improvement
7. Get the facts before making decisions
8. Work with your suppliers

3.5.3 Maturity Level

The Capability Maturity Model (CMM) in its many variants is based on the original model developed by the Software Engineering Institute in the mid-1980s. It is a process improvement approach based on a process model. A process model is basically a structured collection of practices that have proven effective over time. CMM uses a scale of five process maturity levels, ranking any process according to its level of maturity in terms of good practices with demonstrated effectiveness.

The subject areas can be as diverse as software engineering, systems engineering, project management, risk management, system acquisition, services, and personnel management.

CMM is based on a description of the attributes of five levels of "maturity" of organizational structures and processes. A number of variations have been developed based on the original. While quite descriptive and easy to use, almost intuitive, it is fairly subjective.

ISACA has developed a version of CMM used in CobiT based on the following five levels:

1. Ad Hoc: Risks are considered on an ad-hoc basis, and no formal processes exist.
2. Repeatable but Intuitive: There is an emerging understanding of risk and the need for security.
3. Defined Process: Company-wide risk management policies and security awareness.
4. Managed and Measurable: Risk assessments are standard procedure. Roles and responsibilities are assigned. Policies and standards have been developed.
5. Optimized: Organization-wide processes implemented, monitored, and managed.

While software development was the original focus of CMM, the approach works for any set of processes. NIST uses a modified version of CMM, which is available on their Web site.

A complete sample description for security of each of the five maturity levels can be found in Appendix F.

3.5.4 Benchmarking

Benchmarking is essentially the process of comparing performance, operations, or any other factors against a group of other similar organizations to provide a measure of where the organization stands. It can be used as a process for improving certain aspects of security or, as is more common, to provide justification for doing more or not. If another organization is achieving better results at lower costs, it can serve as guidance for a security program as well.

From a regulatory compliance perspective, management may consider it sensible to benchmark other organizations to satisfy the "standard and customary" aspect of due care and avoid being the least compliant, thereby risking regulatory enforcement actions. The risk posed by this approach is that many organizations may be subject to a common threat if they rely on having similar processes and levels of security.

3.5.5 Standards

Standards can serve as the baseline for metrics insofar as compliance is measured. A number of them, such as CobiT, have extensive, well-developed frameworks for management and IT security metrics primarily using a version of the Capability Maturity Model (CMM). The prevailing commercial standards include

- ISO/IEC 27001:2005 Information Security Standard
- ISO/IEC 17799:2005 Code of Security Practice
- ISO/PAS 28000:2005 Specification for security management systems for global supply chains
- CobiT
- ISMS

3.5.6 OCTAVE

Developed by the Carnegie Mellon Software Engineering Institute, the Operationally Critical Threat, Asset, and Vulnerability Evaluation (OCTAVE) criteria define a standard approach for an operational risk-driven, asset- and practice-based information security evaluation. It uses a three-phase approach to examine organizational and technology issues to assemble a comprehensive picture of an organization's security needs:

1. Identifying critical assets and threats to those assets
2. Identifying the vulnerabilities, both organizational and technological, that expose those threats creating risk to the organization
3. Developing a practice-based protection strategy and risk mitigation plan to support the organization's mission and priorities

Endnotes

1. "Best Practices in Security Governance," Aberdeen Group, U.S.A., 2005.
2. Drucker, Peter. "The Information Executives Truly Need." In *Harvard Business Review on Measuring Corporate Performance*. Harvard Business School Publishing, Boston, MA.
3. Sweeny, Allan (1979). "Return on Investment: The Concept and Its Importance." In *ROI Basics for Nonfinancial Executives*. AMACOM, New York, NY.
4. Formerly titled the CSI/FBI Computer Crime and Security Survey, now titled the CSI Computer Crime and Security Survey. Available free of charge at the Computer Security Institute, http://www/gocsi.com
5. CSI Survey 2007—The 12th Annual Computer Crime and Security Survey, Business Justifications. Computer Security Institute. http://www.gocsi.com
6. Berman, Karen and Joe Knight (2006). "Figuring ROI." *Financial Intelligence—A Manager's Guide to Knowing What the Numbers Really Mean*. Harvard Business School Press, Boston, MA.
7. Formerly titled the CSI/FBI Computer Crime and Security Survey, now titled the CSI Computer Crime and Security Survey. Available free of charge at the Computer Security Institute, http://www/gocsi.com
8. CSI Survey 2007—The 12th Annual Computer Crime and Security Survey, Computer Security Institute.

9. A Guide for Government Agencies Calculating Return on Security Investment, Version 2.0. Lockstep Consulting, June 13, 2004.
10. Herman, Debra (2007). "Measuring Return on Investment (ROI) in Physical, Personnel, IT, and Operational Security Controls." In *Complete Guide to Security and Privacy Metrics*. Boca Raton, FL: Auerbach Publications.
11. Butler, Shawn A. "Security Attribute Evaluation Method: A Cost-Benefit Approach," Computer Science Department, Carnegie Mellon University, Pittsburgh, PA.
12. NASA, *Fault Tree Handbook with Aerospace Applications*, Version 1.1.
13. Jaisingh, Jeevan and Jackie Rees. "Value at Risk: A Methodology for Information Security Risk Assessment." Krannert Graduate School of Management, Purdue University.
14. Schein, Edgar (1992). *Organizational Culture and Leadership*, Jossey-Bass, San Francisco. Cameron, Kim S. and Robert E. Quinn (2006), *Diagnosing and changing Organizational Culture*, Jossey-Bass, San Francisco.
15. Tsohou, Aggeliki, Maria Karyda, Spyros Kokolakis, and Evangelos Kiountouzis, "Formulating Information Systems Risk Management Strategies through Cultural Theory." *Information Management & Computer Security*, Vol. 14 No. 3, 2006.
16. Quinn, Robert E. and John Rohrbaugh (1983). "A spatial model of effectiveness criteria," *Management Science*, 29, 3, 363–377.
17. Kiely, Laree, PhD and Terry Benzel, USC Marshall School of Business, 2006.
18. Kiely, Laree, PhD and Terry Benzel, USC Marshall School of Business, 2006.
19. Quoted from the Web site of the Balanced Scorecard Collaborative at www.bscol.com
20. Strategy-Focused Organization is a concept owned by the Balanced Scorecard Collaborative.
21. CSI Survey 2007—The 12th Annual Computer Crime and Security Survey, Business Justifications, Computer Security Institute. http://www.gocsi.com

Chapter 4

Metrics Developments

The *sine qua non* of metrics would be those that are reliably predictive—leading indicators of security failure or compromise. Today, all that can be said with any certainty is that organizations with substandard security will statistically suffer greater losses. A recent study by Aberdeen demonstrates statistically predictive consequences of good, or deficient, security.

> Firms operating at best-in-class (security) levels are lowering financial losses to less than 1 percent of revenue, whereas other organizations are experiencing loss rates that exceed 5 percent.[1]

While this result is both intuitive and reasonable, there is insufficient detail to know what specifically contributed how much to superior outcomes. In other words, "best-in-class" may mean that security spending was far higher, the culture was more security oriented, the security architecture was superior, it was a low-profile business or unattractive target, they worked smarter, they had better metrics, or they were just lucky.

Without fine-tuning the data, this information is not as useful as it might be. For example, in the area of security spending, a recent CSI/FBI survey showing security expenditure per employee demonstrates that it is not a useful predictive metric. The number and severity of attacks and losses do not track well with security spending (Figure 4.1).

It should be noted that the sample is fairly small and there may be a number of other factors that skew the results. Nevertheless, the range of security spending as indicated is quite dramatic and doesn't correlate well with impacts or compromises.

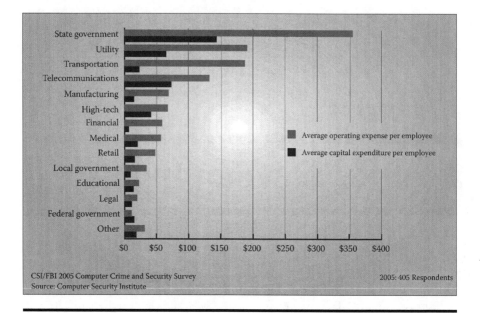

Figure 4.1 Average reported computer security expenditure/investment per employee by industry sector.

4.1 Statistical Modeling

Mathematical risk modeling has seen a great deal of effort and investment during the past decades. The potential for predictive risk analysis is of great interest to numerous industries such as insurance and financial organizations, utilities, and others. There is considerable debate on the actual value of these approaches, and it remains to be seen how well they work in practice.

These models are capable of providing a range of probable outcomes where the risk universe can be bounded and will probably become increasingly useful over time. Currently, mathematical modeling is likely to be well beyond the expertise of most security managers but is included here to suggest that it is possible and evolving. For those inclined to explore this approach in greater depth, following are three recent papers addressing operational risk and approaches to modeling.

"Phase Transitions in Operational Risk" (Kartik Anand and Reimer Kühn, Department of Mathematics, King's College London, London UK. Dated September 12, 2006). In this paper we explore the functional correlation approach to operational risk. We consider networks with heterogeneous a-priori conditional and unconditional failure probability. In the limit of sparse connectivity, self-consistent expressions for the dynamical evolution of order parameters are obtained. Under equilibrium conditions, expressions for the stationary states are also obtained. The consequences of the analytical theory developed are analyzed using phase diagrams. We find co-existence of operational and non-operational phases, much as in liquid-gas systems. Such systems are susceptible to discontinuous phase transitions from the operational to non-operational phase via catastrophic breakdown. We find this feature to be robust against variation of the microscopic modeling assumptions.

"Adequate Capital and Stress Testing for Operational Risks" (Reimer Kühn and P. Neu, *Operational Risk Modeling and Analysis: Theory and Practice*, M. Cruz, Ed., Risk Waters Group, 2004, pp. 273–289). We describe how the notion of sequential correlations naturally leads to the quantification of operational risk. Our main point is that functional dependencies between mutually supportive processes give rise to non-trivial temporal correlations, which can lead to the occurrence of collective risk events in the form of bursts and avalanches of process failures, and crashes of process networks. We show how the adequate capital for operational risk can be calculated via a stochastic dynamics defined on a topological network of interacting processes. One of the main virtues of the present model is the suitability for capital allocation and stress testing of operational risks.

"Functional Correlation Approach to Operational Risk in Banking Organizations" (R. Kühn and P. Neu, *Physica* A 322 650–666 [2003]). A Value-at-Risk-based model is proposed to compute the adequate equity capital necessary to cover potential losses due to operational risks, such as human and system process failures, in banking organizations. Exploring the analogy to a lattice gas model from physics, correlations between sequential failures are modeled by as functionally defined, heterogeneous couplings between mutually supportive processes. In contrast to traditional risk models for market and credit risk, where correlations are described as equal-time-correlations by a covariance matrix, the dynamics of the model shows collective phenomena such as bursts and avalanches of process failures.

4.2 Systemic Security Management

A current effort underway at the USC Marshall School of Business at University of Southern California attempts to model risk from a three-dimensional viewpoint in terms of "tensions." Figure 4.2 represents the typical organizational entity, key elements of its security system, and, perhaps for the first time in the discussion of national security issues, the dynamic relationships or "tensions" among these elements.

The diagram identifies the three traditional elements of people, process, and technology and then adds a fourth "node" of organizational strategy and design to create a three-dimensional working model, best visualized as a pyramid. The connections between the nodes are shown as six dynamic interconnections, which

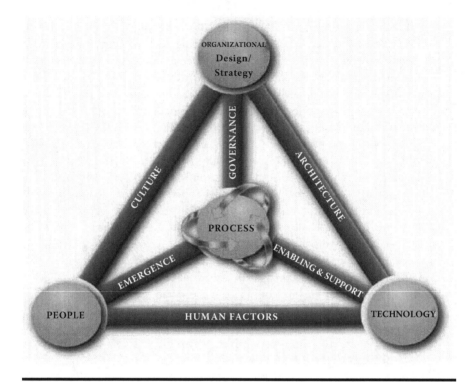

Figure 4.2   Systemic management model.

are referred to as *tensions*, a term chosen to underscore the dynamic and often competing and conflicting roles each plays among the others. These tensions are governance, culture, architecture, enabling and support, emergence, and human factors.

The notion is that security is a dynamic interconnected multidimensional activity rather than a collection of separate and independent issues. It must consider all the elements shown in Figure 4.2 including organizational structure, culture, and emergence and how all these elements interact.[2]

4.3 Value at Risk Analysis

In economics and finance, value at risk (VAR) is the maximum loss with a given probability over a specific period of time. It is commonly used by investment firms and banks to measure the market risk of their asset portfolio although it is a general concept with broad application. For example, a paper prepared at Purdue presents value at risk as a new methodology for information security risk assessment.

VAR summarizes the worst loss due to a security breach over a target horizon, with a given level of confidence. More formally, VAR describes the quantile of the projected distribution of losses over a given time period. Most of the tools that are used for ISEC risk assessment are qualitative in nature and are not grounded in theory. VAR is a useful tool in the hands of an ISEC expert as it provides a theoretically based, quantitative measure of information security risk. Using this measure of risk, the best possible balance between risk and cost of providing security can be achieved. Most organizations, especially those heavily invested in eBusiness, already have determined the acceptable level of risk. The dollar amount of this risk is then computed. When the total VAR of an organization exceeds this amount, the organization is alerted to the fact that an increased security investment is required.

Once the risks are measured, choosing the optimal security is a standard cost-benefit analysis. VAR is an estimate of maximum potential loss to be expected, over a given period, over a certain percentage of time. It has gained rapid acceptance as a valuable approach to risk management in the financial arena (Beder 1995). VAR has been used for a long time to measure the risk of an entire portfolio in a single number. It expresses in dollar terms, the major concern of risk management—the potential loss to portfolio value. VAR has primarily been applied to market risk, though applications have recently been expanded to incorporate corporate risk. VAR holds promise of combining all quantifiable risks across the business lines of an institution, yielding one firm-wide measure of risk (Simons 1996).[3]

4.4 Factor Analysis of Information Risk (FAIR)

A promising approach to decomposing risk and understanding the components is called *factor analysis of information risk* (FAIR).[4] Offering a reasoned, detailed analysis process, a whitepaper is available for understanding and implementing this process.[5]

FAIR provides a reasoned and logical framework:

- A *taxonomy* of the factors that make up information risk. This taxonomy provides a foundational understanding of information risk, without which we couldn't reasonably do the rest. It also provides a set of standard definitions for our terms.
- A *method for measuring* the factors that drive information risk, including threat event frequency, vulnerability, and loss.
- A *computational engine* that derives risk by mathematically simulating the relationships between the measured factors.

- A *simulation model* that allows us to apply the taxonomy, measurement method, and computational engine to build and analyze risk scenarios of virtually any size or complexity.

There are four primary components of our risk taxonomy that we want to identify threat agent characteristics for—those characteristics that affect

- The frequency with which threat agents come into contact with our organizations or assets
- The probability that threat agents will act against our organizations or assets
- The probability of threat agent actions being successful in overcoming protective controls
- The probable nature (type and severity) of impact to our assets (Figure 4.3)

4.5 Risk Factor Analysis

Other approaches to decomposing and analyzing risk include work being undertaken at Los Alamos National Laboratory and presented in a whitepaper titled, "Risk Factor Analysis—A New Qualitative Risk Management Tool"[6] (Figure 4.4).

4.6 Probabilistic Risk Assessment (PRA)

This is a systematic and comprehensive methodology to evaluate associated with a complex engineered technological entity (such as airliners or nuclear power plants).

Risk in a PRA is defined as a feasible detrimental outcome of an activity or action.

In a PRA, risk is characterized by two quantities:

1. The magnitude (severity) of the possible adverse consequence(s)
2. The likelihood (probability) of occurrence of each consequence

Consequences are expressed numerically (e.g., the number of people potentially hurt or killed), and their likelihoods of occurrence are expressed as probabilities or frequencies (i.e., the number of occurrences or the probability of occurrence per unit time). The total risk is the sum of the products of the consequences multiplied by their probabilities. The spectrum of risks across classes of events are also of concern, and are usually controlled in licensing processes. (It would be of concern if rare but high consequence events were found to dominate the overall risk.)

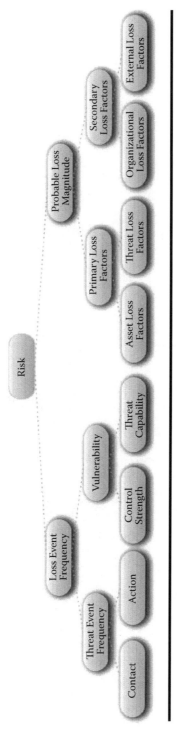

Figure 4.3 Basic risk assessment guide. *Source:* Jack Jones, Risk Management Insight LLC, 2006.

Exhibit 1. Example Qualitative Risk Factor Ranking Criteria

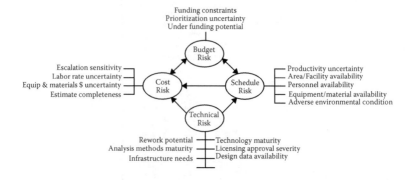

Exhibit 1. Risk Categories and Generic Risk Factors for Risk Factor Analysis

Risk Factor	Risk Category		
	Non/Low (0/1)	Medium (2)	High (3)
Technology Maturity	Facilities & equipment involve only proven technology or new technology for a non-critical activity.	Facilities or equipment require the *adaptation* of new technology from other applications to critical construction or operating functions for this project.	Facilities & equipment require the *development* of new technology for critical construction or operating functions for this project.
Productivity Uncertainty	The planned rate of progress needed to reach completion as planned is conservative and well within benchmarks observed for similar tasks.	The planned rate of progress needed to reach completion as planned is aggressive but still within benchmarks observed for similar tasks.	The planned rate of progress needed to reach completion as planned is extremely aggressive or no benchmark experience is available to judge the reasonableness of the planned progress rate.
Equipment/ Material Cost Uncertainty	Equipment/Material costs are well established and regulated by contracts or competitive market forces.	Equipment/Material costs are not well established but should be regulated by competitive market forces.	Equipment/Material costs are not well established and not subject to competitive market forces.

Figure 4.4   Risk factor analysis.

Probabilistic risk assessment usually answers three basic questions:

1. What can go wrong with the studied technological entity, or what are the initiators or initiating events (undesirable starting events) that lead to adverse consequence(s)?
2. What and how severe are the potential detriments, or the adverse consequences that the technological entity may be eventually subjected to as a result of the occurrence of the initiator?
3. How likely to occur are these undesirable consequences, or what are their probabilities or frequencies?

Two common methods of answering these questions are event tree analysis and fault tree analysis.

In addition to the above methods, PRA studies require special but often very important analysis tools such as human reliability analysis (HRA) and common-cause-failure analysis (CCF). HRA deals with methods for modeling human error whereas CCF deals with methods for evaluating the effect of intersystem and intrasystem dependencies that tend to cause simultaneous failures and thus significant increases in overall risk.

PRA studies have been successfully performed for complex technological systems at all phases of the life cycle from concept definition and predesign through safe removal from operation. For example, the Nuclear Regulatory Commission required that each nuclear power plant in the United States perform an individual plant examination (IPE) to identify and quantify plant vulnerabilities to hardware failures and human faults in design and operation. Although no method was specified for performing such an evaluation, the NRC requirements for the analysis could be met only by applying PRA methods.

Endnotes

1. "Best Practices in Security Governance," Aberdeen Group, U.S.A., 2005.
2. Kiely, Laree, PhD, and Terry Benzel. *Systemic Security Management,* Libertas Press, 2006.
3. Jaisingh, Jeevan, and Jackie Rees, Krannert Graduate School of Management, Purdue University, 1999.
4. Jack Jones, Risk Management Insight LLC, 2006.
5. http://www.riskmanagementinsight.com/media/docs/FAIR_introduction.pdf
6. Kindinger, John P., and John L. Darby, Probabilistic Risk and Hazards Analysis Group, Los Alamos National Laboratory, September 7–16, 2000, Houston, TX.

Chapter 5

Relevance

A discussion of security metrics suggests it is critical to understand what we are attempting to measure, why we want to measure it, and what it means to our organization. Is it a degree of safety? Are we looking for statistical certainty? Predictions? Or do we merely want feedback about what works and what doesn't?

The literature is full of approaches to security metrics. Vendors have dozens of offerings around security metrics. The questions that don't seem to be asked or answered are, "What are we measuring, what does it mean, and who needs to know?"

No doubt some will say, "Hold on. We know what we are measuring. We measured how many people tried using invalid logons to get into our systems."

What is that a measure of? What relevance does it have to managing, operating, or maintaining the security infrastructure? What does it mean? Is it predictive? More importantly, are we certain that no unauthorized person did in fact log on?

That is not to say the foregoing metric doesn't have any meaning, just that no one knows what it is. The historical problem is that companies have not been eager to report security failures or divulge the specifics of their security infrastructure for obvious reasons such as the impact of bad publicity on reputation and share value. However, the net result is that there is a dearth of data about security infrastructures, metrics, and outcomes. In other words, we are not able to correlate any specific security designs, components, or metrics with consequences or outcomes. Vendors cannot support a claim that if you install their box, your impacts from security events will be reduced by X percent. Few will contend that any particular security metric is predictive of a particular outcome or impact.

Most networks and certainly the majority of security infrastructures have grown organically in response to a crisis or other current perceived need. It is likely that never in history have such complex systems been constructed ad hoc with so little design and knowledge of outcomes. As one pundit quipped, "If we built airplanes this way, we wouldn't have a population problem."

As has often been repeated, security is a process, not an event. As with any process, we must have feedback to know if the process is functioning as intended and to be able to manage it, whether to step on the gas or hit the brakes.

> The rationale is that you measure to manage. You manage for outcomes. That suggests a reasonable correlation between measurement and outcomes. That typically doesn't exist today.

What is even less certain is whether there are predictors for nontechnical security failures such as fraud, embezzlement, and theft.

But, to quote Nobel Laureate and nuclear physicist Niels Bohr, "Prediction is very difficult, especially about the future."

5.1 Problem Inertia

One reason to consider tracking trends as critical to effective assurance management is that developing problems inevitably have a certain amount of inertia. That is, they will typically continue to get more troublesome even after efforts to address them have begun. Solutions are never instantaneous and the events giving rise to the problem will probably continue. For example, phishing and its variants have been a rapidly growing form of compromise. Their success has given rise to emulation, and the number and sophistication of attacks continues to rise even as countermeasures increase.

Absent consistent standards for adequate and effective security—as opposed to "best practices"—and a reliable "security yardstick," the most reliable metric for security will be trends. Observing trends requires feedback, or metrics, directly indicating proximity to clearly defined outcomes. Approaching the target indicates things are on the right track.

Unfortunately, trends are a lagging indicator and provide a fine picture of where we have been. Given the dynamic and volatile nature of information and systems, it is not certain that events of the past will provide a reliable path to the future. However, all other things remaining equal, they may still constitute one of the best available management metrics insofar as it is usually a fair assumption that trending will continue in the direction it is headed as long as drivers and context don't change significantly.

5.2 Correlating Metrics to Consequences

Ideally, metrics should provide a direct indication of the type and nature of consequences. A simple example would be that if the measurement of the quantity of gasoline pumped into your car is significantly wrong, the number of miles you can predictably travel will be directly affected.

In IT security, for example, we cannot make a direct correlation between the number of open vulnerabilities *we discover* and the probability of a successful attack. For one thing, with any given process, it is a virtual certainty that some vulnerabilities are still unknown. While intuitively we understand that fewer vulnerabilities probably will result in fewer successful attacks, that knowledge by itself will say nothing of possible impacts. If, after all, there is no impact from the exploitation of a particular vulnerability, there is little purpose in spending resources correcting it. In addition, not knowing all possible threats makes it unpredictable whether a risk actually exists or not. The point is, finding vulnerabilities is a standard practice in large part because *we can* and we can do it with an automated process. That does not make it a useful metric for any but those charged with plugging vulnerabilities. And that information by itself will not provide guidance on which vulnerabilities are a priority or which are of little potential consequence.

We may, for example, attempt to measure the effectiveness of our antivirus controls by the number of viruses or malicious code detected. We may also keep record of the trends and show that more are being caught over time. This is a commonly used metric, but it is virtually useless. The question that we cannot answer that is far more important is "How many were not detected?" The result is that the best although not very desirable metric in this case is actual infections and their consequences. A more useful indicator might be the number and trend of infections. It is only an indicator unless clear determinations can be made as to the source of the infection, which is often not the case.

Some organizations track the number of security incidents with the notion that a decrease in incidents is a good metric on the effectiveness of the security monitoring efforts. Unless other factors are constant, which they generally are not, it is not clear what is being measured. It could be the threshold that triggers an incident or investigation has changed or personnel security awareness has decreased and incidents are not being discovered.

Compliance metrics have become commonplace in recent times in response to legal and regulatory requirements. It is not uncommon to see these measures being confused with security effectiveness and used as a security metric. While it is very probable that a greater degree of compliance with ISO 27001 or the PCI standards will result in better security, it will by itself not be determinative of whether the security program optimally addresses the needs of the organization. The level of compliance will also not be a functional metric to guide day-to-day security management or operations any more than an aircraft meeting airworthiness standards is a measure of whether it is flying in the right direction.

The conclusion that must be considered carefully is whether the metrics chosen can, over time or through experiences of others, provide any indication of possible or even better probable consequences. Some recent studies indicate that to some extent that may be possible. In the near term, however, the challenge faced by the majority of organizations is simply to find a way to develop the most rudimentary metrics that can provide basic guidance on security management and operations.

Chapter 6

The Metrics Imperative

It is generally agreed that there are few activities that can be managed well without decent metrics. The fact that many information security managers do manage adequately with just technical metrics, some notion of good or best practices coupled with experience, a modicum of intuition, and a bit of luck would seem to suggest that isn't entirely true. If in addition, trends show that the overall results from security activities are consistent with expectations, impacts are acceptable, and costs are reasonable, this may seem adequate to the majority of organizations. However, this often results in a dangerous underestimation of actual risks. A prime example is the recent poster child for virtually every aspect of deficient security, TJX, with the loss of some 46 million credit records. The sheer magnitude of this breach, coupled with the facts that it wasn't discovered until some 18 months later and that some 80 gigabytes of protected data had been transferred out on its own networks, can to some significant extent be attributed to poor or nonexistent monitoring and metrics. The ultimate costs of this particular debacle remain to be seen but has as of this writing exceeded 250 million dollars.

An examination of this and numerous other breaches and compromises suggests that poor security is not justified by low costs. It also argues strongly for adequate and effective metrics and monitoring around risks and impacts to indicate potential consequences and the degree and effectiveness of mitigation measures.

Another consideration supporting the need for metrics is the ability of a security organization to provide consistent and adequate security relative to an ever-changing risk landscape based on ongoing feedback on requirements and effectiveness. Effective management metrics serve to address issues of resource allocation based on measures of criticality, risk, and potential impact. The alternative has been shown not to be cost-effective in that the majority of security programs are, at best, only marginally related to risk and potential impacts. Given the never-ending quest for greater productivity and lower costs coupled with greater risks and costs of compromise, it is unlikely that successful organizations can continue to manage security on an ad-hoc reactive basis.

6.1 Study of ROSI of Security Measures

An interesting study that indicates the typical problem of achieving respectable rates of return on investment in security was published in a whitepaper from the security firm @Stake.

An analysis of the ROSI of various security-related activities of over 600 organizations determined that many practices did not provide a positive return from a purely financial perspective (Figure 6.1).

These results will undoubtedly be controversial and lead to energetic protests from many practitioners. Given that central access control and nightly backups are sacrosanct, the results of this analysis will be soundly criticized. Nevertheless,

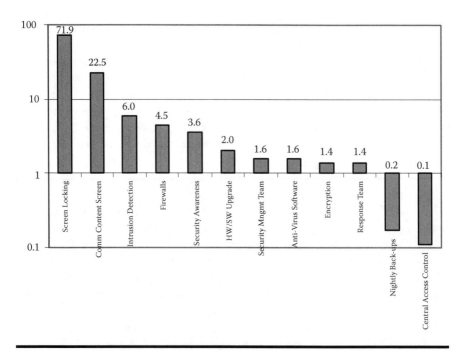

Figure 6.1 Safeguard savings to cost ratio. *Source:* Kevin J. Soo Hoo @Stake, May 16, 2002.

given the immature state of information security, it may be wise to independently assess whether this type of analysis is valid and possibly reconsider standard "best practice" approaches.

ROSI does suffer several weaknesses in terms of possibly speculative estimates of risk frequency and magnitude, the reduction in losses, and effectiveness of mitigation measures among others. Nevertheless, the fact that most security managers are faced with justifying the costs of security initiatives to senior management, this sort of analysis may serve to support a reasonable business case.

Another ROSI study that indicates the value of the approach as a potentially important metric for security management analyzed the cost-effectiveness of addressing software flaws early in the development cycle. Based on data amassed by @Stake from nearly 100 companies over an 18-month period, a study of security defects in software development revealed that

> Overall, the average company catches only a quarter of software security holes. On average, enterprise software has seven significant bugs, four of which the software designer might choose to fix. Armed with such data, the researchers concluded that fixing those four defects during the testing phase cost $US24,000. Fixing the same defects after deployment cost $US160,000, nearly seven times as much.
>
> The ROSI breakdown: building security into software engineering at the design stage nets a 21 per cent ROSI. Waiting until the implementation stage reduces that to 15 per cent. At the testing stage, the ROSI falls to 12 per cent.[1]

6.2 Resource Allocation

Research shows that resource allocation in most organizations has little if any relationship to risk and potential impacts. How then are resources allocated in these organizations? The extent to which resources are misallocated will be a measure of the lack of governance, clear information security objectives, and management metrics. PGP/Vontu performs an annual in-depth analysis of organizations that have been breached. A recent study[2] of 31 companies that suffered a range of security breaches resulting in losses of over 148 million dollars exemplifies this problem (Figure 6.2).

If resources were in fact allocated based on good metrics, the relative losses of these organizations from all sources should be approximately equal. Significant impacts such as those from the loss of portable devices suggests that no one was aware of the risk or potential impact, and if they were, no effective action was taken to address this risk.

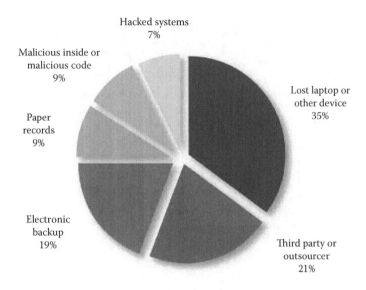

Figure 6.2 Source of data breach.

That the losses from malicious insiders and paper records were greater than those from hacking suggests that most efforts are taken to control access to the network but little effort is expended on equally important paper records.

6.3 Managing without Metrics

A recent study of over 700 global CIOs and CEOs by Price Waterhouse Coopers indicates that most do not employ metrics for managing security. Only 15 percent use some sort of financial metrics and only 20 percent acknowledge monitoring IT performance. Nevertheless, many of these organizations function reasonably well some of the time. Given sufficient budget and utilizing a systematic approach of best practices such as offered by ITIL, it is likely that reasonably effective security can exist. However, if security is effective, it is invariably not cost-effective, and given appropriate metrics to provide information for effective management decisions, these operations can achieve better security at a lower cost.

However, a persuasive argument can be made that "best practices" are ultimately just *a poor substitute for adequate knowledge.* That is, without metrics to determine functionality, performance, and progress toward defined objectives, best practices provide an approach and defensible justification. Whether best practices provide too much security at too great a cost or insufficient security for critical applications or processes cannot be determined except perhaps in retrospect after some adverse event.

Endnotes

1. Berinato, Scott. *CIO Magazine*, April 8, 2002.
2. 2006 Annual Study: Cost of a Data Breach, PGP/Vontu.

Chapter 7

Attributes of
Good Metrics

Metrics serve only one purpose. *We measure to manage.*

Metrics, measures, and monitoring processes exist only to provide decision support. They serve no other purpose. The information they provide is only useful to the extent it serves that purpose.

Given that criteria, to determine what information is needed and the required characteristics and attributes of measuring and monitoring processes, we must know answers to the following questions:

1. What is being managed?
2. What are the objectives?
3. What are the decisions that must be made?
4. What information is needed to make those decisions?
5. What processes can provide the required information?

From this we can evaluate what constitutes useful metrics, measures, and monitoring processes necessary for management. Much that is monitored and measured related to security has the singular attribute of availability—we measure it because we can. Often, this results in overwhelming quantities of technical data that may or may not contain useful information.

Largely unexamined firewall and system logs that by virtue of their sheer bulk are usually ignored except in the event of an incident are typical. And then it is not unusual for the logging granularity having been set to minimize storage requirements, rendering it insufficient for effective forensics.

So, the first important attribute is *manageability*. The information should be available, concise, and understandable.

The next attribute might be *meaningful*. It must be understandable and relevant to the recipient and provide a basis for the decisions.

The information must be *actionable*. Useful metrics information makes it clear what response is needed, as a compass makes it clear whether to turn left or right to stay on course provided we know where we are and where we are going.

Information should lack *ambiguity*. Ambiguous information from metrics that can have a number of meanings may be misleading, of little use, or downright dangerous.

Information from metrics must be *reliable*. The ability to trust the "instruments" is conditioned on the reliability of the measures.

Another critical attribute is *accuracy*. Concomitant with reliability, a reasonable and known degree of accuracy is essential. The compass showing north when we are in fact going south can be fatal.

Metrics and monitoring information must be *timely*. Measures that warn of a disaster after it has happened are not useful

Finally, an attribute is useful if it is *predictive*. Some metrics information will signal impending problems much as a drop in oil pressure is the harbinger of engine failure.

A good start on metrics, measurements, and monitoring information attributes can be summarized as being

- Manageable
- Meaningful
- Actionable
- Unambiguous
- Reliable
- Accurate
- Timely
- Predictive

Other descriptive attributes can undoubtedly be arrived at, but the foregoing attributes are the most significant. The question then may be whether these attributes can be prioritized or whether any metrics or combinations of metrics that do not include most or all of the foregoing characteristics should be discarded.

In other circumstances, such as flying an airplane, any instrumentation that does not meet all of these criteria wouldn't find space on the dashboard. Given the immense criticality of many of our information systems, it is surprising that the same standards are not applied to them.

The acronym SMART is often used to describe metrics requirements: simple, measurable, accurate, repeatable, timely. Although memorable shorthand and perhaps useful notions, this acronym doesn't address all the required attributes.

7.1 Metrics Objectives

Metrics, measures, and monitoring efforts must be in relation to something to be of any use. As with any other organizational activity, there is the *requirement for defined objectives*. Determining the objectives for information security that will ultimately drive metrics selection and development is discussed in Chapter 8, "Information Security Governance." For the purpose of determining suitable criteria and attributes of metrics, measures, and monitoring processes, it is assumed that objectives can be defined.

The necessity of defining objectives can be illustrated using the analogy of piloting an aircraft. This may seem a remote relationship to a security manager, but aircraft are particularly illustrative of effective metrics and the tasks of a pilot are functionally similar to any other manager. To successfully navigate an airplane or a security department to its destination, the necessary information includes

- Objective (or destination)
- Current location (relative to the destination)
- Direction (heading toward the destination)
- Speed (how long to reach the destination)

For the pilot, or security manager, it is also necessary to have information regarding

- Intervening obstacles (constraints that may require a change of course)
- Operational health/malfunctions (knowing whether the equipment is working properly)
- Cost/effectiveness (affordability)

This group of information is a fundamental requirement for navigation and operation of aircraft and information security programs. Examining each will provide insight into the kinds of measures and metrics that can provide the necessary information. Each of these elements is discussed in the following chapters.

7.2 Measurement Categories

There are essentially three fundamentally different kinds of information required for managing and operating an aircraft—or a security program. They are

Navigation (Strategic, Directional): For aircraft, this is the exclusive purview of a central set of instruments concerned with information about location, heading, and distance to the destination. This is the "linkage" to business objectives—that is, steering the ship to the destination that meets the business objectives of operating an airline. It is analogous to the requirement for setting objectives consistent with the business goals for an information security program and then developing metrics to provide the same information in terms of heading to the destination as well as information on current location.

Program Management (Tactical, Administrative): For our airplane analogy, this is the information required to manage the actual flying, which includes aircraft heading, altitude, speed and so forth, which is provided by the main instrumentation located directly in front of the pilot. For managing an airplane or an information security program, this information must be real-time or near real-time. It is the feedback that allows effective day-to-day management and administration while maintaining a heading that will achieve the destination.

Operational (Technical, Procedural): On the typical aircraft dashboard (called the *instrument panel*), technical information regarding the operation of the machinery is off to one side and referenced occasionally for assurance that the systems are operating in the "green" and that there are adequate resources such as fuel. This information is of no value in determining direction or flight management or whether the destination will be reached except to the extent that failure of the power plant can inform us that we are not capable of reaching the destination.

While navigation and administration are the main security management components, they are dependent on higher-level strategic decisions about the underlying mission of the "flight." The oft-mentioned notion of strategic alignment therefore is achieved when the operation of the "flight," or the security program, serves a higher-level organizational purpose such as operating an airline—in other words, when the information security program provides the elements essential to the successful operation of the organization.

The operational component of metrics from a technical perspective are available and commonly deployed. Operational metrics at the physical and process levels are more scarce and less automated. The components that are poorly addressed if at all are navigation and management.

After identifying the broad categories of the types of information required, we can consider what sort of processes can be used to provide feedback that meets the necessary criteria previously identified. There is a large array of choices, but many will not provide the necessary information or meet the previously named criteria of being

- Manageable
- Meaningful
- Actionable
- Unambiguous
- Reliable
- Accurate
- Timely
- Predictive

Some of the things that can be measured include

- Performance
- Results
- Cost
- Quality
- Percentages
- Frequency
- Quantity
- Magnitude
- Trends
- Probabilities

Many other possibilities exist but these are the typical ones. The ability of any of these to serve as metrics must be carefully considered to make certain of what is actually being measured. For example, good process metrics won't ensure good processes. Effective performance contrary to desired outcomes is counterproductive. Cost absent value or effectiveness is wasteful. High quality of deficient processes won't ensure good results.

7.3 Effective Metrics

Effectiveness of metrics is the extent to which they provide information that meet our previously defined criteria for a particular recipient. If we consider one of the most commonly used security metrics provided by network vulnerability scanners such as ISS or NESSUS, in terms of our criteria of being:

- Manageable
- Meaningful
- Actionable
- Unambiguous
- Reliable
- Accurate
- Timely
- Predictive

We find that most of the criteria are not met. For example,

- It is manageable.
- It is only marginally meaningful for security management.
- Without considerable additional information, it is not actionable.
- It will typically not be unambiguous.

- It may be fairly reliable.
- It will typically not be accurate.
- It may be timely.
- It is not very predictive.

In fairness, applying this set of criteria to most current security metrics will yield a similar result. It may be useful to apply a scalar quantity to these metrics evaluations to achieve a relative score that can be used to rank metrics usefulness for security management.

For example, we could use a 1 to 10 scale, with 10 being the highest.

Example 1

Vulnerability scans in terms of usefulness for information security management might be

Manageable	10
Meaningful	3
Actionable	2
Unambiguous	2
Reliable	8
Accurate	6
Timely	10
Predictive	2

resulting in a total score of 44 out of a possible 80.

These scores could be used to prioritize comparative metrics relevance, which, if combined with TCO, could itself be a useful metric for management.

Example 2

Let's consider another typical metric, the percentage of servers patched within some time period, and what it might mean to a CISO.

Manageable	10
Meaningful	2
Actionable	4
Unambiguous	1
Reliable	9
Accurate	9
Timely	5
Predictive	2

In this case, the total score would be 42 out of a possible 80.

Many technical metrics, perhaps most, evaluated using this approach in the context of a CISO recipient will suffer equally poor numbers.

Example 3

Let's consider the metric of the percentage of servers patched within some time period from the perspective of an IT security manager.

Manageable	10
Meaningful	10
Actionable	10
Unambiguous	10
Reliable	10
Accurate	10
Timely	5
Predictive	2

The score in this case 67 out of 80.

The point is, from an operational standpoint, operational metrics are useful. From a strategic or management standpoint, they are not.

Example 4

Consider another type of qualitative metric. Given these criteria and considering the recipient is the CISO, how would a balanced scorecard fare?

Manageable	10
Meaningful	10
Actionable	10
Unambiguous	7
Reliable	8
Accurate	6
Timely	10
Predictive	8

Total score would be 69 out of a possible 80. The multidimensional approach provided by the balanced scorecard (Section 3.4.2) dealing with management issues provides far more information needed for management of information security, but it would be fairly useless to a system administrator.

7.3.1 What Is Being Measured?

If the primary measures needed for navigating security management toward its objectives are direction, current location, and perhaps "speed," we can translate these notions into terms relevant to what needs to be accomplished.

- Speed is translated to project or other activities schedules.
- Direction is moving toward objectives based on current location.
- Location is current state of security in relation to where we want to be.

The "what" is actually being measured may not be obvious. For example, consider a common metric, failed logon attempts. What is actually being measured? It could be the complexity and difficulty of remembering perhaps several complex passwords that cannot be written down. It could be breach attempts. Or, it could be a defective keyboard or other technical malfunction. The point is that what may appear to be one thing may in fact be something totally different. This will obviously have significant relevance in terms of the decisions that need to be made and the actions required.

What is being measured can be categorized in various ways including the *methods* used to provide information. Methods can include such things as

- Quantity
- Trends
- Maturity
- Quality
- Cost
- Value
- Benchmarking/percentages
- Probability
- Frequency
- Magnitude

Some combinations of methods may be used for "rolled up" or correlated metrics or when using a multidimensional approach such as balanced scorecards or CMM. Unreliable, ambiguous, or uncertain metrics may make it prudent to use several methods to measure the same thing. The bottom line is that care must be exercised in metrics design to ensure the information provided is what is needed and expected or at least well correlated in some manner. For example, while oil pressure in an automobile is not a measure of engine performance, its absence is consistently predictive of engine failure.

7.3.2 Why Is It Measured?

Security managers are often not able to provide an answer when asked why a particular activity is measured. Some probing usually results in the answer being "because we can." In addition to meeting the criteria mentioned at the beginning of the chapter, the reasons to measure a particular activity must be to provide the information needed to make management decisions. Anything else is likely to be just clutter. An illustrative example can once again be provided by the instrumentation used in aircraft. There is no instrument on the panel that does not provide useful or essential information needed for the pilot to manage the flight. This includes navigational information to achieve the objectives, management information to control the aircraft, and technical information to ensure the proper operation of the various systems.

7.3.3 Who Are the Recipients?

Depending on roles and responsibilities, the information needed to make informed decisions will be quite different. The fundamental question to be asked is "Who needs to know what when?" Those charged with IT security may want to know detailed information on the status of patches, whereas the information security manager may just want to know that the approved procedure consistent with standards—in other words, compliance—is being performed. Senior management will typically want only assurance that risks are managed to an agreed level.

7.3.4 What Does It Mean?

Technical metrics can supply far more data than information given that a working definition for information is data with meaning and purpose. For data to have meaning, it must be appropriate and relevant to the recipients as discussed above. For it to have purpose, it must be useable and useful.

For managing information security, knowing that 81 percent of employees have had awareness training or that 72 percent of servers are patched will be useful only if the numbers are relevant to some defined objective and meet most or all of the aforementioned metrics criteria.

As in the discussion of what is being measured, it is important to gain clarity on the meaning of any particular information supplied by metrics, or for that matter, monitoring. Meaning always requires context. One part in a million may have little meaning, whereas one part in two could be very significant depending on what those parts are, such as if it is in the context of unauthorized access or the loss of revenues due to compromise.

7.3.5 What Action Is Required?

Any metric, measure, or monitoring process that provides information that is not actionable—that is, prescriptive of a response—is by definition not useful or meaningful. A compass heading is useful only if the direction to the destination and current location—that is, the context—is known. If the context is known, the compass heading is prescriptive. It may be that the response will be to do nothing because everything is on track, or it may indicate that everything is not and a particular corrective reaction such as turning left or right is necessary. Most current information security metrics and measures do not meet this standard and generally are merely an invitation for further examination.

Chapter 8

Information Security Governance

Governance is defined by the Information Security and Control Association (ISACA) as

> The set of responsibilities and practices exercised by the board and executive management with the goal of providing *strategic direction*, ensuring that *objectives are achieved*, ascertaining that *risks are managed* appropriately and verifying that the enterprise's *resources are used responsibly.*[1]

The Organization for Economic Co-operation and Development (OECD) in its 1999 publication "OECD Principles of Corporate Governance" adds the requirement that governance includes the "structure through which the objectives of the enterprise are set, and the means of attaining those objectives and monitoring performance are determined."

Structure and means include strategy, policies, and their corresponding standards, procedures and guidelines; strategic and operational plans; awareness and training; risk management; controls; and audits and other assurance activities. Monitoring performance includes metrics, measures, and monitoring.

Good management requires governance as a foundation. Developing effective metrics for information security management rests on defining the role of security and security management in the organization including

1. *What is to be managed?* This will include defining the scope of security activities as well as roles and responsibilities.
2. *How will it be managed? How* will be dependent on the *what* and will include the available resources and constraints as well as control objectives.
3. *To what end will it be managed?* This encompasses the requirement for determining acceptable risks and defining desired objectives and outcomes of the security program.
4. *How do we know it is managed?* This is the necessity for agreed-upon key goal and performance indicators, overall objectives for the program, and success measures.

The bottom line is that meaningful security management metrics cannot be developed without developing information security governance. It should be obvious that if you don't know where you're going, there is no measure capable of telling you when you have arrived.

Developing governance will include a strategy for implementation. Whether the strategy has been fully implemented is not as critical, but the strategy is a necessity because developing a security governance strategy provides two key elements needed for management metrics: *scope* and *objectives*. Objectives for the information security program will provide the necessary point of reference to determine the necessary metrics for guidance toward those goals—and the necessary navigational requirement of having a defined destination. Scope will determine what the metrics must encompass to ensure objectives are achieved, risks are managed, and resources are used responsibly. So, while effective information security management is not possible without the superstructure of governance, the requirements for information security governance also cannot be met absent adequate metrics.

8.1 Security Governance Outcomes

Considerable effort has been devoted at ISACA and the ITGI to define the expectations of security governance. The result is six defined outcomes for information security governance[2] including

- Strategic Alignment—Aligning security activities in support of organizational objectives
- Risk Management—Executing appropriate measures to manage risks and potential impacts to an acceptable level
- Business Process Assurance/Convergence—Integrating all relevant assurance processes to improve overall security and efficiency

- Value Delivery—Optimizing investments in support of organizational objectives
- Resource Management—Using organizational resources efficiently and effectively
- Performance Measurement—Monitoring and reporting on security processes to ensure objectives are achieved

Defining the desired outcomes provides a basis to develop the specific objectives needed to achieve them to an acceptable extent and what the practical considerations are. Various questions must be answered in the process of defining objectives for each of the six outcomes, such as

1. What is an optimal and effective level for each of these outcomes?
2. How can the objectives to achieve them be defined?
3. What metrics must be developed to gauge whether the objectives are being achieved?
4. What are the costs and level of effort required to achieve these objectives?
5. Can a persuasive business case be made for achieving each of the objectives?

If objectives can be determined that will result in a satisfactory level of these outcomes, they will provide a picture of the "desired state" of security at a high level. Since it isn't possible to quantify an information security program to any significant extent, the suggested approach is to determine a "desired state"—essentially a snapshot at some future point of the essential elements and aspects of the program—in terms of characteristics and attributes. These can include elements such as control objectives, acceptable risk and impact levels, and performance levels.

8.2 Defining Security Objectives

Once high-level outcomes for information security have been decided, it will be necessary to "drill down" and define in detail the characteristics and attributes of the "desired state" for an information security program capable of achieving the desired objectives. There are a number of approaches available to accomplish this. The methods selected should be chosen carefully to attempt maximum integration into the existing methods used by the organization.

If, for example, CMM is standard in the organization, then it makes sense to employ it for the purposes of defining security objectives. If architectural approaches are the common practice, it may be that the SABSA architectural model is most appropriate. If the focus is to establish suitable control objectives, CobiT or ISO 27001 might be used.

8.2.1 Sherwood Applied Business Security Architecture (SABSA)

A detailed approach to defining information security attributes is provided by the architectural model, SABSA, as shown in Figure 8.1. This can provide a checklist of attributes and a framework for various aspects of security to define the "desired state" of virtually all aspects of security. In essence, this approach can be used to develop a taxonomy of security characteristics and attributes for an organization. Attributes are the desired business characteristics or "virtues" that can be seen as the opposite of risk and that must be managed and measured.

8.2.2 CobiT

CobiT is a well-developed comprehensive system that can provide both an approach and a methodology for defining the objectives of security governance. While the focus is primarily on IT, it is possible to cover most information security requirements as well.

The focus for CobiT is defining IT control objectives and developing the controls to meet them. The CobiT framework sets out 34 processes to manage and control information and the technology that supports it (Table 8.1). The processes are divided into four domains:

- Plan and Organize: This domain covers strategy and tactics, and concerns the identification of the way IT can best contribute to the achievement of the business objectives. Furthermore, the realization of the strategic vision needs to be planned, communicated, and managed for different perspectives. Finally, a proper organization as well as technological infrastructure must be put in place.
- Acquire and Implement: To realize the IT strategy, IT solutions need to be identified, developed, or acquired, as well as implemented and integrated into the business process. In addition, changes in and maintenance of existing systems are covered by this domain to make sure that the life cycle is continued for these systems.
- Deliver and Support: This domain is concerned with the actual delivery of required services, which range from traditional operations over security and continuity aspects to training. To deliver services, the necessary support processes must be set up. This domain includes the actual processing of data by application systems, often classified under application controls.
- Monitor and Evaluate: All IT processes need to be regularly assessed over time for their quality and compliance with control requirements. Thus, this domain addresses management's monitoring and evaluation of IT performance and increased control, ensuring regulatory compliance, and providing IT governance oversight.

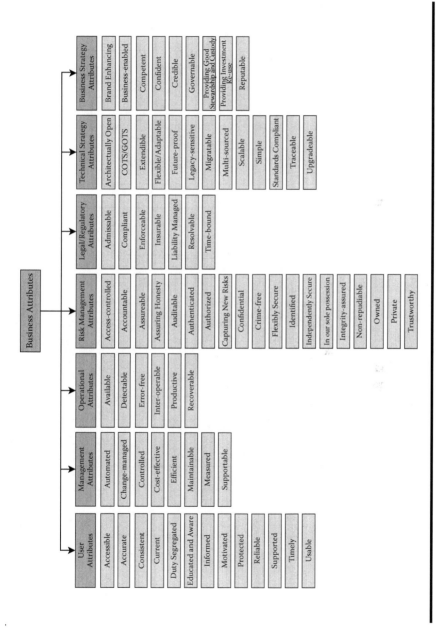

Figure 8.1   SABSA business attributes for security.

Table 8.1   CobiT High-Level Control Objectives

Plan and Organize	
PO1	Define a strategic IT plan and direction
PO2	Define the information architecture
PO3	Determine technological direction
PO4	Define the IT processes, organization, and relationships
PO5	Manage the IT investment
PO6	Communicate management aims and direction
PO7	Manage IT human resources
PO8	Manage quality
PO9	Assess and manage IT risks
PO10	Manage projects
Acquire and Implement	
AI1	Identify automated solutions
AI2	Acquire and maintain application software
AI3	Acquire and maintain technology infrastructure
AI4	Enable operation and use
AI5	Procure IT resources
AI6	Manage changes
AI7	Install and accredit solutions and changes
Deliver and Support	
DS1	Define and manage service levels
DS2	Manage third-party services
DS3	Manage performance and capacity
DS4	Ensure continuous service
DS5	Ensure systems security
DS6	Identify and allocate costs

(Continued)

Table 8.1   (continued)

Deliver and Support	
DS7	Educate and train users
DS8	Manage service desk and incidents
DS9	Manage the configuration
DS10	Manage problems
DS11	Manage data
DS12	Manage the physical environment
DS13	Manage operations
Monitor and Evaluate	
ME1	Monitor and evaluate IT processes
ME2	Monitor and evaluate internal control
ME3	Ensure regulatory compliance
ME4	Provide IT governance

Source: Wikipedia.

8.2.3 ISO 27001

The security standard and code of practice currently published—ISO/IEC 27001 and 27002—can provide the basis for defining a desired state of security. There are 134 control objectives in the 11 domains of 27001, and 2 can be generally mapped to CobiT but are more focused on security.

The 11 domains include

1. Security Policy
2. Organizing Information Security
3. Asset Management
4. Human Resources Security
5. Physical and Environmental Security
6. Communications and Operations Management
7. Access Control
8. Information Systems Acquisition, Development, and Maintenance
9. Information Security Incident Management
10. Business Continuity Management
11. Compliance

8.2.4 *Capability Maturity Model*

The "desired state" of security can be described in narrative form such as one version of the ISACA Capability Maturity Model. As an example that may serve most organizations well, CMM level 4, Managed and Measurable, states the following 15 requirements:

1. The assessment of risk is a standard procedure, and exceptions to following the procedure would be noticed by security management.
2. Information security risk management is a defined management function with senior-level responsibility.
3. Senior management and information security management have determined the levels of risk that the organization will tolerate and have standard measures for risk/return ratios.
4. Responsibilities for information security are clearly assigned, managed and enforced.
5. Information security risk and impact analysis is consistently performed.
6. Security policies and practices are completed with specific security baselines.
7. Security awareness briefings have become mandatory.
8. User identification, authentication, and authorization are standardized.
9. Security certification of staff is established.
10. Intrusion testing is a standard and formalized process leading to improvements.
11. Cost-benefit analyses, supporting the implementation of security measures, are increasingly being utilized.
12. Information security processes are coordinated with the overall organization security function.
13. Information security reporting is linked to organizational objectives.
14. Responsibilities and standards for continuous service are enforced.
15. System redundancy practices, including use of high-availability components, are consistently deployed.

Different organizations may find the 15 elements adequate, but many will require some additional elements to flesh out their specific requirements. This list nevertheless highlights many of the attributes and characteristics of a mature security operation and provides a useful model for defining a "desired state" for information security.

The full text of CMM is included in Appendix A.

In any of the approaches, the gap between the current state and the desired state can then be assessed to determine the required direction. Periodic use of gap analysis can subsequently serve to determine progress toward objectives.

Having defined where we are, where we are going, how far it is, and how fast we're traveling provides some of the basic elements for determining relevant metrics on operational, management, and strategic levels.

8.3 Current State

Once the processes for defining the "desired state" are selected, the same processes are used to assess the current state for each defined attribute. For example, if CMM 4 is the process selected, item 1 describes the desired state:

1. The assessment of risk is a standard procedure, and exceptions to following the procedure would be noticed by security management.

The current state typical of many organizations might be as follows:

There is no policy requirement for risk assessments and the IT manager considers them a waste of time, contending that the risks are already well known. Both the security manager and the IT manager report to the CIO. The CIO supports the IT manager's position citing resource constraints as the reason.

Gap analysis is then employed to determine what steps are needed to move from the current state to the desired state. In this example, the gaps include

- Policy that mandates risk assessment as a standard procedure must be developed and supported by management.
- Security management authority resides with the CIO who must seek resources to assess risk consistent with standards of good practice.
- The reporting structure presents a potential conflict of interest between the regulatory functions of a security manager and the operational performance requirements of IT.

Once all of the attributes have been subjected to analysis and the gaps determined, a strategy can be developed to address them over time. These gaps represent the unmitigated risks that the strategy must address.

8.4 Information Security Strategy

The original military definition for strategy is simply the plan to achieve an objective.

The development of a security strategy is essentially the plan for closing the aforementioned "maturity gaps" utilizing the available resources within existing constraints. Detailed information on strategy development is beyond the scope of this book but is available at little or no cost in a publication from the ISACA bookstore by this author titled *Information Security Governance—Guidance for Information Security Managers*.

Metrics required for the development of a security program to implement the security strategy are quite different from the ongoing management metrics required for managing a security department, which is covered in Chapter 13. Program development metrics will typically be project-oriented as needed to manage the lifecycles of implementation and deployment activities. Several accepted project management methodologies such as PRINCE 2, ISO 10006, and HERMES can be used for this purpose and will provide suitable metrics for tracking progress and providing the necessary information for making implementation and deployment decisions.

Endnotes

1. 2008 CISM Review Manual, Information Security and Control Association. Emphasis added.
2. Brotby, Krag. *Information Security Governance, A Guide for Boards of Directors and Executive Management*, 2nd ed. ITGI, 2005.

Chapter 9

Metrics Development—A Different Approach

Metrics' only purpose is decision support. There is little other reason to implement them. Whether it is to provide the basis for determining a particular course of action or response, or to implement a particular solution, or whether, in fact, everything is operating appropriately and moving in the right direction, we measure to provide a basis for decisions. *We measure to manage.*

The useful metrics, therefore, are the ones that are relevant to the level and type of decisions that must be made. The first question to be answered in metrics development then is "What kind of decisions are being made by whom in the organization?"

This is a different approach to metrics in that it starts with analysis of the scope of responsibilities, authority, and accountabilities for each organizational role involved in some aspect of security. This is followed by an examination and analysis of job functions and the types of decisions a particular organizational role undertakes.

This can be complemented by interviews to gain an understanding of the kinds of security-related operational, tactical, and strategic decisions that are required for a particular function. It will also be important to understand the kinds of information and basis currently used and/or desired in making decisions. That is, executives and managers have preferred types of information and presentation by which they undertake to understand issues and decide on a course of action. Combined with an examination of the types of decisions delegated to each management level, this will provide a basis for the determination of the *kinds of information* that are needed for decision support. This in turn will provide the basis for designing appropriate monitoring and metrics that can provide the necessary information.

To examine how this might work in practice, let us consider the typical information security manager responsibilities, the decisions that need to be made, and the information needed, and examine the types of metrics or monitoring that might be useful.

9.1 The Information Security Manager

While the scope and authority of security managers varies significantly, a representative job description for the majority of information security managers might read as follows:

- **General Purpose.** The information security manager serves as the process owner for all ongoing activities that serve to provide appropriate access to and protect the confidentiality, integrity, and availability of customer, employee, and organization information in compliance with policies and standards.
- **Position Responsibilities.**
  - Serves as an internal information security consultant to the organization
  - Develops and documents security policies, standards, and procedures guided and ratified by the Information Security Committee
  - Provides direct training and oversight to all employees, affiliate marketing partners, alliances, and other third parties, ensuring proper information security clearance in accordance with established organizational information security policies and procedures
  - Initiates, facilitates, and promotes activities to create information security awareness within the organization
  - Performs information security risk assessments and serves as an internal auditor for security issues
  - Implements information security policies, standards, and procedures for the organization
  - Reviews all system-related security plans throughout the organization's network, acting as a liaison to Information Systems
  - Monitors compliance with information security policies, standards, and procedures, referring problems to the appropriate department manager
  - Coordinates the activities of the Information Security Committee
  - Advises the organization with current information about information security technologies and related regulatory issues
  - Monitors the internal control systems to ensure that appropriate access levels are maintained
  - Prepares the disaster recovery plan

Each of these responsibilities can be analyzed in terms of determining the kinds of information needed for effective decision making and to provide guidance for managing the information security program.

Serves as an internal information security consultant to the organization. The effectiveness of internal consulting will be a function of how well various parts of the organization determine their requirements have been met. Essentially, standard measures of customer satisfaction are likely to be the most useful metric.

Develops and documents security policies, standards, and procedures guided and ratified by the Information Security Committee. Policy development requires an understanding of the threat profile for the organization and, to be relevant and effective, must be based on the development of information security objectives and a strategy to achieve them as discussed in Chapter 8.

Provides direct training and oversight to all employees, affiliate marketing partners, alliances, and other third parties, ensuring proper information security clearance in accordance with established organizational information security policies and procedures. The training required for various stakeholders will be a function of an assessment of what they know and what they need to know. What they know is information provided by a skills assessment and what they need to know will be the relevant policies, standards, and various control procedures.

Initiates, facilitates, and promotes activities to create information security awareness within the organization. The level of security awareness is information that can be provided by sampling representative groups using quizzes and interviews.

Performs information security risk assessments and serves as an internal auditor for security issues. The information provided by risk assessments is essential to security management decisions and must be kept current by various means. Reasonably accurate information requires a comprehensive approach along the lines of various business and administrative processes from input into the organization to the point of exit, including all physical and technical processes. In addition, geopolitical and environmental factors must also be considered, and business impact assessments are required to determine potential impacts of manifested risks.

Implements information security policies, standards, and procedures for the organization. The necessary information will be whether the policies meet the criteria for supporting the organization's overall business goals and implement the information security strategy. Necessary information about standards is whether they meet control objectives and whether there is adequate compliance, as well as any policy exceptions and possible mitigation options.

Reviews all system-related security plans throughout the organization's network, acting as a liaison to Information Systems. The security manager will require some process to provide information about what security plans are in the works or an approval process that mandates it. The standards of review must be known as well.

Monitors compliance with information security policies, standards, and procedures, referring problems to the appropriate department manager. Measures of technical compliance can often be automated and are generally straightforward. Procedural and physical compliance will be harder to get good information about, but depending on criticality, can be essential. Acceptable risk is also information the security manager must have to determine the level of necessary compliance and whether the cost of continuous real-time monitoring is warranted.

Coordinates the activities of the Information Security Committee. Coordinating the activities of the security committee will require information about the participants, scope, charter, and expectations of management and the committee, and about the most effective ways to operate it.

Advises the organization with current information about information security technologies and related regulatory issues. Current information about security and regulatory matters requires the development of relevant sources. Information about the recipients and organizational culture will be important to determine effective packaging and dissemination.

Monitors the internal control systems to ensure that appropriate access levels are maintained. Information about entitlements and access controls will be needed on an ongoing basis. Information about access control reliability and effectiveness will be required, as well as incidents involving unauthorized access and other security incidents.

Prepares the disaster recovery plan. Creating business continuity and disaster recovery plans requires a great deal of information to make decisions about approaches and viable options including risk assessments, business impact assessments, recovery time objectives, maximum tolerable outages, and costs of alternate site options.

9.2 Activities Requiring Metrics

Virtually all significant organizational security- or assurance-related activities will require some form of metrics, measurements, and/or monitoring. The most cost-effective approaches will in some manner aggregate these to present a level of information suitable for the recipient.

The question then is "What are the 'significant' activities that must be the subject of some form of measures or monitoring?" Key controls certainly merit some form of monitoring, but what about others? There is probably not a universal answer, but rather the security manager will want to consider and perhaps rank:

- The criticality or sensitivity of the activity
- The aspects and degree of risk or potential impact the activity creates

- The degree of risk or potential impact as a function of time
- The cost-effectiveness of metrics or monitoring options

9.2.1 Criticality and Sensitivity

Asset classification, in addition to providing the basis for access controls and other protection measures, also provides a guide for whether and what level of metrics or monitoring is appropriate. Obviously, any activity, process, or technology that is highly critical or sensitive must have some form "gauge" attached to it. The prudent approach is to develop some standards for the types of monitoring or metrics required at various criticality and sensitivity levels.

Whether an activity is critical or sensitive will be a factor in determining the approach to monitoring and metrics. For example, critical functions essential to keeping the business functioning can benefit from some form of automated redundancy, which lessens the need for immediate action. Sensitivity, such as disclosure of confidential information, cannot benefit from failover processes resulting in greater immediacy for notification and reaction.

9.2.2 Degree of Risk or Potential Impact

High criticality functions at any level of risk require some monitoring process. But, even a less critical function at high risk or one that has the capability of significant impact will require a greater degree of instrumentation.

9.2.3 Risk over Time

The rapidity with which a risk might be exploited or a potential impact realized must be considered in terms of the type and immediacy of feedback needed. An example is a fire alarm. It will be useless if it doesn't respond to the outbreak of a fire until an hour after it starts. Other types of events do not have the same immediacy, and delayed response may be entirely adequate.

9.2.4 Options and Cost-Effectiveness

Some activities will have obvious metrics or monitoring options and be very cost effective. Others, much less so. Intrusion detection on the internal network is a cost-effective approach to detecting compromise. Detecting and reacting to social engineering is far less direct and effective.

Options for measuring things like compliance levels are more complex and will often not be real-time, and the failure to monitor can be costly since a lack of procedural compliance can result in serious compromise or system failure.

9.3 Ranking Metrics and Monitoring Requirements

If the aforementioned four elements constitute the main considerations for determining whether metrics or monitoring is required, and if so, what an effective approach is, then a scoring system can be used to guide the selection process based on risk tolerance and risk management objectives. As we have discussed, well-instrumented systems monitor and measure only those elements that are useful or essential to the required management tasks. Assuming a determination has been made of critical activities and the potential for serious impacts and tolerance for risk, then the issue of effectiveness must be considered in terms of the necessity for certain specific types of information. Just as a fuel gauge won't provide a clue to which direction to head the ship, so will the number of viruses detected and eradicated not help with setting the direction for strategic alignment.

Consider the case of an internal IDS detecting an intruder. This is likely to be the sort of event that requires immediate, decisive action. But, additional information is required to make the best decisions such as the location and extent of the intrusion, the criticality and sensitivity of the impacted systems, the available methods for shutting down the attack, and perhaps the options for containment. Without this additional information, the most effective approach to dealing with the incident cannot be determined.

The point is that metrics, measures, and monitoring processes must be designed, in addition to the other requirements, with consideration for the context and any other information needed to make appropriate decisions. If the additional information requirements cannot be obtained in a timely fashion for whatever reason or are too costly, another approach may need to be devised.

9.3.1 Monitoring, Measures, or Metrics?

Monitoring can be applied in several ways. Metrics or measures can be monitored, meaning that they are being watched in some way. Monitoring of emerging threats by staying current with trade publications is an approach to staying current on the current threat landscape. Direct monitoring of any activity requiring compliance or that may constitute a threat can also be done. In the context of this section, consideration is of the latter, with the assumption that any critical metric or measure either will provide reliable notification or is in some manner monitored. The issues of timeliness, criticality, and the inability to devise cost-effective real-time metrics or measures is generally the basis for selecting monitoring as appropriate. From a controls perspective, real-time monitoring may provide the strongest preventive control, such as for access to a highly critical area. Obviously, cameras that are not monitored in real time but recorded are not preventive but rather detective controls. Biometrics coupled with smart cards may serve as inherently strong preventive controls but still lack the reactive capability provided by real-time monitoring by guards.

General guidance on the suitability of various approaches and the selection of whether metrics, measures, or monitoring is the best choice will depend on a number of considerations. Direct monitoring is generally the most expensive approach for providing information, but in some circumstances it is the best or only option, for example, critical configuration processes for a nuclear reactor or the key generation ceremony for a root certificate authority. So, the criteria is typically when the impact of procedural failure is so onerous or costly that not having real-time monitoring is not an option. For most organizations, there are usually processes that meet this requirement. The manufacture of critical components is invariably subject to quality control processes that serve as the requisite monitoring. On this basis, any critical security process or procedure should be considered for ongoing quality control monitoring beyond periodic audits. As with other information needed for decision making, standards for quality must be established and sampling rates providing acceptable assurance levels determined.

As previously discussed, metrics are measures based on one or more reference points. The question is whether measures absent any reference will be useful for making information security management decisions. Countless measures are possible, but without a point of reference, they will typically not be useful. Are there any exceptions? In many circumstances, measures may be sufficient for low criticality matters insofar as there are implied reference points or at least norms serving the same purpose.

Metrics that adequately meet the criteria defined in Chapter 7 and provide the specific actionable information needed for management are generally the preferred option if they provide some process for notification upon exceeding definable limits, that is, automated monitoring.

Chapter 10

Information Security Governance Metrics

We discussed approaches to developing metrics for implementing a security governance strategy in Chapter 8. In this chapter, we will examine the decisions that will typically need to be made and the information needed to support them from a strategic perspective from the viewpoint of managing an effort to develop and implement a strategy and from an operational standpoint for strategy development. This will provide the basis for determining what metrics will be needed to provide decision support information.

For the development of metrics, the intended recipients must always be considered. Many of these measures and metrics will be destined for governing board members and executive management. This means that it will be critical to understand what decisions they make and what information will provide the basis for those decisions. It will also be important to consider how to aggregate, or roll-up, information for conciseness as well as the best presentation options for presenting the information.

10.1 Strategic Security Governance Decisions

Strategic information security decisions are all business-related. In the SABSA architecture this domain is termed *contextual*. A review of the Business Strategy Attributes column in Figure 8.1 shows some examples. At the governance level, as with all other major activities of the organization, the issues, and therefore decisions, will revolve around integrating the various functions of the organization in a manner that promotes the efficient and effective operation of the business.

The information required to determine what decisions need to be made at the strategic level regarding information security will include

- The business of the organization
- The objectives and strategic direction of the organization
- The risks associated with current and anticipated activities
- The degree of acceptable uncertainty

The business of the organization will be relevant in terms of regulatory and legal requirements. It will determine the sorts of social and geopolitical elements that will need to be considered as well as help define the threat landscape.

The objectives and strategic direction of the organization will set the ultimate reference points for the security program in terms of its support for and enablement of organizational goals.

Determination of potential risks will feed back into strategic plans for feasibility analysis and cost estimates. It will help determine appropriate pricing strategies that take into consideration potential losses.

Many organizational endeavors can succeed only within certain operational parameters. Those parameters will determine the risk tolerance of the organization or of any particular initiative. This will in turn provide much of the information needed to determine the requirements for how risk must be managed.

10.1.1 Strategic Security Governance Decision Metrics

What metrics if any are useful in guiding information security decisions at the strategic level?

The business of the organization must be understood by the security manager. While this seems a simplistic requirement, for large multinational organizations, this may prove to be a formidable task. For example, one well-known home supply company has 64 subsidiaries located in dozens of countries, each with its own security manager. Most of these subsidiaries in turn have multiple lines of business. All report to a corporate security department, but, clearly, keeping track of and current with the overall organization's activities is not a simple matter. The relevance is that risks for each line of business will be different, as will the legal, regulatory, and risk environments in which they operate. In this situation, defining an overall security governance approach and an inclusive security strategy will be difficult, but without the information about all of the organization's business activities, it will be impossible.

Depending on the organization, there may be centralized planning activities that can serve as a central source of information about current and prospective business activities. Absent a central information source, the challenge will be to develop monitoring processes that will keep the information security manager informed about business activities as well as legal and regulatory matters that may impact the organization. This monitoring effort must be supported by enterprise-wide reporting policies and standards as well as effective communication channels to every part of the organization.

A primary set of metrics or monitoring processes needed for strategic decision support will relate to current and potential organizational risks and changes to those risks. The primary metric will be some form of risk assessment to establish the baselines, coupled with a robust method of tracking changes typically through the organization's change management processes. Metrics for vulnerabilities and threats must also be developed so that changes to either can be addressed by modifying or adding controls as needed to maintain acceptable levels of risk.

Acceptable or tolerable risk must also be established and then tracked or monitored for changes likely to occur over time. Most organizations determine acceptable risk only after some adverse event that proves to have unacceptable consequences. It will typically be more effective to have management decide what level of impact, usually in terms of cost, will require consideration for remediation. In the alternative, processes to define recovery time objectives will ultimately define rather precisely acceptable risk when the tradeoffs between shorter recovery times are balanced against costs of achieving those targets.

10.2 Security Governance Management Decisions

The governance process itself must be managed. Governance is effected through a system of rules—primarily in the form of policies, standards, and procedures.

If we consider the four requirements of governance as defined by ISACA for the governing board and executive management—(1) providing strategic direction, (2) ensuring objectives are achieved, (3) ascertaining risks are managed, and (4) verifying resources are used responsibly—we have set the general targets for what must be monitored and measured from a governance point of view. To devise metrics for this level of abstraction, it is necessary to reduce these four statements into specific requirements for the organization.

10.2.1 Strategic Direction

Let's consider the first item of providing strategic direction. In many organizations, strategic direction is often stated in aspirational terms such as "we will strive to increase the trust and confidence of stakeholders and customers," or as an example of "strategies" taken from a recent government tax authority publication, "Compliance—Helping People to Pay Tax and Get Their Entitlements," and "Human Resources—The Right People with the Right Tools."

While this form of "strategy" is more like a vague goal than an actual strategy, it can provide a starting point for considering a strategy. To repeat a previous definition, *strategy* means the plans to achieve an objective. Considerably more information will be needed, however, before these "strategies" can be translated into actionable information capable of being implemented and measured.

A lack of reasonable clarity of strategic direction for an organization will make it difficult to determine a strategic direction for a security program, which in turn will limit the possibilities of developing a security strategy. While clarifying this matter may not fall under the purview of the typical security manager, it might nevertheless make sense to attempt it. In some cases it may simply be a case where senior management has failed to document a strategic direction or has reason to keep it in confidence. It may be a case where there is a general "vision" for "the way forward" that has resulted in a series of departmental "strategies." In this situation it may be possible to gain sufficient clarity from each department to provide overall objectives for security activities.

While there may not be metrics for strategic direction, that direction may change and it can be monitored. Since significant changes in the organization's direction can have major impact on security operations, it is prudent to determine how and where in the organization these matters are considered and to devise an approach to stay informed.

10.2.2 Ensuring Objectives Are Achieved

Ensuring objectives are achieved requires first and foremost that objectives are defined and that there are agreed-upon measures to determine when those objectives have been met. As discussed in Chapter 5, for security, objectives must be defined in terms of characteristics and attributes in sufficient enough detail and precision that it is possible to know whether activities are heading in the right direction and when objectives have been achieved. In the aforementioned examples, how would anyone know that you have achieved the objective of "helping people to pay tax and get their entitlements"? Or conversely, how would anyone determine that you haven't? What is the measure? What level of help would be suitable?

Metrics for making decisions about the management of governance require, in addition to clear objectives, knowledge of the current state of security. The metrics are then simply the trajectory and velocity toward those objectives. These metrics can be developed by gap analysis, achievement of milestones, percentage of goals completed, extent of progress from current state to desired state, numeric score on a CMM analysis, and so on.

10.2.3 Managing Risks Appropriately

How can it be determined whether risks are managed appropriately?

Only management can decide an appropriate level of risk management by defining what constitutes acceptable or tolerable risks and impacts and then allocating adequate resources to accomplish those goals. The primary metrics for whether this is occurring are regular risk assessments, security reviews, and audits. The complexity arises out of the fact that there are numerous ways risk can be managed and whether those options are considered "appropriate." The conventional approach to control risk is generally through preventative controls, but other options could focus less on prevention if they proved not to be cost-effective and more on corrective approaches such as containment or better incident management and response. It is conceivable that under some circumstances the most "appropriate" approach would rely mostly on restoration or on business continuity and disaster recovery options. In many other circumstances analysis would show that insurance would be more cost-effective. The point to consider is that the term *appropriate* allows for many options that may best serve the requirement to manage risk for a particular organization or under specific conditions.

10.2.4 Using Resources Responsibly

What measures can provide evidence that resources are used responsibly?

Most practitioners will have some notion as to what this governance objective means, but there is likely to be substantial disagreement when it comes to specifics. Substantial elements of determining the notion of "responsibly" will be cultural and situational. In most cases, the overall "tone at the top" will set the standards for "acting responsibly," and it will often be evident in policies and standards as well. It is a reasonable assumption that in most cases providing persuasive business cases and financial analysis to support resource usage will suffice to meet the criteria.

A variety of cost-effectiveness approaches that should be suitable to demonstrate that this requirement is met are covered in Chapter 2. These include various possible financial metrics and others such as resource utilization metrics and statistics, and perhaps benchmarking. Including the demonstration of specific business linkages and support for business objectives will also aid in meeting this requirement.

10.3 Security Governance Operational Decisions

During the design, development, and implementation phases of information security governance, there will be a number of operational elements that will require metrics, measures, and monitoring. Some of the operational requirements will be to develop the means of providing the necessary information for strategic feedback discussed in Section 7.2. However, the main operational activity of information security governance will be the development of a security strategy. If strategy is the plan to achieve an objective, the outcome is some form of roadmap or, in fact, a high-level architecture.

What decisions must be made in developing a security architecture and what metrics are needed? The discussion of the SABSA business attributes approach in Section 3.4.3 provides a useful methodology for determining in great detail what must be addressed in a strategy that is directly tied to the relevant business drivers.

Each of the attributes in turn has suggested metrics enumerated in the table in Appendix E.

If a CobiT or ISO 27001 approach to developing control objectives is utilized, the relevant metrics for strategy development will be the extent to which those objectives are addressed by the strategy.

If the capability maturity approach is used to set objectives, the metrics for strategy development will be the improvement in maturity that will occur as a result of implementing the strategy.

In other words, at this level, the metrics are tied to the methodology used for setting and dissecting the information security objectives that the strategy is developed to address. A review of Chapter 2 should provide guidance on the approach or combination of approaches available that will meet the requirements for setting both objectives and options for devising meaningful metrics to support the required decisions.

Chapter 11

Information Security Risk Management

Risk management responsibilities are usually split between a number of organizational entities with the consequence that the biggest risk may well be a lack of continuity and integration between these efforts. The fact that all parts of any organization are required to operate in some fashion related to managing risk further complicates the problem. While many of these risk management concerns may be the responsibility of an organizational risk manager, many will also have a direct impact on information security. This includes most elements of physical security including how every user of information systems behaves, how physical information is handled, how laptops and other portable devices storing information are managed, and how access to facilities is controlled, to mention a few.

Good metrics that are directly informative of risk are virtually nonexistent at least in the area of information security. While we can get more-or-less direct metrics on technical vulnerabilities, most other components of risk including procedural vulnerabilities, threats, frequency, probability, and magnitude will not be as simple. Risk assessments are the primary approach to ascertaining risks but are only a snapshot in time and just a form of monitoring. They are also subjective and imprecise, which results in the likelihood that some risks will be overestimated and excessive precautions will be taken or that the underestimation of risks will result in unfortunate consequences.

While the increasingly sophisticated approaches such as value at risk (VAR) computations and other analysis methods offer promise of providing better risk management metrics, most are not ready for general implementation and their utility remains to be demonstrated. In most situations, technical vulnerability scans,

107

security reviews, and monitoring are typically the only viable options for the feedback needed for risk management decision support. This will require processes for gathering, analyzing, synthesizing, and correlating the necessary information. The question then is, "What information can be collected and processed that will effectively guide risk management decisions?"

11.1 Information Security Risk Management Decisions

The decisions that must be made by an information security manager about managing risk are numerous, complex, and generally lacking information of sufficient clarity and precision for any degree of certainty. These decisions are often guided by intuition and experience. They are, of course, also often wrong.

Typically the most important decisions relate to the type and level of protection that should be afforded various information-related assets and whether the protection provided is in fact adequate. The whole notion of layered security is to compensate for the inherent uncertainty in the entire risk assessment and management process.

Though well known to practitioners, it may be useful to dissect the kind of information needed to make rational decisions about managing risks including

- Criticality of assets
- Sensitivity of assets
- The nature and magnitude of impact if assets are compromised
- The extent and types of vulnerabilities and conditions that may change them
- The extent and nature of viable and emerging threats
- The probability or likelihood of compromise
- Strategic initiatives and plans
- Acceptable levels of risk and impact

Most of this information will be needed whether considering management or operational risk metrics. The difference will be that, typically, operational concerns will deal with current specific risks, often technical, and ways to provide remediation. At a strategic, or management, level the scope of information and assets will be broader, possibly more forward looking, and more concerned with control design and implementation as well as governance issues. The responsibilities are well described in the ISACA 2008 *Certified Information Security Manager Review Manual*:

> The objective of this job practice area (risk management) is to ensure that the information security manager understands the importance of risk management as a tool for meeting business needs and developing a security management program to support these needs. While information security governance defines the links between business goals and

objectives and the security program, security risk management defines the extent of protection that is prudent based on business requirements, objectives and priorities.

The objective of risk management is to identify, quantify and manage information security-related risks to achieve business objectives through a number of tasks utilizing the information security manager's knowledge of key risk management techniques. Since information security is one component of enterprise risk management, the techniques, methods and metrics used to define information security risks may need to be viewed within the larger context of organizational risk. [. . .] [I]nformation security risk management also needs to incorporate human resource, operational, physical and environmental risks.

11.2 Management Requirements for Information Security Risk

From a management perspective, risk must be managed proactively to the extent that it is cost-effective. Risk must be assessed and analyzed for new business initiatives and strategic plans as well as current activities. Remediation must be considered in terms of overall acceptable risk for the organization and prioritization of available resources. Baselines for acceptable risks must be developed across the enterprise, and business impact assessments must be performed for all critical business activities. Business continuity and disaster recovery must be planned for and hopefully tested.

Considering the primary, necessary information listed below, let's consider the decisions that will need to be made and possible sources of supporting information:

- Criticality of assets
- Sensitivity of assets
- The nature and magnitude of impact if assets are compromised
- The extent and types of vulnerabilities and conditions that may change them
- The extent and nature of viable and emerging threats
- The probability or likelihood of compromise
- Strategic initiatives and plans
- Acceptable levels of risk and impact

11.2.1 Criticality of Assets

Any information resource upon whose performance the organization depends is critical. It goes without saying that all resources needed to maintain those operations will require substantial protection if they are (1) in any way vulnerable and (2) there exists some potential threat that can exploit those vulnerabilities.

It will be necessary to determine which combination of operations is in fact required for the organization to function. The assets necessary for those operations will determine which assets are critical.

The usual metric will be a business impact assessment or a resource dependency analysis. The costs of the loss of essential resources can be determined with fair accuracy and will provide the basis for rational decisions about the level of protection warranted.

11.2.2 Sensitivity of Assets

Sensitivity refers to the possible harm to the organization that would result from the inadvertent disclosure of confidential information. Many types of information will meet the criteria, such as personally identifiable information (PII), which would include credit or bank account information and medical information, as well as strategic plans for products or acquisitions, perhaps accounting information and information considered trade secrets.

Determining with any precision what costs or other impacts might result from such disclosures is speculative. The best indicators or measures of possible impacts are historical trends of similar organizations. Given the level of well-publicized breaches and the consequences, monitoring the trade journals and news reports will likely serve as the best measure.

11.2.3 The Nature and Magnitude of Impacts

Security compromise can lead a variety of possible impacts ranging from the demise of the business (e.g., card systems, a payments processor that was compromised and lost 46 million credit card records) to regulatory sanctions, to class action lawsuits resulting in millions of dollars in damage. Determining the potential impact of a particular event is likely to be at best educated guesswork. As discussed above, a business impact analysis will provide insight into the direct impact on the organization's activities and how critical they are. What will be more ephemeral will be external factors such as lawsuits or regulatory sanctions, share market, and customer reaction. Again, the best overall measures are likely to be consequences for other organizations as reported in trade journals and the news media.

11.2.4 Vulnerabilities

Information on vulnerabilities other than technical can be difficult to acquire easily or in an automated fashion. Organizations requiring high security will test for physical vulnerabilities using tiger or red teams to attempt to gain unauthorized access to various parts of the organization by various means such as impersonation, false credentials, tail-gating, and social engineering. Most commercial organizations don't practice this sort of penetration testing and typically have little awareness of physical vulnerabilities. The information security manager can seek information from those responsible for physical security about what measures are in place, to what extent they have been tested for robustness and reliability, and what sort of metrics and monitoring is utilized. Another source of information will be historical breach and incident events caused by physical vulnerabilities. If it is evident that information assets are at risk from physical vulnerabilities and there are inadequate measures available to provide the ongoing information needed, the decision is clear—improve metrics and/or monitoring of physical vulnerabilities and improve controls.

11.2.5 Threats

Threats typically don't lend themselves to any sort of measurement. In addition, they are so numerous and diverse, it will be a challenge to monitor all possibilities. Typically, the best option for threat monitoring will be trade associations, the trade press, vendors, CERT, AusCert, and other governmental entities. While this information is readily available, it must still be analyzed to determine if it is of significance to any particular organization.

11.2.6 Probability of Compromise

The probability of attack is more subject to calculation than the probability of compromise. This information will primarily be subjective guesstimates based on thorough analysis. Keeping an eye on the information about vulnerabilities and threats will provide the information to feed the analysis and provide a vague indicator of likelihood.

It appears that a prevalent threat meeting significant vulnerabilities is likely sooner or later to result in compromise. Over sufficient time, experience shows that what can go wrong will. This, of course, is the reason all prudent security managers have a plan B, such as an effective, well-trained incident management capability as well as business continuity and disaster recovery plans and resources—which means that a comprehensive risk analysis needs to factor in response and recovery capabilities to determine the bounds of impacts.

11.2.7 Strategic Initiatives and Plans

Most organizations have some form of strategic planning activity. Sometimes it is ad hoc, perhaps centered in the marketing department, and in many instances it is a formal department charged with charting a course to the future. To be proactive and provide strategic guidance for security, the information security manager must have visibility into these functions.

11.2.8 Acceptable Levels of Risk and Impact

Throughout this work, we have discussed the necessity for senior management to decide on acceptable levels of risk and impact. Information security cannot be managed effectively and efficiently with this information. It will not be clear what we are managing to or when we have achieved our objectives. Various approaches to arriving at this information have been previously mentioned such as utilizing business access assessment (BIA) to define recovery time objectives that will ultimately define rather precisely acceptable risk when the tradeoffs between shorter recovery times are balanced against costs of achieving those targets.

Collecting the information discussed above in the foregoing Section 11.2 will provide the foundation for analysis of the requirements for making the necessary management decisions to guide risk management and strategic planning activities.

11.3 Information Security Operational Risk Metrics

Operational risk management (ORM) goals are tactical rather than strategic, and the time horizons are generally much shorter. Operational risk management generally has a financial focus brought about by the Basel II accords and do not include market and credit risk. While most efforts in this direction have been with a financial institution focus, the broad relevance for all organizations is clear. But, regardless how risk management is sliced and diced, many areas will either fall to information security management or impact it.

Operational risk management is largely concerned with the failure of internal controls and corporate governance. According to the Basel Committee on Banking Supervision, this includes seven areas of loss events, including

Internal Fraud—Loss due to acts of a type intended to defraud, misappropriate property, or circumvent regulations, the law, or company policy, excluding diversity, discrimination events, which involve at least one internal party.

External Fraud—Losses due to acts of a type intended to defraud, misappropriate property, or circumvent the law by a third party. These activities include theft, robbery, hacking, and phishing attacks.

Employment Practices and Workplace Safety—Losses arising from acts inconsistent with employment, health, or safety laws or agreements, from payment of personal injury claims, or from diversity/discrimination.

Clients, Products, and Business Practice—Losses arising from unintentional or negligent failure to meet a professional obligation to specific clients (including fiduciary and suitability requirements), or from the nature of design of a product.

Damage to Physical Assets—Losses arising from loss or damage to physical assets from natural disaster or other events.

Business Disruption and Systems Failures—Losses arising from disruption of business or system failures. This includes loss due to failure of computer hardware, computer software, telecommunications failure, or utility outage and disruptions.

Execution, Delivery, and Process Management—Losses from failed transaction processing or process management, from relations with trade suppliers and vendors. This includes transaction capture, execution and maintenance miscommunication, data entry, maintenance or loading error, missed deadline or responsibility, model/system misoperation, accounting error, entity attribution error, delivery failure, collateral management failure, reference data maintenance, monitoring and reporting failed mandatory reporting obligation, inaccurate external report (loss incurred), customer intake and documentation client permissions/disclaimers, missing/incomplete legal documents, customer/client account management, unapproved access given to accounts, incorrect client records (loss incurred), negligent loss or damage of client assets, trade partners, nonclient vendor misperformance, and vendor disputes.

Operational risk management decisions for a security manager will essentially revolve around ensuring controls are operational and functioning as intended. It may include designing or modifying controls and implementation as well to meet control objectives. Ensuring operation of controls will require metrics and monitoring with characteristics of reliability, robustness, accuracy, timeliness, and so on, as discussed in Chapter 4.

As with the foregoing management section, much of the same information about assets, risks, and impacts will be needed to properly allocate resources and prioritize monitoring and metrics activities. These include knowing

- Criticality of assets
- Sensitivity of assets
- The nature and magnitude of impact if assets are compromised
- The extent and types of vulnerabilities and conditions that may change them
- The extent and nature of viable and emerging threats
- Acceptable levels of risk and impact

At the operational level, many of these issues should already have been determined, and this information should be available to guide tactical activities in alignment with strategic objectives.

The decisions a security manager at the operational level needs to make will mainly be based on whether controls are

1. Adequate to ensure risks are managed to acceptable levels
2. Operating as intended

This may seem an oversimplification, but the assumption is that risks have been assessed, a risk management strategy and approach are in place, and controls have been devised at the management level and are implemented and operational.

What metrics or monitoring will be needed to provide this assurance at the operational level?

Penetration tests both electronic and physical will provide some level of assurance of vulnerability to compromise.

Live tests of BCP/DR and incident response plans will provide the likely limits of risks and impacts at a point in time. That is, to the extent these tests are realistic and meet design criteria, the limits of risk can be measured and impact evaluated.

Audits will usually provide some reasonable assurances that controls are functioning and risks are managed as well.

While all three are a means for providing assurance, they are limited to being a snapshot in time and prudent operational risk management requires a more or less continuous approach of the operational capabilities of at least key controls.

As discussed in Chapter 4, at the technical level, continuous monitoring can be achieved using the many tools available. Key physical and procedural controls will typically require monitoring processes. Both will require periodic testing for reliability and accuracy.

Chapter 12

Information Security Program Development Metrics

Information security program development is considered the process of implementing strategy into operational use. This will typically result in a series of projects or initiatives as the result of developing a strategy that meets the strategic objectives of the organization. It is the series of activities that over time results in achieving the "desired state" of the information security program, as discussed in Chapter 7.

The projects undertaken to achieve program objectives can utilize standard project management approaches such as Prince II and metrics not unique to information security. This will typically include GANNT and PERT charts and perhaps critical path charts. Assuming preconditions such as specific objectives having been defined, adequate resources committed, and a roadmap or architecture developed, the relevant question is "What decisions must be made and what metrics will be needed to provide the information required to manage security program development?"

This will in large part depend on the scale and nature of security program implementation. If it is a major initiative and highly complex with many moving parts such as implementing an enterprise resource planning (ERP) system, there will be many dependencies and serious consequences for poor planning, inadequate metrics, and ineffective management. As a result, adequate monitoring and metrics becomes a crucial element in managing for satisfactory outcomes.

12.1 Program Development Management Metrics

From a management perspective, what information will a security manager need to make implementation decisions, and what metrics will provide the required information? Numerous minor operational decisions will typically relate to resolving particular problems encountered during implementation. The more important management decisions will relate to whether implementation is meeting budget and time objectives and ultimately whether the project performs as anticipated. Time and budget issues can be crucial if they are in the critical path of other initiatives. Decisions may need to be made whether to increase or reallocate resources or perhaps whether to reschedule dependent activities. These aspects can be very important if major organizational activities are dependent on timely completion of a security initiative and its meeting the required performance objectives. An example might be an online business such as banking or product merchandising initiative dependent on an adequate and functional security implementation or achieving regulatory compliance mandates within an allotted time frame.

Key goal indicators (KGIs) and key performance indicators (KPIs) are likely to be the most useful approaches to measuring program development progress. There are a number of variations of system development life cycle (SDLC) methods, but they all generally include

- Determining feasibility
- Establishing requirements
- Solution architecture and design
- Proof of concept
- Full development and coding
- Integration testing
- Deployment
- Quality and acceptance testing
- Maintenance

If the SDLC approach is used in security program development, each phase can include KGIs and KPIs.

For example, a feasibility study goal indicator will be the completion of an analysis determining whether or not an initiative is likely to meet the defined business objectives at acceptable costs and risks within required time frames. Performance indicators for this phase will be whether the study provides answers with adequate certainty, progresses at the desired pace, and is completed on time at anticipated costs.

Establishing requirements goals could include ensuring that all critical business needs can be addressed. Performance will revolve around whether necessary specifications are achievable, affordable, and can meet requirements.

Solution architecture and design goals will relate to completion times, incorporating all required elements, design efficiency, meeting control objectives, and so on.

Proof of concept goals will be to prove feasibility and to provide evidence that the required performance objectives can be achieved.

Full development and coding will be a project to be managed in conventional ways with standard project metrics in terms of milestones, costs, resources, and so on, as will integration testing.

Deployment objectives and performance goals will also include time, cost, and effectiveness measures.

Quality and acceptance testing (UAT) will include metrics on the outcomes and deficiencies encountered as well as conformance to specifications.

Maintenance metrics will be gathered over time, and the performance indicators will be set by the original specifications.

While this may seem to be a highly granular approach, for important and/or complex projects, it is prudent to set goals and performance indicators for each phase to manage project risks and ensure development proceeds at the necessary pace.

12.2 Program Development Operational Metrics

Operational metrics for program development will center on specific project-related issues. Typically, decisions required will deal with project progress, meeting milestones, unforeseen impediments, inadequate performance, and so on. The necessary information will in like fashion be about milestones and project performance-related issues. They will deal with design problems and implementation issues. The goals at this level will hopefully be clear and in terms of SDLC, the issues will be far down on the list of requirements for projects—that is, objectives, feasibility, and design elements will already be in place.

Chapter 13

Information Security Management Metrics

Managing information security will typically require a variety of decisions including those involving strategy and management as well as those in administration and operational areas. Clearly, the information or feedback needed will be very different for making prudent decisions in the various areas and, consequently, the metrics needed will be quite different.

> Metrics serve only one purpose: decision support. We measure to manage.
> We manage to meet objectives in order to achieve desired outcomes.

Strategic measures and metrics for governance are discussed in Chapter 10 and are basically the navigational tools to keep the program on track.

It is a good idea to keep in mind what well-known management consultant Peter Drucker said: "What gets measured, gets managed." Tony Murphy points out that the corollary is just as true: "What does not get measured, does not get managed."[1] In pointing this out, Murphy explains that the lack of a measurement culture has surely been responsible for the poor returns of IT in terms of business value. The same thing can be said of information security. It is the contribution to the business value that matters, and we need management metrics for those calculations.

Management metrics discussed here are concerned with the effectiveness of the program and providing the information needed to fly straight and level and operating within acceptable limits. These will be tactical metrics that are needed to keep the program operating at acceptable levels guided by the strategic objectives—the destination. Just as operational metrics can be "rolled up" to provide assurance to the security manager that the machinery is performing within acceptable ranges, so too can management metrics be abstracted to provide assurance to executive management that the entire security program is operating within prescribed limits so that strategic objectives will not be compromised.

While technical metrics for information security have seen significant gains in the operational area, strategic and management measures remain virtually nonexistent. The consequence is that there is scant information to provide the basis for the decisions needed to manage an information security program on an ongoing basis.

Some practitioners contend that abstractions of technical operational information can be effective for security management, but this argument is flawed. There is simply no way of putting technical operational information together to navigate or manage a security program. It is not unlike attempting to operate an aircraft using a fuel gauge, oil pressure, engine temperature, and so on. From a predictive perspective, the only thing known from operational information will be that objectives cannot be achieved if operations fail.

As an example, the manager of an aircraft, the pilot, requires three types of information in order to accomplish his responsibilities:

1. Strategic information, which is provided by navigation systems
2. Management, or tactical, information such as attitude, airspeed, turn, and bank
3. Operational information, including oil pressure, temperature, and fuel level

Navigation information is strategic for the flight as it tells the pilot which direction to go and how far it is to the destination as well as the current location. The destination is set by senior management based on the strategic requirements and operation of the business and can be considered the business objectives of the flight needed to operate an airline.

The pilot needs management information regarding the aircraft attitude, altitude, airspeed, and direction of flight to operate it safely within acceptable limits and headed toward the destination set by senior management. It will also be important to keep an eye on operational metrics such as fuel, oil pressure, temperatures, and so forth to ensure they are within acceptable ranges, which are analogous to technical IT metrics to ensure progress isn't disrupted by mechanical failure.

The requirements for a security manager operating a security department are not much different.

13.1 Security Management Decision Support Metrics

Management metrics differ from strategic governance and program development metrics in several ways. Just as the metrics for running an airline or building an airplane are quite different from the ones that are used to fly it, so too are the metrics needed for day-to-day management and administration of a security program.

The information needed for management of a security department is also quite different from information needed for operational security management. Operational security will be concerned with information about such things as server configurations, intrusion detection systems, and firewalls.

For managing a corporate security department, let's consider the types of decisions that are typically made by someone serving in the CISO role regardless of the actual title. This role should generally report to senior management or the audit committee of the board of directors. The role of a CISO will usually be involved in strategic activities such as developing policies and standards, incident management, developing or implementing security strategy, budgets, personnel issues, and regulatory and contractual matters.

As a part of an oversight function, a CISO may also monitor some operational information, perhaps in summary form, to ensure that the "machinery" is performing within normal limits just as a pilot wants to know that engines are operating normally and there is adequate fuel. This information is important only from the aspect that "mechanical" failure can cause operational failure, which will result in the objectives not being realized. But, this operational information tells the pilot nothing about whether the aircraft is headed in the right direction to arrive at the desired destination.

Management of information security will be primarily concerned with strategic business outcomes, ensuring that security activities properly support the organization's objectives and alignment with the overall business strategy. As a result, the types of information needed must be indicative of things like the effectiveness of risk management, the appropriateness of resource allocation and utilization, and the degree of overall policy compliance. The problem is that most organizations have few if any useful metrics that provide this sort of information. Given that reality and if we accept the notion that decisions can only be as good as the information they are based on, then it follows that, for most organizations, management of security is far from optimal as evidenced by the ongoing security failures continuously reported in the press.

The starting point for determining the kinds of measures, metrics, and monitoring needed is understanding the scope and responsibilities of those who make the decisions. This provides the basis for determining the information required, which in turn defines the kinds of measures and monitoring processes that must be developed. The areas that should be the focus for security managers will include the aforementioned six outcomes including:

1. Strategic Alignment—Aligning security activities in support of organizational objectives
2. Risk Management—Executing appropriate measures to manage risks and potential impacts to an acceptable level

3. Assurance Process Integration/Convergence—Integrating all relevant assurance processes to improve overall security and efficiency
4. Value Delivery—Optimizing investments in support of the organization's objectives
5. Resource Management—Using organizational resources efficiently and effectively
6. Performance Measurement—Monitoring and reporting on security processes to ensure organizational objectives are achieved

If these are the outcomes that good security management should achieve, then defined objectives must be devised for each of them, and there must be information provided by appropriate metrics, measures, or monitoring for each of them as well.

In previous chapters, key goal indicators (KGIs) and key performance indicators (KPIs) are discussed in the context of security program development. For ongoing information security management, performance measures are generally not as relevant. Rather, information about location, direction, and speed will be more useful in guiding the overall security program to achieve the defined objectives. In other words, performance measures, while useful for managing operational activities, do not provide navigational information needed at the tactical and strategic levels.

13.2 Security Management Decisions

Effective security management in the majority of organizations relies primarily on the experience of the security manager coupled with a shotgun approach to plugging all perceived vulnerabilities to the extent possible and employing "best practices." Given a modicum of luck and adequate resources, this approach can be reasonably effective much of the time. However, as witnessed by the near continuous reports of increasingly costly compromises, this approach fails all too often. Typically, these failures are not a surprise to security managers and are often the result of organizations failing to support and implement recommended security measures. What is considered an adequate level of security is frequently an area of contention between IT, business owners, and security managers. In part, this is a consequence of security managers failing to make a persuasive business case for controls seen as too restrictive or costly. It is also in part due to the fact that lacking effective metrics, there is a tendency for cautious security managers to adopt excessively restrictive controls much as the lack of an accurate speedometer will cause a cautious individual to drive too slowly. The uncertainty caused by a lack of adequate metrics drives prudent security managers to attempt to increase safety margins that may be seen as overkill by those focused on performance.

Effective information security management metrics, then, are those that provide the right kind of information for the security manager to make appropriate decisions. The key to developing these metrics is *defined objectives,* which provide the reference points against which to measure.

If the previously stated six outcomes for information security are to be achieved, it will be necessary to provide clear objectives for each of them. This will in turn provide the reference points by which information security management metrics can be developed. The decisions that a CISO must make are then determined by whether security activities are headed in the right direction to achieve those objectives.

While the six outcomes are readily understood, reducing them to concise objectives will vary considerably between different organizations and requires some effort. Achieving consensus on the extent and degree that these outcomes should be attained will provide the basis for the objectives needed to design useful measures, metrics, and monitoring activities.

13.2.1 Strategic Alignment

—aligning security activities in support of organizational objectives

The concept of aligning security to support the organization's objectives is readily understood, but the questions raised are more complex. What degree of alignment is adequate? How can it be measured?

More alignment is arguably better than less alignment, so the metric shouldn't be binary—that is, aligned or not aligned. The metric will also be subjective and not quantitative. Nevertheless, the extent that security activities are *perceived as hindering any particular organizational activity* is likely to be a useful measure whether true or not. But the metrics for strategic alignment must extend beyond just perception and deal with reasonably quantifiable measures to manage those perceptions. To accomplish this, it will be necessary to determine

1. Clearly defined objectives of the organization
2. The risks and security implications for those objectives
3. The boundaries of acceptable risk

For example, if one of the objectives of the organization is to provide online banking, the risks and implications can be assessed and potential impacts of compromise determined. Management must then determine the extent to which various risks associated with the activity are acceptable or not. Alignment of security with this objective is fairly straightforward although likely to result in some tension between usability by customers and adequate safety of the process. The perception of alignment is likely to be the result of how great an impediment to implementation security considerations are seen to have.

Another example of a more tactical nature is a scenario where a security manager determines that eliminating e-mail attachments will significantly reduce virus infections of the organization's systems. From a purely safety perspective, this might be prudent but from a business perspective is likely to adversely affect operational efficiency and be perceived as an unnecessary nuisance and even contrary to the notion of strategic alignment.

What information is needed to make this decision?

To a large extent, this will be determined by the industry sector. It is common in manufacturing and retail to preclude any security activity that has a noticeable negative impact on operations. In this case, the information needed by the security manager is simple—for example, the metric can be the number of complaints from users. Any increase in complaints mandates the requirement to make controls less restrictive.

The regulated financial sector is more balanced in considering the tradeoffs between performance and safety and might require the development of a business case assessing the range of options and the costs and benefits. The information needed to support a decision in this regard includes

1. The costs of infections from e-mail attachments
2. The value of benefits to users and/or cost of inconvenience
3. The cost of incremental limitations
4. The costs of remedial processes as a result of attachments

The metrics for the cost of infections are relatively straightforward. There are no consistent methods used across industries, but any reasonable approach should be satisfactory as long as the methods used are consistent. This will allow trends to be determined that might be a basis for different decisions.

Metrics for inconvenience and incremental restrictions can be against a baseline of user complaints or the result of periodic surveys. Incident costs resulting from infectious attachments can be based on information from incident reports and response and resolution costs from postmortems.

Decisions around strategic alignment regarding appropriate risk baselines, acceptable impacts on the organization from security activities, and acceptable tradeoffs between performance and safety pose more of a challenge. In part, this is because these will often be dynamic elements and in part because it will be difficult to achieve consensus among stakeholders with very different perspectives and agendas. Often, this results in highly subjective or reactive decisions and a focus solely on quarterly financial performance. The focus on profit regardless of risk is a typical result of misaligned incentives and inadequate governance.

Case Study

Consider the approach undertaken by a major bank to align security with its business objectives. The organization was clear that it wanted to expand its operations online because the efficiencies gained from online banking had proven persuasive. It was also demonstrated by surveys and analysis undertaken by the CISO that customer trust was the single most important factor in driving growth and the factors that most affected that trust were primarily in the information security domain. In response to these findings, senior management implemented a plan whereby several hundred of the top managers have a substantial portion of their compensation tied to evaluation of their adherence to security requirements and compliance of their respective organizations.

The revelation in this instance is that the most significant security metric had nothing to do with security. Rather, it was customer satisfaction. In the case of this bank, careful analysis made it clear that this was the best correlation with growth, and inadequate security was one of the main causes of unhappy customers.

The important idea to take away is that for many organizations, at the strategic and management levels, the best security metrics may only be related to the impact of security, not any measure of security itself. Decisions related to strategic alignment will often be strategic as well.

For example, the decision to make standards more restrictive to increase security baselines over time may affect the entire organization and is likely to be costly. What information is needed by the CISO to make that decision and be able to support it? Here is how the CISO might proceed:

1. Gather evidence in the form of studies or surveys that security compromise would result in a loss of business. An example is the PGP/Vontu analysis of a number of breach losses showing that 19 percent of customers immediately ceased doing business with the affected organizations and another 40 percent were considering doing so.[2]
2. Based on the evidence, determine probable lost revenues and profits.
3. Perform an analysis to estimate the decrease in security failures based on historical evidence of preventable breaches.
4. Determine costs of modifying and implementing new standards, the modification of procedures, and new technical control measures.

Analysis of this information can be made using ROSI, or other means will determine the optimal level of security baselines based on costs and benefits. If it is determined that increased security baselines make business sense, other measures will be required to measure progress of the initiative as well ultimate success in achieving the objectives. These could include project management metrics of implementation against plan and budget. Subsequent surveys could assess customer satisfaction and the correlation with sales or perhaps a decrease in customer turnover.

13.2.2 Risk Management

—executing appropriate measures to manage risks and potential impacts to an acceptable level

For the purposes of this book, the definition of risk is the probability of a threat exploiting a vulnerability causing an impact. The level of risk will be a function of both frequency and magnitude.

To devise effective metrics for risk management, it must be determined what constitutes "appropriate" risk management measures and what are considered "acceptable" risk levels. Without fairly concise definitions, it is difficult to make decisions about what levels risk must be managed to and in what direction the program should be headed. Wide variances in these elements between different organizations, sectors, and cultures will affect what is considered appropriate and acceptable.

The organization's "risk tolerance" is the major determinant in what is considered acceptable risk, and the prudent security manager will determine this level by some measure. Determination of acceptable risk levels is often easier to achieve by discussing impact levels in terms of the range of likely costs of disruptions and the probability of occurrence. If, for example, management decides that any event costing less than 10,000 dollars that will occur less than once a year is an acceptable impact not worth mitigation efforts, the security manager has a defined target and a reference point for a useful metric.

The extent that the culture of the organization is risk adverse is a major factor in what is ultimately determined as "acceptable." This in turn will likely be the main determinant of the level of support for risk management activities. While it is possible in an organization with a high aversion to risk to require an excessive level of risk management resulting in low cost-effectiveness, the more common problem is just the opposite. The undermanagement of risk coupled with good fortune resulting in a lack of incidents is typically a greater problem. This is because it may suggest to management that existing risk management efforts are adequate and as a result management may opt to allocate resources to areas perceived as more pressing or offering greater returns.

For most organizations, risk management for information security is generally ad hoc and haphazard. This is borne out by studies showing that security resource allocation is generally unrelated to risks or impact and is often narrowly focused only on IT risks. The lack of a mature security governance structure with the resultant absence of defined objectives is often the cause and the result is that some risks typically in IT are managed reasonably well whereas others are not addressed until there is a compromise. The analysis of breach losses inventoried by PGP/Vontu in 2006 highlights this situation (Table 13.1).

While the usual emphasis on purely preventive IT perimeter controls appears to have been generally effective at keeping intruders out, it can be inferred that baseline security of the organizations studied were highly inconsistent and most non-IT risks were not managed effectively. Consistent security baselines would arguably result in roughly equal losses and, of course, all would be within defined acceptable levels.

13.2.2.1 Metrics for Risk Management

It is clear that a requirement for developing effective metrics for risk management, as for all other aspects of information security, is to define and develop clear objectives

Table 13.1 Breach Losses from Compromise of 33 Companies

Lost laptops	35%
Third party or outsourced	21%
Electronic backup	19%
Paper records	9%
Malicious insider or malware	9%
Hacking	7%

Source: 2006 Annual Study: *Cost of a Data Breach,* PGP/Vontu.

to serve as the reference point against which to measure. From a risk management standpoint, the question then arises, "What information will the security manager require to make the decisions to effectively guide risk management activities?"

1. Determination of the organization's risk tolerance
2. Comprehensive resource valuation
3. Complete risk assessment
4. Business impact assessment of important systems
5. Tests of control effectiveness and reliability
6. Known level of metric accuracy

The information from metrics around each of these six items will provide the basis for determining both the priority of risk management efforts and the level of effort required to achieve the objective of acceptable risk and impact levels.

In the next section we will examine what types of metrics, measures, or monitoring can be used to provide this information.

Organizational Risk Tolerance

The level of risk or impact that management considers acceptable must be determined as a prerequisite to an effective risk management effort. Impact in financial terms is usually the best way to arrive at this determination as organizations operate on numbers. It should be considered that there is a risk associated with any activity as well as with not doing something. While risk management is usually considered in terms of preventing loss from adverse events, in some cases it may also be concerned with not achieving some potential gain.

For any organization, there is some level of financial impact small enough that no expenditure to address the risk is warranted. There will also be some level of potential loss that will not be acceptable and will be dependent to some extent on the probability of occurrence. If the probability of even a major event is vanishingly small, the risk may still be accepted. It should be noted that acceptable risk may differ for various parts of an organization, and it may change over time under different circumstances, consequently requiring periodic revisit.

The determination for acceptable information security impacts is not significantly different from determining suitable levels of insurance. In both cases, less impact is generally more costly. Consequently, the exercise boils down to a cost-benefit analysis. The rational point to arrive at is where the mitigation cost of a particular risk is equal to the cost of that risk's impact. When graphed, this is the point where the curve of the increasing cost of mitigation crosses the curve of decreasing cost of impacts.

In these determinations, the enterprise's risk manager is the information security practitioner's best friend. Specialists in total quality management (TQM) and Six Sigma can be helpful, and allies in legal and internal audit departments should be sought. Certainly, the chief financial officer is both an audience for the completed analysis and an ally in its completion.

An innovative approach to risk management is the cost of self-insurance, which has been introduced by Russell Cameron Thomas.[3] The notion of this is that money would be set aside each year into a reserve fund that would offset the expense of low-probability, high-impact losses such as

- Budget-busting losses such as severe outages, delays in new products, losses of contracts
- Long-lasting business disruptions, regulatory action, and punitive damages

Thomas points out that in all cases, top management sets the risk threshold and the time horizon, presumably based on input that includes the work of the information security practitioner. The idea of self-insurance grows out of the fact that insurance, such as cyberinsurance, may not be available for the transfer of particular risks. As Thomas points out, a "self-insurance premium" must be calculated in such circumstances. This is done using models and organizational and industry experience. The insurance industry is increasingly seeking new markets and is rising to the challenge of information security–related risks by offering new products in this space. In the meantime, calculating a "self-insurance premium" can help in determining the cost of risk mitigation.

Depending on the organization, there may be a number of reasons that the determination of risk tolerance may not be entirely rational, however. These reasons can range from "it hasn't happened here and we'll deal with it when it does" to skepticism about the accuracy of risk assessments or the level of threat. There may also be financial constraints that preclude appropriate mitigation activities such as conserving funds to improve quarterly results.

In some cases, it may be more effective to go through the process of developing recovery time objectives (RTOs) for critical organizational activities. The process of negotiating acceptable RTOs at an acceptable cost provides a direct financial value of what the organization is willing to spend to address the risk of system failure. This serves as a clear indicator of risk tolerance based on acceptable impacts. This approach is, of course, also dependent on the credibility of the prerequisite risk assessment in terms of the probability of an event and its potential magnitude (i.e., whether it can cause system failure).

Defining risk tolerance in measurable terms provides the objectives the security manager can manage to as well as the reference point for metrics needed to guide risk management efforts. This can also be useful in that risks that fall below this measure can provide the basis for reducing controls and costs, while risks in excess of the mark will require additional mitigation efforts.

Resource Valuation

Resource valuation is an obvious requirement. However, surprisingly, this is often not the case in many organizations and the result is that the value of most or all information resources is not known. For risk to be managed appropriately, it is essential that actual or relative value of information assets is determined. For assets of little value, there is obviously not a significant reason to manage risks to them.

The underlying principle of proportionality requires that the cost of protection never exceed the value of the asset and that assets of equal value subject to similar risk should have the same level of protection.

Many information assets will be difficult to value with any precision. Some organizations use a simpler process of valuing assets, which has just three or five levels of relative value. While inexact, this approach may be sufficient to determine the necessary levels of risk management effort as well as the priority.

For example, in Chapter 3, we presented a brief discussion of Debra Herman's security return on investment (security ROI.)[4] As with most such systems of relative value assignment, she uses qualitative groupings. She assigns a range of values to each one of the qualitative labels:

- Ultra high: 164–200
- High: 128–163
- Medium: 92–127
- Low: 55–91
- Little to none: 17–54

The value of a particular asset is determined by adding up weighting factors for several categories:

- Asset importance
  - Criticality
  - Sensitivity

- Impact of asset loss
  - Loss sensitivity
  - Scope of loss
  - Loss duration

Each category has a scale that is reflective of it. Each category has a qualitative value associated with it. For instance, in her scheme, the Scope of Loss category has the following values:

- 40—Beyond the enterprise (critical infrastructure)
- 32—Enterprise-wide
- 24—Region-wide
- 20—Campus-wide
- 16—Facility-wide
- 4—Single work area
- 2—Single device

The other categories have a similar value scale assigned to them.

To get the relative value of an asset, the scores are added to determine the final score in the qualitative groups. For instance, if the final score for an asset is 200, the relative value of an asset is labeled *Ultra High* because its score is in the identified range for that label (164–200).

As discussed in Chapter 3, most ROI methods fail because of the amount of guesswork that is involved in arriving at a final significant score and the arbitrary nature of the individual category values. While asset valuation is far from a settled art, this form of relative asset valuation can be useful as long as it is grounded in some reality. For instance, using Herman's asset valuation scheme, a database that directly supports emergency responders (fire, police, search and rescue, etc.) would merit the highest score of 40 for the Scope of Loss category because its loss would have an effect beyond the enterprise, and it is a part of the critical infrastructure.

Comprehensive Risk Assessment

Risks that are not known are not likely to be managed. Effective risk management is not possible without the information provided by comprehensive risk assessment and analysis. Risk assessment and analysis must be comprehensive in the sense that the entire business process is assessed from initial entry into the organization until the final output. The assessment must include all related physical and technical processes that are related. In addition, external factors such as environmental, cultural, legal, and geopolitical risks, to name just a few, must be considered insofar as they may pose a viable risk that may impact the organization.

Business Impact Assessment

Potential impacts from compromise must be understood in order to manage risk. Impact is the bottom line in risk management, and it might more accurately be called *impact management*. Even enormous risks that have little or no impact do not need to be managed. It must be acknowledged that there continues to be disagreement among security practitioners about the exact meanings of the terms *risk*, *impact, exposure*, and so on.

As explained, for the purposes of this book the definition of risk is the probability of a threat exploiting a vulnerability causing an impact. The level of risk will be a function of both frequency and magnitude.

The information obtained from business impact assessments (BIAs) will be critical for effective risk management decisions in terms of the level of mitigation required as well as prioritizing security resource allocations. BIAs are central to business continuity planning (BCP), continuity of operations (COOP), and disaster recovery planning (DRP). Therefore, it is important to involve an organization's BCP, COOP, and DRP specialists in the risk assessment and analysis. If the organization is not large enough to have such specialists, the information security practitioner needs to either have these skills or consider engaging external expertise. For a good overview, refer to NIST Special Publication 800-34—*Contingency Planning Guide for Information Technology.*[5]

Control Effectiveness and Reliability

Control effectiveness and reliability must be determined to consistently manage risks to acceptable levels. The degree of effectiveness will determine to what extent layering of controls is necessary to achieve acceptable mitigation levels. The information security manager can also use this information to support decisions to replace or modify controls that are not sufficiently effective or reliable. Technical controls usually fare much better than procedural controls in this regard. Metrics on effectiveness can be obtained by periodic testing or some process for regular or continuous monitoring.

Metrics on incident detection, response times, impacts, and effectiveness of response activities will also provide useful information to provide a basis for risk management decisions.

Metrics Accuracy

If they are to be useful, metrics developed to provide information for risk management must be tested for accuracy. Inaccurate or misleading metrics may be worse than no metrics and likely to lead to faulty decisions. The accuracy needs not be extreme provided that the limits of the range are known and can be factored into the decision-making processes. Other attributes of metrics are discussed in Chapter 7.

13.2.3 Assurance Process Integration

—integrating all relevant assurance processes to improve overall security and efficiency

Organizations typically have a number of departments and functions that are in some manner charged with ensuring the safety and security of various elements of the enterprise. Most or all of these assurance-related functions have relevance for information security risk management. Since many aspects of risk will cut across a number of these segmented functions, the effectiveness of risk management will likely be limited to the extent to which these functions are integrated. In large organizations, these assurance-related activities can include

- Audit
- Legal
- HR
- Risk management
- Insurance
- Training
- Privacy
- Compliance
- Quality assurance
- Facilities
- Physical security
- IT security
- Project management
- Help desk
- DR/BCP
- Forensics
- Architecture

Typically, the scope of activities and reporting structures of these various functions is arbitrary and will have evolved organically over time without benefit of governance or a security strategy that might serve to integrate them. In most cases, there exists no framework or architecture providing overarching assurance of safety, security, and effective risk management. The problem is exacerbated by the fact that these functions generally speak their own language, have their own terms of art (i.e., buzz words) and associations, see risk issues narrowly from their own perspectives, and report to different parts of the organization. The results are all too often that various departments are working at cross-purposes and have contradictory security initiatives, and failures in one area can cause failures of physical security causing compromise of security in another. An example is when a failure of physical security causes a compromise of information or IT security.

It is this fragmentation, and the realization that it markedly degrades the ability to provide overall assurance of safety, that has led to the notion of "convergence" of physical, IT, and information security, which is the focus of a group composed of ASIS, ISACA, and ISSA. On a national level, it is the driver for the creation of the U.S. Department of Homeland Security, which has the mandate of integrating a number of previously independent security- and safety-related departments. This concept is not yet widely recognized or supported, but a number of factors will drive integration over time, including the ever-growing requirement for more cost-effective security. For the CISO considering initiating efforts to leverage through some process to drive integration of the organization's various assurance functions, there are several questions that need to be answered, including the following:

- What would constitute an effective level of integration?
- What benefits can be achieved by this course of action at what cost?
- What approaches can be used to achieve a level of functional or actual integration?
- What metrics or measures can gauge the level of integration on an ongoing basis?

The answers will vary from one organization to another, but if the decision is made that some degree of functional or operational integration of assurance function is beneficial, a plan can be devised to achieve the objective in a number of ways over time. Some possibilities to consider can include

- Explicit policy directives mandating interplay and communications between departments
- Modification of reporting structures of some assurance functions to a common management point
- Appropriate representation on a steering committee

As with other aspects of risk management, objectives for the desired level of assurance integration must be devised. Measures or indicators of the need for better integration could include

- Incidents traceable to a lack of integration. The Australian Customs office example where two people appearing to be service personnel simply entered a supposedly high-security area and walked out with several highly sensitive servers would certainly qualify as an indicator.
- Another indicator is significantly different levels in the organizational structure of physical and information security and other major regulatory functions. In organizations that have not achieved a level of maturity in security, it is common to see the head of physical security hold the rank of vice president while the information security manager is many levels lower in an operational role.

■ Inconsistencies or contradictions in the objectives, policies, and standards applied to various assurance functions is a common indication of a lack of integration and can result in operating at cross purposes.

■ The higher in the organization the common reporting point for assurance processes exists, the lower the level of integration is likely to be. In part, this is a result of the observation made by well-known management consultant Peter Drucker nearly two decades ago that for every level of management, the noise doubles and the amount of information is cut in half.

■ The degree of communications between assurance providers correlates well with the level of integration between these activities.

These indicators and measures can both serve to develop a business case for better assurance process integration and provide the basis for how better integration can be accomplished. Some possible approaches include

■ Developing or modifying policy to mandate integration supported by standards for minimum requirements, and procedures for how that will be accomplished

■ Modifying reporting structures to lower the organizational level where the responsibility for various related assurance functions converge to a single authority

■ Defining roles and responsibilities to explicitly interface with other assurance providers

■ Ensuring that an effective steering committee with high-level representation from major assurance providers regularly addresses integration issues

13.2.4 Value Delivery

—optimizing investments in support of the organization's objectives

Optimizing value is a fundamental management function. For information security, this can be a challenge absent many of the financial metrics and analysis tools available for other types of organizational activities. It is nevertheless important to make inroads into developing financial metrics and indicators for value in the security domain. Corporations run on numbers, and it will increasingly be a requirement for security as well.

As with other aspects of a security program, objectives must be developed that will result in the desired outcomes of optimizing investments. Metrics and indicators can then be developed using the objectives as the reference point to provide guidance to the effort. There are a number of areas that can be considered.

One aspect that may pay considerable dividends is measures or metrics of the cost-effectiveness of existing controls. Effectiveness must be measured by some process, as must the total costs associated with the control. Effectiveness metrics can be the extent to which control objectives are met, or how often a control fails or how often it is circumvented. Cost of a control should be computed to include the costs of acquisition, deployment, management, training, and maintenance as well as its impact on productivity and perhaps end-of-life decommissioning.

Another measure is the level of standardization, as multiple solutions to the same problems are generally more costly in deployment, training, management, and maintenance. For example, standardized access controls across. the enterprise are easier to manage and monitor than a number of different implementations. However, the benefits of standardization are to some extent offset by the increased risk of a single compromise affecting the entire system. To address the aggregated risk posed by homogeneity, it may be necessary to incur some additional cost to increase control robustness or provide additional preventive or compensatory controls.

Financial returns on security investments are often the most difficult to arrive at with any certainty. However, if they are well supported, they will also generally be useful and persuasive. To the extent that they are reasonably accurate, financial measures provide the best information to guide decisions ranging from priorities to the allocation of resources and achieving the most effective security investment strategy.

Some practitioners maintain that security is similar to insurance and attempting to calculate a return on investment is not useful. As discussed in Chapter 3, numerous efforts to determine return on security investments have been developed during the past few decades with mixed results. But, as previously mentioned, organizations run on financial numbers. Accordingly, security activities must ultimately run on them as well.

For certain security investments, return on investment is straightforward while other methods will be much more speculative. The automation of certain manual processes is an example that readily lends itself to computing ROI. Return on investment of prevention activities will be much more difficult but not impossible. ROSI, discussed in Section 3.2.2, is an effort to address the return on investment of preventing certain adverse events. While subject to a significant degree of estimation and possibly speculation, the approach is supportable in some circumstances where either there are fairly consistent documented losses over time or industry data provides the same information. The return on investment of any particular mitigation method is calculated by the expected reduction in losses divided by the cost of doing so. In other words, if a particular security solution can be reasonably shown to save two dollars and it costs one dollar to implement, the formula will show a 100 percent return on investment.

Other metrics for the value of security activities may be largely perceptual. This suggests that if the organization generally perceives security as effectively meeting its requirements, as not excessively intrusive, and as providing for consistent, reliable operations, these factors may ultimately be the most important metric for delivering value. The conclusion is that monitoring and managing expectations is an important component for the CISO to consider.

13.2.5 Resource Management

—using organizational resources efficiently and effectively

Resource management is related to value delivery but is focused primarily on resource utilization. Typically, the resources that are managed and the processes used will be similar to most other departments. The resources will be personnel and various physical and technical assets.

The requirement for efficiency and effectiveness means that the necessary security services are delivered at the lowest cost commensurate with achieving the defined objectives. This is largely an area of operational concern insofar as the metrics needed will be around ongoing utilization of resources and related management costs. There are obviously some prerequisites to achieving high levels of resource utilization such as knowing all of the available resources. Many organizations still do not maintain accurate information asset registers, which creates difficulties in efforts to manage them effectively.

Once again, it will be necessary to develop utilization objectives for both personnel and systems in order to develop useful metrics. While measures of personnel utilization rates can be achieved with time sheets or other monitoring, absent targets that might be based on industry statistics or historical information, this will be a less useful metric. The argument could be made that as long as productivity continues to rise and utilization is high, objectives are not required. While to some extent this may be true, measuring against a clearly defined target will provide better, more consistent information upon which to base management decisions.

Another possibly useful metric might be benchmarking against comparable organizations although it may be difficult to get valid comparisons. However, if a similar organization achieves better security effectiveness such as fewer losses related to security failures at a lower cost, it could be indicative of better resource management.

13.2.6 Performance Measurement

—monitoring and reporting on security processes to ensure organizational objectives are achieved

Measuring the performance of security processes in a broader sense than the specifics detailed in this book can involve determining if the overall range of metrics at the strategic, tactical, and operational levels is sufficient to provide the information needed for effective decision making. In addition, it must be determined if these metrics are in the right mix for a specific organization.

Performance measurement can include an assessment of whether all key controls are monitored in some manner to ensure they are functional and operating as intended. Performance measures can include metrics on the metrics themselves in terms of reliability and accuracy, as well as their failure modes.

This information can be used by the CISO to guide the development of additional metrics or monitoring as needed, and it can be usefully summarized in reports to senior management.

13.3 Information Security Management Operational Decision Support Metrics

Operational security roles at various levels of the organization have different responsibilities and are required to make different decisions in the process of discharging their duties. The information needed for decision support will come from operations as opposed to strategic sources. As an example, consider a typical IT or information security manager who reports directly or indirectly to the CIO and often has a system administrator background. Activities are generally focused around operational issues involving the data center, network, and desktop computers. Responsibilities usually include such things as firewall configuration and management, antimalware activities, patching, IDS/IPS-related activities, pen testing, vulnerability scanning, configuration management, compliance monitoring and enforcement, and incident response. There are many variations on this theme, and perhaps their responsibilities might include many other specific tasks. Some will be more on the technical side, and some less so. Some have greater responsibilities, and some have less. However, this encompasses the generality. Accordingly, a wide variety of metrics are required. Therefore, it is important to ensure that the mix of metrics that are being used is broad enough to cover both the strategic and the tactical aspects of their responsibilities.

13.3.1 IT and Information Security Management

Many technical metrics are available in the IT environment. The larger problem is often too much data and too little information. What decisions does this manager make and what information is needed to ensure that an appropriate conclusion is reached? Even with the vast amounts of data available for efforts to secure the IT environment, it is not an easy task to determine what might serve as useful metrics that meet the previously mentioned criteria:

- Manageable
- Meaningful
- Actionable
- Unambiguous
- Reliable
- Timely
- Predictive

Applying these criteria can serve to eliminate a great deal of the less relevant measures and focus on the metrics that provide the most useful information.

13.3.2 Compliance Metrics

Compliance with policy and technical standards is typically an area of responsibility for security managers. Procedural compliance is an important component of providing effective security. Even well-developed and -tested procedural controls are only as good as the level of compliance.

The objective will normally be full and consistent compliance with mandated procedures. The decisions that the manager must make related to compliance will generally revolve around either training and education or, alternatively, enforcement, or perhaps both. That is, it may require training in procedural controls to ensure personnel know what to do, or it may require enforcement activities to ensure compliance takes place. It may also be necessary to test the functionality of the procedure itself or determine whether a particular function requires additional staff or resources.

For the manager to make decisions regarding which direction to take, specific additional information will be needed, such as the actual level of compliance and whether individuals understand how to perform the control procedures. Without these metrics, it cannot be determined whether education or enforcement is required, or whether additional resources must be allocated. If the problem is indifference or carelessness, training might be a waste of time and money. In some cases, the best decision may be that a particular procedure is too cumbersome, impractical, or ineffective and must be changed.

To provide the information needed to make an informed decision in this case, we need to monitor or measure several elements including compliance levels, performance proficiency, and awareness levels. It may also be necessary to test and evaluate a procedure to measure its functionality, efficiency, and appropriateness. There will be varying degrees of sensitivity and criticality of various activities that mandate different degrees of security effort to ensure that acceptable levels of risk are maintained. The assets involved will be subject to varying levels of risk exposure as well. Obviously, highly critical functions with significant exposures whose security is dependent on fully functioning controls will need better and more timely metrics or monitoring than those that are not so important. The reliability of the metrics themselves may also be an important consideration to factor into any decision process.

In this situation, the relevant information required for management decisions can include

1. The criticality and sensitivity of assets involved
2. The level of risk the assets are exposed to
3. The state of compliance with the relevant procedure
4. The degree of procedural competence of personnel
5. The adequacy of resources
6. The reliability and accuracy of the metrics themselves
7. The functionality, efficiency, and appropriateness of the procedure

Let's consider how the required information may be acquired for each of these elements.

Criticality and Sensitivity

The level of compliance that may be satisfactory from a purely risk-based view will hinge on the level of criticality and/or sensitivity of the procedural activity under consideration. For procedures that are not critical or sensitive, a low level of procedural compliance may pose little risk. A broader issue may be the difficulty in structurally, operationally, and culturally mandating and enforcing vastly different levels of compliance. One risk is that personnel in the habit of cutting corners while performing some procedures are likely to do so in others as well.

For activities that are highly critical or sensitive, procedural compliance at anything less than 100 percent will be unacceptable. Regardless, realities and limited resources may force priorities to be set for monitoring and metrics activities, and, obviously, the highest concern will be for the most critical functions with significant degrees of exposure.

From a management standpoint, the level of criticality or sensitivity is required information for informed decision making. While compliance failure for noncritical functions may still need to be dealt with and decisions made, the urgency will be less and the required decisions might suffer from excessive postponement.

Determining Criticality and Sensitivity—Various approaches can be used to determine the sensitivity and criticality of assets. Some form of asset classification is typically used and it may also include performing a business impact analysis or a resource dependency assessment. Asset owners will need to be engaged to make these determinations.

Sensitivity can be measured by the extent to which there are adverse consequences, or impact, from unplanned disclosure. The typical approach is qualitative and quite subjective. As previously explained, asset valuation is often just ranked in three or four categories. Assets may be categorized in only three classifications, such as *confidential* or *in confidence, internal*, and perhaps *public* or *unclassified*.

Criticality is the measure of how important a particular asset is to the business function and the consequences, or impact, of the loss of the use of the asset over time. This is usually measured in terms of some sort of ranking or by recovery time objectives (RTO) based on a business impact assessment (BIA). RTO ranking recognizes that the immediate recovery of all processes and assets is not required. Indeed, immediate recovery of all processes and assets may not even be possible given the limitations of time and budget.

It is obvious that for organizations that haven't performed these classifications, it will be difficult to determine appropriate metrics for compliance since they should arguably be related to the relative importance of the assets.

Sensitivity and criticality are not likely to change quickly, and once their classification is determined by a classification process, a change management process should in most cases inform security management of any significant changes that would affect either of those dimensions. Nevertheless, either sensitivity or criticality may change over time for reasons that aren't reflected in change management processes. For example, a database supporting a new service may initially have only a few items of sensitive information in it, but over time, this may grow to include a great deal of sensitive information whose compromise might pose a major risk. The growth in the quantity of information wouldn't be subject to change management processes, but the risk and potential impacts may increase substantially. Of course, this potential change should have been anticipated and compensatory activities undertaken at appropriate times. But it would be a prudent practice to plan some form of monitoring or review process to identify significant changes in risk for assets where a change in utility or value may occur over time.

Risk Exposure

The level of exposure will be a major factor in making decisions regarding compliance. If the level of exposure is very low for even a highly critical asset, the need for real-time metrics or monitoring is diminished. If, on the other hand, a critical asset is exposed to considerable risk, metrics or monitoring that provides a high level of assurance of procedural compliance is warranted. In addition, it may also be justified to provide inherently strong controls such as dual controls.

Risks — Risks are measured by risk assessments. These are, of course, also qualitative, subjective, and generally speculative. Nevertheless, relative risk to the assets under consideration will need to be known for effective decision support. Compliance with control procedures will be more critical for highly critical assets at substantial risk than for unimportant assets at little risk. Precision is not a necessity for decision making. However, it is necessary to have a process that will provide a consistent relative risk ranking in relation to other assets since the objective is to ensure the highest levels of compliance for the most critical assets at the most risk.

Risk will change over time or with the advent of new threats. A risk assessment combined with effective change management processes will often provide much of this information. But, threats, vulnerabilities, and potential impacts will change and must be monitored.

The State of Compliance

The next element to consider is what unit of measurement is useful for compliance. Percentage is a common measure and would seem obvious, but on consideration it proves to be inadequate. In some cases, only 90 percent compliance with the steps required in a critical procedure can be fatal. So, for important or critical procedures we need 100 percent compliance with all the steps, 100 percent of the time. Accordingly, the metric doesn't need to be scalar, just binary—either the procedures are consistently followed or they are not.

It can be argued that a 100 percent compliance is unrealistic and high percentages might be adequate. For noncritical procedures, that might be sufficient, but in the case of heart surgery or flying jumbo jets, the argument is not persuasive, and procedural failures have resulted in fatalities and huge negligence awards. Given potentially catastrophic consequences, few knowledgeable managers would accept only high percentages of critical procedural compliance as acceptable.

If procedural compliance for critical systems is an absolute requirement, the unit of measurement can then be simply yes or no, green or red. The issue, then, is how to acquire the information on an ongoing, real-time basis. Compliance with technical controls can generally be reliably automated, but procedural controls pose a greater challenge. In many instances, procedures that interact with technical elements might provide the possibility of automated compliance metrics. In other instances there may be no options other than some form of monitoring, such as CCTV. But, direct observation or monitoring is inefficient and expensive, and it is not the preferred option if other avenues exist. For trusted personnel, a common approach is the use of a signed manual checklist as a reminder of accountability.

A variety of possibilities exist that can be considered for purely physical procedures. A typical physical access control procedure in highly sensitive or critical areas is some combination of guards, ID badges, proximity cards, and sign-in logs. For handling critical backup tapes, procedures might include elements such as secure containers, identification and authentication of personnel transporting the tapes, and signed receipts, as well as CCTV recordings at pick-up and delivery points. While these sorts of procedures are common and generally effective, providing real-time metrics on compliance with the procedures is not straightforward and not typically done. The reality is that the compliance metrics in these cases involve after-the-fact reviews of logs and tapes, which is both troublesome and rarely performed unless there is a discovered incident.

Audits are the primary metric for compliance. However, they suffer from the lack of timeliness. In the case of the backup tapes, possible approaches could include secured GPS tracking devices or RFID chips and scanners at particular points. The required information could be gathered by a series of reporting checkpoints. These methods lend themselves to automated compliance management, but an additional investment is required to knit these individual measures together for monitoring and reporting purposes. Finally, a management system would need to be instituted to ensure that each component and the system as a whole are functioning as designed.

Compliance may pose the greatest challenge in terms of monitoring or metrics. Compliance monitoring or metrics, may be available from automated sources or may require physical or electronic observation in some fashion. Most organizations measure compliance primarily through audits, which may not provide information that is timely enough to meet risk management objectives. The decision on a reasonable level of monitoring will be a factor of the other foregoing elements. In cases where operating personnel with low proficiency are working in areas of high risks and with assets of high criticality or sensitivity, it is obvious that more monitoring and/or better metrics will be required. On the other hand, highly trained, experienced personnel performing consistently and reliably over time may not require more than a periodic check to provide adequate levels of assurance.

Cultural, psychological, and organizational structural aspects will be a factor in the human dimension that in many circumstances can be quite important. While these dimensions are likely to be too esoteric for most organizations, they must be considered where potential impacts can be catastrophic, such as dealing with nuclear weapons or the kinds of rogue currency trading that bankrupted Britain's largest merchant bank (Barings Bank) some years ago in 1995. Individual "world-views" of personnel involved in highly critical or sensitive activities is an additional dimension that might be usefully considered. Employees with a "hierarchical" perspective are more likely to follow rules than are individuals with an "individualist" outlook. Approaches to testing these dimensions are discussed in Appendix B.

Compliance measures for technical control procedures can generally be obtained from logs. The problem of reviewing the immense amounts of data from the typical logging activities can to some extent be addressed through so-called security information management (SIM) or security information management systems (SIMS), which are log-reading and correlation tools. Essentially, through data mining of the logs, these tools can be configured in a number of ways that can address many metrics requirements.

However, these tools are still lacking in a number of respects. For instance, security maven Bruce Schneier is critical:

> Analyzing log messages can determine how the attacker broke in, what he accessed, whether any backdoors were added, and so on. The idea behind log analysis is that if you can read the log messages in real time, you can figure out what the attacker is doing. And if you can respond fast enough, you can kick him out before he does damage. It's security detection and response. Log analysis works, whether or not you use SIMS. Even better, it works against a wide variety of risks. Unlike point solutions, security monitoring is general. Log analysis can detect attackers regardless of their tactics.
>
> But SIMS don't live up to the hype, because they're missing the essential ingredient that so many other computer security products lack: human intelligence. Firewalls often fail because they're configured and maintained improperly. IDSs are often useless because there's no one to respond to their alerts—or to separate the real attacks from the false alarms. SIMS have the same problem: unless there's a human

expert monitoring them, they're not defending anything. The tools are only as effective as the people using them.

SIMS require vigilance: attacks can happen at any time of the day and any day of the year. Consequently, staffing requires five fulltime employees; more, if you include supervisors and backup personnel with more specialized skills. Even if an organization could find the budget for all of these people, it would be very difficult to hire them in today's job market. And attacks against a single organization don't happen often enough to keep a team of this caliber engaged and interested... The key to network security is people, not products. Piling more security products, such as SIMS, on our network won't help. This is why I believe that network security will eventually be outsourced. There's no other cost-effective way to reliably get the experts you need, and therefore no other cost-effective way to reliably get security.[6]

It should be pointed out in this piece, Bruce Schneier promotes the company that he started to do outsourcing of network security: Counterpane. Large organizations do, in fact, employ high-caliber teams that are quite busy defending their networks. Nevertheless, Schneier's comments illustrate some of the problems with the automation of some metrics and measurements.

Measures of compliance with physical procedures may require, in addition to periodic audits, random inspections, security reviews, video monitoring, supervisory oversight, or guards.

Compliance metrics can often be obtained from procedures that interface with technology. An example would be the procedures for hardening a server. Activities can be logged and the required steps can be verified or the configuration can be tested automatically to conform to specifications. Checking the configuration does not ensure the steps were followed exactly but may nevertheless be adequate to ensure the desired outcomes. Much work on the automation of automated configuration and vulnerability testing continues. This work by both the research and vendor communities has made it possible to compare configurations and scan for vulnerabilities in an automated fashion, and report those results in a standardized manner.[7] Indeed, work continues on a language that can be used to describe business rules:

The Semantics of Business Vocabulary and Business Rules (SBVR) is an adopted standard of the Object Management Group (OMG) intended to be the basis for a formal and detailed natural language declarative description of a complex entity, such as a business. SBVR is intended to formalize complex compliance rules, such as operational rules for an enterprise, security policy, standard compliance, or regulatory compliance rules. Such formal vocabularies and rules can be interpreted and used by computer systems. SBVR is an integral part of the OMG's Model Driven Architecture (MDA).[8]

As this work continues, more and better capabilities will continue to be developed and made available as products and services.

So, we can monitor a process by some means to ensure all steps required by a procedure are followed. We can provide some type of outcome metrics to ensure we achieve the desired results. For processes that engender risks if steps are not followed (such as mixing nitroglycerine to make dynamite or flying jets), either monitoring at critical stages or creating metrics that warn of impending danger can be used.

Are there elements of managing security that create hazardous situations at various points even if final outcomes can be verified as being satisfactory? A number of situations come to mind, and the answer is in the affirmative. An example would be the event of a breach not being responded to according to the correct procedures and consequently escalating into a full blown catastrophe. Events at a major financial institution involving the Slammer worm serve to illustrate this possibility:

Case Study

Personnel monitoring the Network Operations Center (NOC) noticed unusual network activity on a Sunday evening. Deciding there was no imminent danger and certain that they could handle any eventuality, they decided to watch the event. By the early morning traffic continued to increase at both the main facility and then suddenly began to grow dramatically at the mirror site hundreds of miles away. By 7 a.m. they notified senior IT managers that there was a problem and the network was becoming saturated. An hour later when the external CIRT team arrived, the network was totally inoperative and the team determined that they had in fact been compromised by Slammer. The CIRT team manager informed the network manager that Slammer was memory resident and restarting the entire network and mirror facility would resolve the issue. The manager stated he did not have the authority to do so and it would require the CIO to issue that instruction. The CIO could not be located and current phone numbers were kept in an emergency paging system that required network access. When asked about the disaster recovery plan and what it had to say regarding declaration criteria, three different plans were produced that had been prepared by teams in different parts of the organization unbeknownst to each other. The final resolution ultimately required the CEO, who was also not immediately available to finally issue instructions the next morning to shut the expletive-deleted non-functioning network down. Over 30,000 people could not perform their work, and the institution was

inoperative for a full day and a half. The final direct costs were estimated by the postmortem team to exceed 50 million dollars despite the
stonewalling and lack of cooperation from most employees fearful of
being found somehow at fault.

The author managed the postmortem team that found literally hundreds of deficient processes, a dysfunctional culture, and an array of
useless metrics in addition to a fatally flawed lack of adequate governance. For those monitoring the NOC, metrics indicated a problem,
but they were not sufficiently meaningful to the employees for them
to make any active decisions, much less the correct ones. Either better metrics or greater proficiency of the personnel could have resolved
the issue quickly in the initial stages of the incident before it became
a problem. Better governance would have vested adequate authority in
the network manager to take the appropriate action. Better governance
would have insisted that either the vulnerability patches issued a full
two months prior were applied or suitable compensatory controls were
implemented to address a well-known threat. Even marginally effective risk management would have insisted that a flat network with no
segmentation was unacceptable and that DR/BCP was an integrated
and tested activity.

The conclusions that can be reached that are relevant to metrics is that data is
not information and that incomprehensible information is just data and useless. It
also illustrates that no matter how good the metrics and monitoring providing decision support, it is useless to someone not empowered to make decisions.

As a consequence, to develop useful metrics, it must be clear what decisions
must be made by whom and what information is needed to make them. It is
apparent from this analysis that management metrics will typically require a variety of information from different sources that must then be synthesized to provide meaningful information needed for making decisions about what actions are
required.

Personnel Competence

Metrics around the competence of personnel to perform complex procedures reliably and consistently will be important as well. To some extent the metrics indicating high levels of personnel proficiency, commitment, integrity, and reliability
can to some indeterminate extent, under some conditions, reduce the need for
real-time continuous monitoring or metrics. Complex procedures may require
training and/or periodic refresher courses if metrics indicate inadequate proficiency. The decisions a manager might need to make for the amount and type of
training will benefit from metrics in terms of personnel awareness, proficiency,
and reliability.

Proficiency and Awareness—Proficiency in performing procedures can be tested in a variety of fairly obvious ways. Written tests, quizzes, direct observation, and tracking errors or omissions would be some of the possibilities. Performance records over a period of time may be useful measures as well.

Security awareness can be measured by simple questionnaires or quizzes administered periodically.

Resource Adequacy

The adequacy of resources can be determined by observation, by analysis, or by questioning the individuals involved. Inadequacy of resources is often a function of misallocation, underutilization, or a productivity issue. Standard approaches can be utilized to determine which is the case.

In the case of personnel, a typical approach to measurement would be detailed time sheets to determine how time is utilized. It is likely that high-value individuals are spending too much time on low-value activities. This would support the decision for better task and time management or, possibly, outsourcing low-value activities.

Metrics Reliability

Metrics on the reliability and accuracy of the metrics themselves will be needed in order to make appropriate decisions. If the metrics of a critical function are only 90 percent reliable and 60 percent accurate, additional actions will be required to achieve high assurance levels since the information can be relied on only 45 percent of the time. Another consideration for the decision maker will be whether the metrics will indicate false positives or false negatives, or whether in some cases they will merely fail to show anything.

Metrics need to be tested periodically to provide assurance of functionality, reliability, and accuracy. Depending on the metric, reliability can be measured in a number of ways. Repeatability and consistency would be useful for measuring both reliability and accuracy. For technical metrics, testing can usually be automated to provide assurance of consistency. Other gauges of reliability can range from statistical sampling and analysis over a large number of measurements to comparison to some sort of standard.

Measures may be evaluated against outcomes to determine reliability and consistency. That is to say, if a particular metric value consistently results in the same outcome given the same circumstances, it would be judged as reliable. For instance, if every time the fuel gauge shows empty, the vehicle ceases operating, there is a level of assurance of the reliability of the gauge. Conversely, if periodically, it shows that an amount of fuel still remains when there is none, prudence dictates some other metric be used such as a dipstick in the gas tank.

Procedure Functionality, Efficiency, and Appropriateness

Finally, it is necessary to consider the possibility that if there are problems with compliance, a particular procedural control is poorly designed, difficult to perform, or inefficient. An analysis of the control objectives may be needed to ensure they are properly aligned with business and security requirements. Research indicates that more often than not, poor performance by employees is the result of bad process design. As a result, the procedure may need to be tested and evaluated from a process standpoint and perhaps be redesigned or possibly automated.

In most organizations, procedures that more or less work are typically not subject to review. If compliance is found to be a problem, a good candidate for the root cause will be poor procedures. If control objectives have not been defined and the assets have not been classified, it will be difficult to determine appropriate procedural controls, however.

With the assumption that procedural controls are documented, measures include the completeness, accuracy, consistency, and conformance to standards (and therefore policy) of the procedure itself. Another measure is the ability of someone unfamiliar with the procedure to accurately accomplish the task using only the written procedure.

Endnotes

1. Murphy, Tony (2002). "P2—Process, Step 3—IT Value Analysis." *Achieving Business Value from Technology—A Practical Guide for Today's Executive*. Gartner Press, John Wiley and Sons, New York, NY.
2. 2006 Annual Study: *Cost of a Data Breach*, PGP/Vontu.
3. Thomas, Russell Cameron (2007). "Total Cost of Cyber (In)Security—Integrating Operational Security Metrics into Business Decision-Making." Presentation to Mini-Metricon, February 5, 2007. Available from http://www.meritology.com
4. Herman, Debra (2007). "Measuring Return on Investment (ROI) in Physical, Personnel, IT, and Operational Security Controls." *Complete Guide to Security and Privacy Metrics*. Auerbach Publications, Boca Raton, FL.
5. National Institute of Standards and Technology, Information Technology Laboratory (2002). NIST Special Publication 800-34: *Contingency Planning Guide for Information Technology—Systems Recommendations of the National Institute of Standards and Technology*. http://csrc.nist.gov/publications/PubsSPs.html
6. Schneier, Bruce (2004). "Schneirer on Security, Security Management Systems (SIM)." http://www.schneier.com/blog/archives/2004/10/security_inform.html
7. "Making Security Measurable—A Collection of Information Security Community Standardization Activities and Initiatives." Mitre Corporation. http://makingsecuritymeasurable.mitre.org/
8. "Semantics of Business Vocabulary and Business Rules (SBVR)." Wikipedia. http://en.wikipedia.org/wiki/Semantics_of_Business_Vocabulary_and_Business_Rules

Chapter 14

Incident Management and Response

Incident management and response are the last step in risk management and the final barrier to what may become an unmitigated disaster. The decisions that must be made require accurate and timely information and will probably include many of the following:

- Is it actually an incident?
- What kind of incident is it?
- Is it a security incident?
- What is the severity level?
- Are there multiple events and impacts?
- Will they need triage?
- What is the most effective response?
- What immediate actions must be taken?
- Which incident response teams and other personnel must be mobilized?
- Who must be notified?
- Who is in charge?
- Is it becoming a disaster?

There may be assistance available for making some of the necessary decisions such as event detection and correlation tools. Specific suggestions for metrics are difficult as individual circumstances are highly variable. Nevertheless, this is a vital area for most organizations and we will attempt to identify the different types of information needed and some possibilities for acquiring it. Once again, management information requirements will differ from operational or incident response needs.

14.1 Incident Management Decision Support Metrics

The answers to the questions above will determine how to proceed in the event of an incident and may prove critical to the organization. Let's consider them individually and what information is required as well as possible sources and metrics.

14.1.1 Is It Actually an Incident?

Nontechnical personnel encountering unusual events on the network or on their computer may suspect an incident is taking place and report it perhaps to the help desk. Help-desk staff unfamiliar with the situation may in turn escalate to IT or security, or ignore it. If the situation is unfamiliar to security staff or IT, how will they determine if the situation constitutes an incident and is in fact posing a risk? What must be done to clarify whether an individual desktop machine has a problem or the situation is a manifestation of a bigger event? It is likely to prove useful to have a defined, systematic approach of "troubleshooting" to quickly determine these answers so that proper response can be initiated. As in medical situations, early detection and proper diagnosis are key to preventing serious impacts. In the majority of organizations, general awareness education about incidents and specific training for key personnel are the proven methods of improving incident detection, management, and response.

Depending on what is monitored and the types of metrics available, there will be information that, if accessible, will be helpful in incident diagnosis. For example, incidents involving intrusions into the network may be detected by network IDS (NIDS) or host IDS (HIDS) or other tools such as SIM tools checking logs. There may be possibilities for detecting anomalies when the ranges of normal operations are known in a manner similar to anomaly-based IDSs. In other words, unusual levels of traffic or certain operations at unusual times can be an indication that something is amiss. This is true of physical access as well, and having visibility into existing physical access controls is essential and, surprisingly, in most organizations, unusual.

A simple and effective monitoring tool is to simply correlate physical presence with login location. Obviously, if someone not shown to be on the premises by physical access controls is found to be logging into the system from the premises (i.e., not remotely), either there's a failure of the access controls or there is some other security incident occurring.

In order for the information to determine whether an event constitutes an incident, personnel monitoring resources must have suitable skills as well as effective communication channels. If skills are not adequate, the decision will be to either provide training or acquire personnel with the necessary skills. If it is not clear who needs to communicate what to whom when and how or the channels are not available, the decisions will revolve around addressing those issues.

Understanding that this information is required to make appropriate decisions makes it straightforward to determine what metrics or monitoring are needed for management.

The necessary skills must be determined and then skills assessment testing is required to determine the gap that must be addressed. Communication channels can be tested by simulated incidents perhaps starting with a table-top walk-through to ensure personnel have the right information and understand their responsibilities. The metric will be binary—that is, personnel either have the skills and know what to do or they don't. Effective incident response is pretty much all or nothing.

14.1.2 What Kind of Incident Is It?

There are generally few metrics likely to directly identify the type of incident, and what remains is monitoring and diagnostic capabilities. An example of a physical event that will have technical manifestations such as lost connectivity is when a ditch-digging machine severs the fiber link to the data center or a wiring closet burns up. Whether the organization considers these to be security events varies although arguably this will impact availability, which usually has security implications of one sort or another. If emergency services cannot be contacted, air traffic control cannot communicate with aircraft, or credit cards cannot be authorized, it is difficult to argue that availability isn't a security issue.

Validating that an incident has occurred in the foregoing paragraph will generally result in the determination of the kind of incident it is. Additional information will usually be required, such as the scope and possible impact of the incident as well.

14.1.3 Is It a Security Incident?

There is little consensus on exactly what constitutes a "security" event, although many organizations have developed internal criteria and definitions. Organizations often consider the cause of an incident to be determinative, that is, a deliberate disruptive act would be a security matter whereas an accident would not. This distinction suffers from the fact that it is easy to imagine many accidental situations that can have major security implications and impacts. It may be more prudent to consider a security incident *any event that has the potential of compromising security or elevating risk regardless of cause.*

14.1.4 What Is the Severity Level?

Severity of an incident must be determined quickly and hopefully with a degree of accuracy. Declaring a full-fledged disaster as the result of a minor incident is not likely to be a good career move and neither is failing to declare a disaster and reacting inappropriately when there is one.

Severity levels must be defined and agreed upon, and personnel must be educated or trained on making the determination. Authority to declare the various severity levels must be assigned and escalation procedures defined. Other preconditions exist such as information asset classification, which is required so that the criticality and/or sensitivity of affected assets can be quickly determined, which along with the level of impact will be largely determinative of severity level.

Once again, good diagnostics will be the key to efficiently gathering the needed information to arrive at a conclusion and initiate appropriate action.

14.1.5 Are There Multiple Events and Impacts?

Incidents can aggregate and cascade. That is, one threat can affect multiple resources concurrently, or an incident can initiate a chain of events causing a "cascade" of failures—the so-called domino effect. It will be critical to determine scope of impact or whether there are other resources at risk as a result of an event. Metrics and monitoring are often helpful in assessing scope, but intimate knowledge of systems, networks, personnel, or facilities is likely to be needed to assess "knock on" eventualities.

14.1.6 Will an Incident Need Triage?

Multiple events that exceed the organization's incident response capacity to address them all will require triage to determine which issues to deal with, which to ignore either because they are not serious or there is no ability to address them effectively, and in which order. This capability requires substantial expertise; systems, personnel, and possibly facilities knowledge; and a variety of real-time operational metrics about what's working and what isn't, performance impacts, and so on. For purely technical events, the typical range of data being monitored in the NOC may be adequate provided there is the expertise to interpret it correctly.

14.1.7 What Is the Most Effective Response?

Determining the most effective response to a security incident requires the right information and knowledge of the available options. For example, if an attacker has breached perimeter security and created an intrusion detection alert, what action should be taken? Perhaps the network is segmented and the attack can be isolated. Perhaps the intruder can be blocked at the firewall, or possibly more drastic action is required such as terminating the connection to the Internet. Without adequate information and an understanding of the systems and architectures, it will be difficult to determine the least disruptive response consistent with security.

Physical compromise such as theft of proprietary information or indications of embezzlement by an insider will present even more challenging response issues. Often the main metrics and sources of information for these types of events will be technical or accounting forensics.

14.1.8 What Immediate Actions Must be Taken?

Some incidents will require immediate action to avoid serious consequences. HIDS or NIDS inside the perimeter signaling an intrusion certainly qualifies. Besides validating that it is in fact an intrusion, operational metrics indicating the scope and nature of activity are critical to deciding the nature and extent of action required.

In many organizations where operations and traffic follows consistent patterns, anomalies may be a useful metrics to warn of incipient incidents.

14.1.9 Which Incident Response Teams and Other Personnel Must be Mobilized?

The type and nature of an incident must be determined to make decisions about which teams or personnel will be required to deal with it.

14.1.10 Who Must be Notified?

Utilizing defined severity criteria will provide the input into the declaration criteria, which if properly developed defines who has what authority and who must be notified.

14.1.11 Who Is in Charge?

Indecision and lack of clear authority to take necessary actions can and has transformed an incident into a disaster.

14.1.12 Is It Becoming a Disaster?

It is clear that one of the metrics the information security manager must develop from an incident management and response perspective is the level of skill and expertise available at a given point in time to address events.

Chapter 15

Conclusions

It is evident that we must measure to manage and yet as we have demonstrated, most approaches to contemporary metrics are not useful for management or strategic purposes and, all too often, not particularly beneficial for operational decisions either. It is the hope that the shift in perspective offered will allow a more focused approach toward developing methods for collecting the information needed for more effective information security management.

15.1 Predictive Metrics

Key performance indicators (KPIs) are sometimes termed *leading indicators* but to a significant extent that can be misleading. Inadequate performance is likely to ensure that objectives are not met but the corollary is not as certain. Adequate performance cannot ensure objectives are achieved just as the failure of performance of the power plant in an aircraft can predict that the destination will not be achieved. But adequate performance of the aircraft has no bearing on proper navigation and is not an indicator of the correct course or the likelihood of arriving at the desired destination.

Acronyms

AES	Advanced Encryption Standard
AESRM	Alliance for Enterprise Security Risk Management
AICPA	American Institute of Certified Public Accountants
AIW	Acceptable interruption window
ALE	Annual loss expectancy
API	Application programming interface
ARP	Address Resolution Protocol
AS/NZS	Australian Standard/New Zealand Standard
ASCII	American Standard Code for Information Interchange
ASIC	Application-specific integrated circuit
ASP	Application service provider
ATM	Asynchronous transfer mode
BCI	Business Continuity Institute
BCM	Business continuity management
BCP	Business continuity planning
BGP	Border Gateway Protocol
BI	Business intelligence
BIA	Business impact analysis
BIMS	Biometric information management and security
BIOS	Basic input/output system
BIS	Bank for International Settlements
BITS	Banking Information Technology Standards
BLP	Bell-LaPadula
BLP	Bypass label process

BMS	Building management systems
BS	British Standard
CA	Certificate authority
CASPR	Commonly accepted security practices and recommendations
CBT	Computer-based training
CCO	Chief compliance officer
CD	Compact disk
CD-ROM	Compact disk read-only memory
CEO	Chief executive officer
CERT	Computer emergency response team
CFO	Chief financial officer
CICA	Canadian Institute of Chartered Accountants
CIM	Computer-integrated manufacturing
CIO	Chief information officer
CIRT	Computer incident response team
CIS	Center for Internet Security
CISO	Chief information security officer
CLC	Chief legal counsel
CMM	Capability Maturity Model
CMU	Carnegie Mellon University
CobiT	Control objectives for information and related technology
COO	Chief operating officer
COOP	Continuity of operations plan
CORBA	Common object request broker architecture
COSO	Committee of Sponsoring Organizations of the Treadway Commission
CPO	Chief privacy officer
CPS	Certification practice statement
CPU	Central processing unit
CRL	Certificate revocation list
CRM	Customer relationship management
CSA	Control self-assessment
CSF	Critical success factor
CSIRT	Computer security incident response team

CSO	Chief security officer
CSRC	Computer Security Resources Center (U.S.A.)
CVE	Common vulnerabilities and exposures
CW	Clark-Wilson
DAC	Discretionary access controls
DBMS	Database management system
DCE	Distributed control environment
DCE	Data communications equipment
DCE	Distributed computing environment
DCL	Digital command language
DDoS	Distributed denial of service
DES	Data Encryption Standard
DHCP	Dynamic Host Configuration Protocol
DLT	Digital linear tape
DMZ	Demilitarized zone
DNS	Domain name server
DNSSEC	Domain name service secure
DoS	Denial of service
DOSD	Data-oriented system development
DR	Disaster recovery
DRII	Disaster Recovery Institute International
DRP	Disaster recovery planning
EDI	Electronic data interchange
EER	Equal error rate
EFT	Electronic funds transfer
EGRP	External Gateway Routing Protocol
EIGRP	Enhanced Interior Gateway Routing Protocol
EU	European Union
FAR	False-acceptance rate
FCPA	Foreign Corrupt Practices Act
FERC	Federal Energy Regulatory Commission (U.S.A.)
FFIEC	Federal Financial Institution Examination Council (U.S.A.)
FIPS	Federal Information Processing Standards (U.S.A.)
FISMA	Federal Information Security Management Act (U.S.A.)

FSA	Financial Security Authority (U.S.A.)
GAISP	Generally accepted information security principles
GAS	Generalized audit software
GASSP	Generally accepted security system principles
GLBA	Gramm-Leach-Bliley Act (U.S.A.)
GMI	Governance Metrics International
HD-DVD	High-definition/high-density digital video disc
HIPAA	Health Insurance Portability and Accountability Act (U.S.A.)
HIPO	Hierarchy input-process-output
HR	Human resources
HTML	Hypertext markup language
HTTP	Hypertext Transfer Protocol
HTTPS	Secure Hypertext Transfer Protocol
HVAC	Heating, ventilating, and air-conditioning
I&A	Identification and authentication
I/O	Input/output
ICMP	Internet control message protocol
ICT	Information and communication technologies
ID	Identification
IDC	International Development Corp.
IDEFIX	Integration Definition for Information Modeling
IDS	Intrusion detection system
IEC	International Electrotechnical Commission
IETF	Internet engineering task force
IFAC	International Federation of Accountants
IIA	Institute of Internal Auditors
IMT	Incident management team
IP	Internet Protocol
IPF	Information processing facility
IPL	Initial program load
IPMA	International Project Management Association
IPRs	Intellectual property rights
IPS	Intrusion prevention system
IPSec	Internet Protocol Security

IRP	Incident response plan
IRS	Internal Revenue Service (U.S.A.)
IRT	Incident response team
IS	Information systems
ISF	Information Security Forum
ISO	International Organization for Standardization
ISO	Information security officer
ISP	Internet service provider
ISS	Institutional Shareholders Services
ISSA	Information System Security Association
ISSEA	International System Security Engineering Association
IT	Information technology
ITGI	IT Governance Institute
JCL	Job control language
KGI	Key goal indicators
KLOC	Kilo lines of code
KPI	Key performance indicators
L2TP	Layer 2 Tunneling Protocol
LAN	Local area network
LCP	Link Control Protocol
M&A	Mergers and Acquisition
MAC	Mandatory access control
MIME	Multipurpose Internet mail extensions
MIS	Management information system
MitM	Man-in-the-middle
MTO	Maximum tolerable outage
NAT	Network address translation
NCP	Network Control Protocol
NDA	Nondisclosure agreement
NetBIOS	Network basic input/output systems
NFPA	National Fire Protection Association
NFS	Network file system
NIC	Network interface card
NIDS	Network intrusion detection system

NIST	National Institute of Standards and Technology (U.S.A.)
OCC	Office of the Comptroller of the Currency (U.S.A.)
OCSP	Online Certificate Status Protocol
OCTAVE	Operationally Critical Threat, Asset and Vulnerability Evaluation
OECD	Organization for Economic Cooperation and Development
OEM	Original equipment manufacturer
OEP	Occupant emergency plan
OS	Operating system
OSI	Open systems interconnection
OSPF	Open shortest path first
PAN	Personal area network
PC	Personal computer/microcomputer
PDCA	Plan-do-check-act
PKI	Public key infrastructure
PMBOK	Project management body of knowledge
POS	Point-of-sale
PPP	People, process, and policy
PPPoE	Point-to-point Protocol over Ethernet
PPT	People, process, and technology
PSTN	Public switched telephone network
PVC	Permanent virtual circuit
QA	Quality assurance
RAID	Redundant array of inexpensive disks
RARP	Reverse Address Resolution Protocol
RCERT	Regional Computer Emergency Response Team (U.S.A.)
ROI	Return on investment
RPO	Recovery point objective
RRT	Risk Reward Theorem/Tradeoff
RSA	Rivest, Shamir, and Adleman (RSA stands for the initials of the developers' last names.)
RTO	Recovery time objective
S/HTTP	Secure Hypertext Transfer Protocol
SABSA	Sherwood Applied Business Security Architecture
SAC	Systems auditability and control
SCADA	Supervisory control and data acquisition

SDLC	System development life cycle
SDO	Service delivery objective
SEC	Securities and Exchange Commission (U.S.A.)
SEI	Software Engineering Institute
SET	Secure electronic transfer/transactions
SIM	Security information management
SLA	Service level agreement
SMART	Specific, measurable, achievable, relevant, time-bound
SMF	System management facility
S-MIME	Secure multipurpose Internet mail extensions
SOP	Standard operating procedure
SPI	Security Parameter Index
SPICE	Software process improvement and capability determination
SPOC	Single point of contact
SPOOL	Simultaneous peripheral operations online
SQL	Structured Query Language
SSG	Security steering group
SSH	Secure shell
SSL	Secure sockets layer
SSO	Single sign-on
TCO	Total cost of ownership
TCP	Transmission Control Protocol
TCP/IP	Transmission Control Protocol/Internet Protocol
TCP/UDP	Transmission Control Protocol/User Datagram Protocol
TLS	Tramspor layer security
UDP	User Datagram Protocol
UPS	Uninterruptible power supply
URL	Universal resource locator
USB	Universal serial bus
VoIP	Voice-over IP
VPN	Virtual private network
WAN	Wide area network
XBRL	Extensible Business Reporting Language
XML	Extensible Markup Language

Appendix A: Metrics Classifications[1]

A.1 IA Program Developmental Metrics

Organizational IA programs are a comprehensive set of program areas that together guide an organization's ability to provide information assurance. IA program developmental metrics measure the extent to which IA is effective in an organization by measuring if the organization has chosen the policies and process. These metrics can be further classified as policy management or process maturity.

A.1.1 Policy Management Metrics

These are measures that management uses as security objectives for an organizational IA program. These metrics are specific to development of security strategy, policy, implementation of policy, and compliance with policy. An example of a Policy Management metric is the appraisal used by the Federal Information Technology Security Assessment Framework (FITSAF), which provides a self-assessment guide for organizations to use to measure the assurance of their security program. (*Note: FITSAF has been replaced by NIST Pub 800-37.*)

A.1.2 Process Maturity Metrics

These metrics assess the maturity of security practices in developing a system. They are used to measure the organizational security process framework required to develop a good information assurance program. Process maturity metrics concentrate on security engineering activities that span the life cycle of secured systems deployed by organizations. Examples here include the common criteria that measure process factors of systems by ranking them in one of the seven evaluation assurance levels (EALs)—primarily by examining the artifacts of the development process. Similarly, the system's Software Security Engineering Capability Maturity Model (SSECMM) measures developers' process and procedure based on artifacts.

A.2 Support Metrics

Support metrics measure an organization's support for security programs and processes in terms of personnel (e.g., awareness, training, experience) and resource (e.g., funding, technical resources).

A.2.1 Personnel Support Metrics

People are a part of any process. Professionals and practitioners developing, operating, defending, attacking, or evaluating a system are critical components for Information System Security Professionals (CISSPs), and certification as Systems Security Certified Practitioners (SSCPs) is a good indicator of individuals' knowledge of best practices, their credibility as practitioners, and their exhibition of a sound working knowledge of security. The number of CISSP professionals in an organization, for example, can indicate that an organization has experienced, knowledgeable personnel support.

A.2.2 Resource Support Metrics

Resource support metrics serve as indicators of an organization's financial support and available resources for IA programs and processes. Such metrics help one to determine if budget allocation is adequate or proper resources are in place. An example of this type of metric can be the budget percentage allocated for security program as a percentage of annual organizational budgets.

A.3 Operational Metrics

These are end-to-end measures of operational support in an organization. Operational metrics for an organization's security program observe the working environment of the organization in terms of its security program and evaluate the organization's operational readiness and effectiveness in providing information assurance. The operational readiness metrics are subdivided into three categories: operational readiness metrics, operational practice metrics, and operational environment metrics.

A.3.1 Operational Readiness Metrics

This concept was drawn from the traditional military readiness measures of combat readiness. The IA posture of an organization can be measured by how well its units (systems, departments) and individuals are prepared to perform their assigned tasks of operating the system in a proper manner. Readiness measures are internally self-assessed or externally assessed by third party. An example of the IA readiness metric exists in a current Joint Chief of Staff Instruction (CJCSI) as a self-assessment checklist of IA-related capabilities (e.g., "if adequate architecture for securing systems and networks is in place"). Operational readiness metrics can be further classified as management readiness related and/or technical readiness related.

A.3.1.1 Management Readiness Metrics

Management readiness metrics measure management's support of information security processes in the organization—for example, commitment, personnel, and resource management, and risk assessment of intellectual property. These metrics are mostly static; that is, these are questionnaire-based assessments and are generated by reviews of organizational policy and procedures with respect to the operations by interviewing management. An example is the frequency of regular audit trail reviews or operational procedure drills.

A.3.1.2 Technical Readiness Metrics

Technical readiness metrics measure the readiness state of technical support that affects the organization's ability to provide information assurance while performing operational missions. They can be static or dynamic. Risk assessment and vulnerability analysis are examples of static technical readiness measurements. Information Assurance Vulnerability Alerts (IAVA) by the Defense Information System Agency (DISA) require organizations to use IA metrics to remediate known vulnerabilities of the technical resources, keep track of remediated systems, and report compliance status. Dynamic technical readiness assessments are like "live-play" exercises that simulate adversarial scenarios. Red team threat-based efforts apply a simulated task force to expose IA vulnerabilities, as a method to assess the readiness of DOD components. A specific example of this type would be the Information Design Assurance Red Team (IDART) methodology used by Sandia National Laboratories, which results in metrics such as attack percent completed, attack probability of success, and time/cost/skill in attacks.

A.3.2 Operational Practice Metrics

Operational practice metrics measure the security practices of people who directly or indirectly affect an organization's IA posture. These metrics assess culture and climate, awareness of existing policy, and socioethical awareness, for example. An example might be the number of users with passwords in compliance with the local password management security policy.

A.3.3 Operational Environment Metrics

Operational environment metrics are used for describing and measuring the security-relevant aspects of the operational environment (i.e., external threats, conditions, objects) that affect the organization's security operations directly or indirectly. An example might be number of systems susceptible to a specific penetration technique.

A.4 Effectiveness Metrics

Effectiveness metrics measure how effective the organization's IA program is in actually providing defense in-depth assurance. Examples include the number of malicious code incidents (measures protection), number of intrusions reported (measures detection), percentage of data recovered after security incident (response). The Air Force Information (On Line Survey Program) uses quantitative effectiveness metrics such as the number of systems root or user privileges that were obtained as a percentage of the total number of systems. The Air Force Communication Agency (AFCA) developed information protection metrics that measures compliance with and the effectiveness of information protection policy in organizations, for example, number of intrusion attempts reported and number of reported successful intrusions with limited access or total control. Another example might be the number of security incidents this month per number of security incidents the previous month.

A.4.1 Metrics for Technical Target of Assessment (TTOA)

This type of metric is intended to measure how much a technical object, system, or product (collectively referred to as TTOA) is capable of providing assurance in terms of protection, detection, and response. This type of metric is often used in comparing or differentiating between alternative and competing TTOA, for example, the EAL ratings of the Common Criteria, DITSCAP certification levels developed by DoD Information Technology Security Certification and Accreditation Process. We further categorize metrics for TTOAs in two classes: metrics for measuring TTOA's strengths and its weaknesses.

A.4.1.1 Metrics for Strength Assessment

The focus here is on how strong the TTOA is. The strength factor is further classified into two categories used for assessing the strengths of the TTOA based on the typical environment when there is no adversarial activity going on to compromise the TTOA and its capabilities and when there is some adversarial force working against the TTOA. We refer to these as normal and abnormal circumstances.

A.4.1.1.1 Metrics for Features in Normal Circumstances

These metrics measure the capabilities that the TTOA should have in order to provide information assurance under normal circumstances. They can be used for assessing the claimed features of a TTOA. For a firewall, metrics in this category might be the number of invalid packets a server can reject per second; for a cryptographic algorithm, this metric might be the number of clock cycles per byte encrypted, number of rounds, or something similar. The resilience assurance index is another example of this metric as it provides a way to evaluate systems in terms of the level of system expectations or assurances one expects from a system to provide defense to attacks.

A.4.1.1.2 Metrics for Features in Abnormal Circumstances

These metrics are used for measuring the TTOA's capabilities in the face of adversarial activities working to compromise the TTOA. They measure the TTOA's strength in resistance to and in response to attacks. Two further refinements of this classification are adversary work factor and survivability metrics.

1. Adversary Work Factor Metrics: Penetration testing is used to assess the strengths of systems, and the concept of adversary work factor metrics was generated from penetration testing. The idea is, the stronger a system is, the more likely it is to withstand attacks. Relative differences in adversary work factor can provide insight to relative assurance of information systems. Adversary work factor is the amount of effort an adversary spends in order to compromise protective measure(s) of a system. It not only incorporates technical factors, but also personnel and operational factors. SRI International developed an adversary work factor metrics known as Red Team Work Factor metrics, which is an estimate of the effort required by a model adversary to achieve adversarial goals. The metric is a function of preparation time, attack time, cost of resource and access, man-hours to break a security policy, and time to penetrate the system.

2. Survivability Metrics: These metrics measure the TTOA's ability to deliver essential services in the presence of attacks and failures and to recover in a timely manner. The survivable network analysis (SNA) methodology was developed by the SEI CERT Coordination Center. This methodology utilizes statistical techniques for assessing the survivable properties of systems. The analysis is carried out from the architectural level to the operational level. An example metric in SNA is actual survivability, which is quantitatively determined by the system's performance at the new state after attack against its normal performance level. SNA also looks at other metrics, such as expected survivability, average damage per unit time, and others.

A.4.1.2 Metrics for Weakness Assessment

These metrics assess the weaknesses of the TTOA in terms of threats, vulnerabilities, risks, anticipation of losses in face of attack, and any operational limitations of the TTOA. This classification of metric is subcategorized into risk and operational limitation metrics.

A.4.1.2.1 Risk Metrics

Risk metrics are those that measure threats, vulnerabilities, and associated risks to the TTOA. Threat is an external or internal circumstance/event that may cause potential harm to the system. Vulnerability is a weakness of an information system or its components that could be exploited to violate assurances in systems. Risk is the probability that a particular threat will exploit a particular vulnerability of the system. The intelligent communities' INFOSEC Risk Management Methodology provides a consistent repeatable measurement method for determining IA risk of a system by observing and analyzing the threats, vulnerabilities, and significance levels. The result is a qualitative subjective measurement of the risk factor of the system.

A.4.1.2.2 Operational Limitation Metrics

These metrics measure the impact of operational limitations that are generated by certain functionality or limitations that might restrict or affect the functionality of evident features of the TTOA. This metric is useful for evaluating competing products.

Acknowledgments

Support by Harris Corporation is gratefully acknowledged. Work conducted at Mississippi State University was supported by the Army Research Laboratory contract DAAD 17-01-C-0011 and the National Science Foundation grant CCR-0085749.

The complete paper is published by the IEEE in the *Proceedings of the 36th Hawaii International Conference on System Sciences* (HICSS'03) 0-7695-1874-5/03.

Endnotes

1. Rayford B. Vaughn, Jr., Associate Professor, Department of Computer Science, Mississippi State University; Ambareen Siraj, Department of Computer Science, Mississippi State University; and Ronda Henning, Harris Corporation, Government Communications, Systems Division, Department of Computer Science. *Information Assurance Measures and Metrics—State of Practice and Proposed Taxonomy.*

References

Vaughn, Rayford B., Jr., Ambareen Siraj, and Ronda Henning, *Information Assurance Measures and Metrics—State of Practice and Proposed Taxonomy.*

Vaughn, R., D. Dampier, and A. Siraj, *Information Security System Ranking and Rating.* A summary of this paper can be found here: CrossTalk the Journal of Defense Software Engineering, May 2002, pp. 30–32. Retrieved May 27, 2008 from: http://www.stsc.hill.af.mil/crosstalk/2002/05/index.html>>http://www.stsc.hill.af.mil/crosstalk/2002/05/vaughn.html

Appendix B: Cultural Worldviews[1]

Hierarchists. Marris et al. (1996) claim that hierarchists, meaning individuals whose worldview corresponds to high grid–high group, are characterized by strong group boundaries and binding prescriptions. These individuals' position in the world is defined by a set of established classifications, based on criteria such as age, gender, or race. These demarcations are considered unquestionable and are justified on the grounds that they enable harmonious life (Douglas and Wildavsky, 1982; Langford et al., 2000; Thompson et al., 1990). Hierarchical cultures emphasize the importance of establishing and preserving the "natural order" of the society. Hierarchists mostly fear things that disrupt this social order, such as social disturbance, demonstrations, and crime. Another important facet of this worldview is that people who share it show a great deal of faith in expert knowledge (Torbjorn, 2004). Hierarchical individuals trust rules and regulations and believe that institutional order and experts will be able to tackle all types of problems (Lima and Castro, 2005). Hierarchical organizations are structured according to the belief that everyone must know one's place, though that place might vary with time (Altman and Baruch, 1998). Another noticeable characteristic of members of hierarchic groups is that when they cheat, steal, or overlook procedures, they operate according to the same criteria and values that apply to their formal work—they act as a group in an orderly, disciplined, and coordinated way, with respect for their own rules, limits, and precedents (Mars, 1996). Finally, hierarchists are characterized by slow adaptability to change and overdependence on regular ways of doing things (Mars, 1996).

Egalitarians. People who can be positioned in the high group–low grid quadrant are also characterized by high degree of the group dimension, but, contrary to hierarchists, their lives are not prescribed by role differentiation. Instead, egalitarians share the idea that individuals should negotiate their relationship with others and that no person is granted authority by virtue of his or her position (Marris et al., 1996; Langford et al., 2000). They also believe that leadership must be charismatic (Altman and Baruch, 1998). Egalitarians are characterized by intense sense of equality; therefore, they mostly fear developments that may increase the inequalities among people. Compared with hierarchists, they tend to be skeptical to expert knowledge, because they suspect that experts and strong institutions might misuse their authority (Torbjorn, 2004). Since, they dislike others deciding for their life and actions, egalitarians prefer to have information provided to them, based upon which they can make their own personal choices (Finucane and Holup, 2005).

Individualists. People with low group–low grid worldview are bound neither by group integration nor by prescribed roles, and assert that all boundaries are subject to negotiation (Karyda et al., 2005; Langford et al., 2000). They barely feel responsible toward other members of society and regard the allocation of power as a matter of own responsibility, not dependent on position or status (Langford et al., 2000). They do not accept enforcements based on ancestry or past, since each person is responsible for oneself (Altman and Baruch, 1998). Individualists are especially concerned for the maintenance of freedom to continue life and business as usual, and they believe that carrying on through the same paths pursued thus far is the answer (Lima and Castro, 2005). They are also particularly afraid of things that might obstruct their individual freedom (Torbjorn, 2004). Mars (1996) claims that individualists are reluctant to accept rules or to follow defined instructions or procedures, especially in the case these appear to obstruct their current autonomy, such as, for instance, maintenance and administrative procedures and manual instructions. They tend to build short-term and instrumental relationships with their superiors. Individualism is also associated with corner cutting, rule breaking, and cheating, which means that people who share this worldview have a propensity to cheat, convert materials to their own use, short-cut procedures for ease of operation, and exploit ambiguities. When they have the choice, individualists prefer to choose short-term personal advantages over long-term corporate consequences. Individualist tendencies are also linked to a high propensity for risk taking (Mars, 1996).

Fatalists. With a low group–high grid worldview, fatalists believe, like hierarchists, that their autonomy is restricted by social distinctions but in contrast to them, they feel excluded from membership in the institutions responsible for setting the rules, and tend to see themselves as "outsiders" (Douglas and Wildavsky, 1982; Langford et al., 2000; Thompson et al., 1990). They believe that the sphere of individual autonomy is minimal and there is little room for personal negotiations (Altman and Baruch, 1998). They also believe that social classification should be based on ancestry (Altman and Baruch, 1998). Fatalists usually take small part in social life; surprisingly, they feel tied and regulated by these social groups although they do not belong to them. This fact makes this worldview quite indifferent concerning the concept of risk; what fatalists fear and what they do not fear is mostly decided by others. These individuals would rather be unaware of dangers, since they assume that they are unavoidable anyway (Torbjorn, 2004). Concerning the type of work they prefer, most of the time, they attach themselves to jobs characterized by high degree of routine (Mars, 1996).

Endnote

1. *Risk Analysis Journal,* Springer Netherlands, ISSN: 0272-4332 (Print); ISN: 1573-9147 (online) Vol.18, No.5, 635–647, October 1998.

Appendix C: The Competing Values Framework

C.1 Cultural Dimensions

C.1.1 Horizontal: In/Out

The horizontal dimension maps the degree to which the organization focuses inward or outward. To the left, attention is primarily inward, within the organization, whereas to the right, it is outward, toward customers, suppliers, and the external environment.

An internal focus is valid in environments where competition or customer focus is not the most important thing, but in competitive climates or where external stakeholders hold sway, then this challenge must be met directly.

C.1.2 Vertical: Stability/Flexibility

The vertical axis determines who makes decisions. At the lower end, control is with management, whereas at the upper end, it is devolved to employees who have been empowered to decide for themselves.

Stability is a valid form when the business is stable and reliability and efficiency is paramount, but when environmental forces create a need for change, then flexibility becomes more important.

C.2 The Competing Values Map

	Flexibility and Discretion		
Internal Focus and Integration	**Clan**	**Adhocracy**	External Focus and Differentiation
	Hierarchy	**Market**	
	Stability and Control		

The four hierarchies are to some extent historical in their development and are presented in this order below.

C.2.1 Hierarchy

The hierarchy has a traditional approach to structure and control that flows from a strict chain of command, as in Max Weber's original view of bureaucracy. For many years, this was considered the only effective way of organizing and is still a basic element of the vast majority of organizations.

Hierarchies have respect for position and power. They often have well-defined policies, processes, and procedures.

Hierarchical leaders are typically coordinators and organizers who keep a close eye on what is happening.

C.2.2 Market

The market organization also seeks control but does so by looking outward, and in particular taking note of transaction cost.

Note that the market organization is *not* one that is focused just on marketing, but one where all transactions, internal and external, are viewed in market terms. Transactions are *exchanges of value*. In an efficient market organization, value *flows* between people and stakeholders with minimal cost and delay.

Market cultures are outward looking, are particularly driven by results, and are often very competitive.

Leaders in market cultures are often hard-driving competitors who seek always to deliver the goods.

C.2.3 Clan

The clan organization has less focus on structure and control and a greater concern for flexibility. Rather than strict rules and procedures, people are driven through vision, shared goals, outputs, and outcomes.

In contrast to hierarchies, clans often have flat organizations and people and teams act more autonomously.

It has an inward focus and a sense of family and people work well together, strongly driven by loyalty to one another and the shared cause. Rules, although not necessarily documented, do still exist and are often communicated and inculcated socially.

Clan leaders act in a facilitative, supportive way and may take on a parental role.

C.2.4 Adhocracy

The adhocracy has even greater independence and flexibility than the clan, which is necessary in a rapidly changing business climate.

Where market success goes to those with greatest speed and adaptability, the adhocracy will rapidly form teams to face new challenges. It will use prototyping and experimenting rather than long, big-bang projects and development.

Leaders in an adhocracy are visionary, innovative entrepreneurs who take calculated risks to make significant gains.

Appendix D: The Organization Culture Assessment Instrument (OCAI)

The OCAI is a simple questionnaire that has six categories in which you distribute 100 points between four subitems for each that represent the four competing values cultures, where

- Type A style indicates a clan culture
- Type B style indicates an adhocracy culture
- Type C style indicates a market culture
- Type D style indicates a hierarchy culture

Category	Style
1. Dominant organizational characteristics	A: Personal, like a family
	B: Entrepreneurial, risk taking
	C: Competitive, achievement oriented
	D: Controlled and structured
2. Leadership style	A: Mentoring, facilitating, nurturing
	B: Entrepreneurial, innovative, risk taking
	C: No-nonsense, aggressive, results oriented
	D: Coordinating, organizing, efficiency oriented
3. Management of employees	A: Teamwork, consensus, and participation
	B: Individual risk taking, innovation, freedom, and uniqueness

Category	Style
	C: Competitiveness and achievement
	D: Security, conformity, predictability
4. Organizational glue	A: Loyalty and mutual trust
	B: Commitment to innovation, development
	C: Emphasis on achievement and goal accomplishment
	D: Formal rules and policies
5. Strategic emphasis	A: Human development, high trust, openness
	B: Acquisition of resources, creating new challenges
	C: Competitive actions and winning
	D: Permanence and stability
6. Criteria for success	A: Development of human resources, teamwork, concern for people
	B: Unique and new products and services
	C: Winning in the marketplace, outpacing the competition
	D: Dependable, efficient, low cost

This is often done twice: once for "now" and once for "preferred."

The scoring is then summed across A, B, C, and D for each category to give axis scores, which are plotted on a chart that then shows the differences between "now" and "preferred" and hence guides actions to close these gaps.

Cultural, financial, and organizational metrics and other theoretical approaches offer new and perhaps improved insights into the issues of effective metrics. They are probably still too immature to be of significant value for practical security management requirements. The notion used by auditors of "tone at the top" is recognition of an aspect of culture insofar as it is set by senior management's attitudes, styles, management approaches, and so forth.

Practitioners are also generally aware of the "culture" issue and how it affects their ability to address risk in the organization. The concepts of *culture* and *organizational structure* raised by the Systemic Security Model are undoubtedly highly significant and must be further developed to a point of practical application. These may turn out to be the most pertinent metrics with the highest correlations to good security and, quite possibly, the most predictive as well.

Appendix E: SABSA Business Attribute Metrics

Business Attribute	Attribute Explanation	Metric Type	Suggested Measurement Approach
User Attributes	**This group of attributes is related to the user's experience of interacting with the business system.**		
Accessible	Information to which the user is entitled to gain access should be easily found and accessed by that user.	Soft	Search tree depth necessary to find the info
Accurate	The information provided to users should be accurate within a range that has been pre-agreed upon as being applicable to the service being delivered.	Hard	Acceptance testing on key data to demonstrate compliance with design rules
Anonymous	For certain specialized types of service the anonymity of the user should be protected.	Hard	Rigorous proof of system functionality
		Soft	Red team review[1]
Consistent	The way in which login, navigation, and target services are presented to the user should be consistent across different times, locations, and channels of access.	Hard	Conformance with design style guides
		Soft	Red team review
Current	Information provided to users should be current and kept up to date, within a range that has	Hard	Refresh rates at the data source and

Business Attribute	Attribute Explanation	Metric Type	Suggested Measurement Approach
	been pre-agreed upon as being applicable for the service being delivered.		replication of refreshed data to the destination
Duty-segregated	For certain sensitive tasks the duties should be segregated so that no user has access to both aspects of the task.	Hard	Functional testing
Educated and aware	The user community should be educated and trained so that they can embrace the security culture and so as to have sufficient user awareness of security issues that behavior of users is compliant with security policies.	Soft	Competence surveys
Informed	The user should be kept fully informed about services, operating procedures, operational schedules, planned outages, and so on.	Soft	Focus groups or satisfaction surveys
Motivated	The interaction with the system should add positive motivation to the user to complete the business tasks in hand.	Soft	Focus groups or satisfaction surveys
Protected	The user's information and access privileges should be protected against abuse by other users or by intruders.	Soft	Penetration test (Could be regarded as "hard," but only if a penetration is achieved. Failure to penetrate does not mean that penetration is impossible.)
Reliable	The services provided to the user should be delivered at a reliable level of quality.	Soft	A definition of "quality" is needed against which to compare
Responsive	The users obtain a response within a satisfactory period of time that meets their expectations.	Hard	Response time

Business Attribute	Attribute Explanation	Metric Type	Suggested Measurement Approach
Supported	When a user has problems or difficulties in using the system or its services there should be a means by which the user can receive advice and support so that the problems can be resolved to the satisfaction of the user.	Soft	Focus groups or satisfaction surveys Independent audit and review against Security Architecture Capability Maturity Model[2]
Timely	Information is delivered or made accessible to the user at the appropriate time or within the appropriate time period.	Hard	Refresh rates at the data source and replication of refreshed data to the destination
Transparent	Providing full visibility to the user of the logical process but hiding the physical structure of the system (as a url hides the actual physical locations of Web servers).	Soft	Focus groups or satisfaction surveys Independent audit and review against Security Architecture Capability Maturity Model[2]
Usable	The system should provide "easy-to-use" interfaces that can be navigated intuitively by a user of average intelligence and training level (for the given system). The user's experience of these interactions should be at best interesting and at worst neutral.	Soft	Numbers of "clicks" or keystrokes required Conformance with industry standards— e.g., color palettes Feedback from focus groups
Management Attributes	**This group of attributes is related to the ease and effectiveness with which the business system and its services can be managed.**		
Automated	Wherever possible (and depending upon cost/benefit factors) the management and operation of the system should be automated.	Soft	Independent design review

Business Attribute	Attribute Explanation	Metric Type	Suggested Measurement Approach
Change-managed	Changes to the system should be properly managed so that the impact of every change is evaluated and the changes are approved in advance of being implemented.	Soft	Documented change management system, with change management history, evaluated by independent audit
Controlled	The system should at all times remain "in the control" of its managers. This means that the management will observe the operation and behavior of the system, will make decisions about how to control it based on these observations, and will implement actions to exert that control.	Soft	Independent audit and review against Security Architecture Capability Maturity Model[2]
Cost-effective	The design, acquisition, implementation, and operation of the system should be achieved at a cost that the business finds acceptable when judged against the benefits derived.	Hard	Individual budgets for the phases of development and for ongoing operation, maintenance, and support
Efficient	The system should deliver the target services with optimum efficiency, avoiding wastage of resources.	Hard	A target efficiency ratio based on: (input value) / (output value)
Maintainable	The system should be capable of being maintained in a state of good repair and effective, efficient operation. The actions required to achieve this should be feasible within the normal operational conditions of the system.	Soft	Documented execution of a preventive maintenance schedule for both hardware and software, correlated against targets for continuity of service (such as MTBF[3])
Measured	The performance of the system against a variety of desirable performance targets should be measured so as to provide feedback	Hard	Documented tracking and reporting of a portfolio of conventional system performance

Business Attribute	*Attribute Explanation*	*Metric Type*	*Suggested Measurement Approach*
	information to support the management and control process.		parameters, together with other attributes from this list
Supportable	The system should be capable of being supported in terms of both the users and the operations staff, so that all types of problems and operational difficulties can be resolved.	Hard	Fault-tracking system providing measurements of MTBF and MTTR[4], with targets for each parameter
Operational Attributes	**This group of attributes describes the ease and effectiveness with which the business system and its services can be operated.**		
Available	The information and services provided by the system should be available according to the requirements specified in the service level agreement (SLA).	Hard	As specified in the SLA
Continuous	The system should offer "continuous service." The exact definition of this phrase will always be subject to an SLA.	Hard	Percentage up-time correlated versus scheduled and/or unscheduled downtime; or MTBF, or MTTR
Detectable	Important events must be detected and reported.	Hard	Functional testing
Error-free	The system should operate without producing errors.	Hard	Percentage or absolute error rates (per transaction, per batch, per time period, etc.)
Interoperable	The system should interoperate with other similar systems, both immediately and in the future, as intersystem communication becomes increasingly a requirement.	Hard	Specific interoperability requirements

Business Attribute	*Attribute Explanation*	*Metric Type*	*Suggested Measurement Approach*
Monitored	The operational performance of the system should be continuously monitored to ensure that other attribute specifications are being met. Any deviations from acceptable limits should be notified to the systems management function.	Soft	Independent audit and review against Security Architecture Capability Maturity Model[2]
Productive	The system and its services should operate so as to sustain and enhance productivity of the users, with regard to the business processes in which they are engaged.	Hard	User output targets related to specific business activities
Recoverable	The system should be able to be recovered to full operational status after a breakdown or disaster in accordance with the SLA.	Hard	As specified in the SLA
Risk Management Attributes	**This group of attributes describes the business requirements for mitigating operational risk. This group most closely relates to the "security requirements" for protecting the business.**		
Access-controlled	Access to information and functions within the system should be controlled in accordance with the authorized privileges of the party requesting the access. Unauthorized access should be prevented.	Hard	Reporting of all unauthorized access attempts, including number of incidents per period, severity and result (did the access attempt succeed?)
Accountable	All parties having authorized access to the system should be held accountable for their actions.	Soft	Independent audit and review against Security Architecture Capability Maturity Model[2] with respect to the ability to hold accountable all authorized parties

Business Attribute	Attribute Explanation	Metric Type	Suggested Measurement Approach
Assurable	There should be a means to provide assurance that the system is operating as expected and that all of the various controls are correctly implemented and operated.	Hard	Documented standards exist against which to audit
		Soft	Independent audit and review against Security Architecture Capability Maturity Model[2]
Assuring honesty	Protecting employees against false accusations of dishonesty or malpractice.	Soft	Independent audit and review against Security Architecture Capability Maturity · Model (see Footnote 9) with respect to the ability to prevent false accusations that are difficult to repudiate
Auditable	The actions of all parties having authorized access to the system, and the complete chain of events and outcomes resulting from these actions, should be recorded so that this history can be reviewed. The audit records should provide an appropriate level of detail, in accordance with business needs.	Soft	Independent audit and review against Security Architecture Capability Maturity Model[2]
	The actual configuration of the system should also be capable of being audited so as to compare it with a target configuration that represents the implementation of the security policy that governs the system.	Hard	Documented target configuration exists under change control with a capability to check current configuration against this target
		Soft	Independent audit and review against Security Architecture Capability Maturity Model[2]

Business Attribute	Attribute Explanation	Metric Type	Suggested Measurement Approach
Authenticated	Every party claiming a unique identity (i.e., a claimant) should be subject to a procedure that verifies that the party is indeed the authentic owner of the claimed identity.	Soft	Independent audit and review against Security Architecture Capability Maturity Model[2] with respect to the ability to authenticate successfully every claim of identity
Authorized	The system should allow only those actions that have been explicitly authorized.	Hard	Reporting of all unauthorized actions, including number of incidents per period, severity, and result (did the action succeed?)
		Soft	Independent audit and review against Security Architecture Capability Maturity Model[2] with respect to the ability to detect unauthorized actions
Capturing new risks	New risks emerge over time. The system management and operational environment should provide a means to identify and assess new risks (new threats, new impacts, or new vulnerabilities).	Hard	Percentage of vendor-published patches and upgrades actually installed
		Soft	Independent audit and review against Security Architecture Capability Maturity Model[2] of a documented risk assessment process and a risk assessment history

Business Attribute	Attribute Explanation	Metric Type	Suggested Measurement Approach
Confidential	The confidentiality of (corporate) information should be protected in accordance with security policy. Unauthorized disclosure should be prevented.	Hard	Reporting of all disclosure incidents, including number of incidents per period, severity, and type of disclosure
Crime-free	Cyber-crime of all types should be prevented.	Hard	Reporting of all incidents of crime, including number of incidents per period, severity, and type of crime
Flexibly secure	Security can be provided at various levels, according to business need. The system should provide the means to secure information according to these needs, and may need to offer different levels of security for different types of information (according to security classification).	Soft	Independent audit and review against Security Architecture Capability Maturity Model[2]
Identified	Each entity that will be granted access to system resources and each object that is itself a system resource should be uniquely identified (named) such that there can never be confusion as to which entity or object is being referenced.	Hard	Proof of uniqueness of naming schemes
Independently secure	The security of the system should not rely upon the security of any other system that is not within the direct span of control of this system.	Soft	Independent audit and review against Security Architecture Capability Maturity Model[2] of technical security architecture at conceptual, logical, and physical layers

Business Attribute	Attribute Explanation	Metric Type	Suggested Measurement Approach
In our sole possession	Information that has value to the business should be in the possession of the business, stored and protected by the system against loss (as in no longer being available) or theft (as in being disclosed to an unauthorized party). This will include information that is regarded as "intellectual property."	Soft	Independent audit and review against Security Architecture Capability Maturity Model[2]
Integrity-assured	The integrity of information should be protected to provide assurance that it has not suffered unauthorized modification, duplication, or deletion.	Hard	Reporting of all incidents of compromise, including number of incidents per period, severity, and type of compromise
		Soft	Independent audit and review against Security Architecture Capability Maturity Model[2] with respect to the ability to detect integrity compromise incidents
Nonrepudiable	When one party uses the system to send a message to another party, it should *not* be possible for the first party to falsely deny having sent the message or to falsely deny its contents.	Hard	Reporting of all incidents of unresolved repudiations, including number of incidents per period, severity, and type of repudiation

Business Attribute	Attribute Explanation	Metric Type	Suggested Measurement Approach
		Soft	Independent audit and review against Security Architecture Capability Maturity Model[2] with respect to the ability to prevent repudiations that cannot be easily resolved
Owned	There should be an entity designated as "owner" of every system. This owner is the policy maker for all aspects of risk management with respect to the system and exerts the ultimate authority for controlling the system.	Soft	Independent audit and review against Security Architecture Capability Maturity Model[2] of the ownership arrangements and of the management processes by which owners should fulfill their responsibilities, and of their diligence in so doing
Private	The privacy of (personal) information should be protected in accordance with relevant privacy or "data protection" legislation, and so as to meet the reasonable expectation of citizens for privacy. Unauthorized disclosure should be prevented.	Hard	Reporting of all disclosure incidents, including number of incidents per period, severity, and type of disclosure
Trustworthy	The system should be able to be trusted to behave in the ways specified in its functional specification and should protect against a wide range of potential abuses.	Soft	Focus groups or satisfaction surveys researching around the question "Do you trust the service?"

Business Attribute	Attribute Explanation	Metric Type	Suggested Measurement Approach
Legal & Regulatory Attributes	**This group of attributes describes the business requirements for mitigating operational risks that have a specific legal or regulatory connection.**		
Admissible	The system should provide forensic records (audit trails and so on) that will be deemed to be "admissible" in a court of law, should that evidence ever need to be presented in support of a criminal prosecution or a civil litigation.	Soft	Independent audit and review against Security Architecture Capability Maturity Model[2] by "computer forensics" expert
Compliant	The system should comply with all applicable regulations, laws, contracts, policies, and mandatory standards, both internal and external.	Soft	Independent compliance audit with respect to the inventories of regulations, laws, policies, etc.
Enforceable	The system should be designed, implemented, and operated such that all applicable contracts, policies, regulations, and laws can be enforced by the system.	Soft	Independent review of 1. Inventory of contracts, policies, regulations, and laws for completeness 2. Enforceability of contracts, policies, laws, regulations on the inventory
Insurable	The system should be risk-managed to enable an insurer to offer reasonable commercial terms for insurance against a standard range of insurable risks.	Hard	Verify against insurance quotations

Business Attribute	Attribute Explanation	Metric Type	Suggested Measurement Approach
Legal	The system should be designed, implemented, and operated in accordance with the requirements of any applicable legislation. Examples include data protection laws, laws controlling the use of cryptographic technology, laws controlling "insider dealing" on the stock market, and laws governing information that is considered racist, seditious, or pornographic.	Soft	Independent audit and review against Security Architecture Capability Maturity Model[2] Verification of the inventory of applicable laws to check for completeness and suitability
Liability-managed	The system services should be designed, implemented, and operated so as to manage the liability of the organization with regard to errors, fraud, malfunction, and so on. In particular, the responsibilities and liabilities of each party should be clearly defined.	Soft	Independent legal expert review of all applicable contracts, SLAs, etc.
Regulated	The system should be designed, implemented, and operated in accordance with the requirements of any applicable regulations. These may be general (such as safety regulations) or industry-specific (such as banking regulations).	Soft	Independent audit and review against Security Architecture Capability Maturity Model[2] Verification of the inventory of applicable regulations to check for completeness and suitability

Business Attribute	*Attribute Explanation*	*Metric Type*	*Suggested Measurement Approach*
Resolvable	The system should be designed, implemented, and operated in such a way that disputes can be resolved with reasonable ease and without undue impact on time, cost, or other valuable resources.	Soft	Independent audit and review against Security Architecture Capability Maturity Model[2] by legal expert
Time-bound	Meeting requirements for maximum or minimum periods of time: e.g., a minimum period for records retention or a maximum period within which something must be completed.	Hard	Independent functional design review against specified functional requirements
Technical Strategy Attributes	**This group of attributes describes the needs for fitting into an overall technology strategy.**		
Architecturally open	The system architecture should, wherever possible, not be locked into specific vendor interface standards and should allow flexibility in the choice of vendors and products, both initially and in the future.	Soft	Independent audit and review against Security Architecture Capability Maturity Model[2] of technical architecture (conceptual, logical, and physical)
COTS/GOTS compliant	Wherever possible the system should utilize "commercial off-the-shelf" or "government off-the-shelf" components, as appropriate.	Soft	Independent audit and review against Security Architecture Capability Maturity Model[2] of technical architecture (conceptual, logical, and physical)

Business Attribute	Attribute Explanation	Metric Type	Suggested Measurement Approach
Extendable	The system should be capable of being extended to incorporate new functional modules as required by the business.	Soft	Independent audit and review against Security Architecture Capability Maturity Model[2] of technical architecture (conceptual, logical, and physical)
Flexible & adaptable	The system should be flexible and adaptable to meet new business requirements as they emerge.	Soft	Independent audit and review against Security Architecture Capability Maturity Model[2] of technical architecture (conceptual, logical, and physical)
Future-proof	The system architecture should be designed as much as possible to accommodate future changes in both business requirements and technical solutions.	Soft	Independent audit and review against Security Architecture Capability Maturity Model[2] of technical architecture (conceptual, logical, and physical)
Legacy-sensitive	A new system should be able to work with any legacy systems or databases with which it needs to interoperate or integrate.	Soft	Independent audit and review against Security Architecture Capability Maturity Model[2] of technical architecture (conceptual, logical, and physical)

Business Attribute	Attribute Explanation	Metric Type	Suggested Measurement Approach
Migratable	There should be a feasible, manageable migration path, acceptable to the business users, that moves from an old system to a new one, or from one released version to the next.	Soft	Independent audit and review against Security Architecture Capability Maturity Model[2] of technical architecture (conceptual, logical, and physical)
Multisourced	Critical system components should be obtainable from more than one source to protect against the risk of the single source of supply and support being withdrawn.	Soft	Independent audit and review against Security Architecture Capability Maturity Model[2] of technical architecture at the component level
Scalable	The system should be scalable to the size of user community, data storage requirements, processing throughput, and so on that might emerge over the lifetime of the system.	Soft	Independent audit and review against Security Architecture Capability Maturity Model[2] of technical architecture (conceptual, logical, and physical)
Simple	The system should be as simple as possible, since complexity only adds further risk.	Soft	Independent audit and review against Security Architecture Capability Maturity Model[2] of technical architecture (conceptual, logical, and physical)
Standards compliant	The system should be designed, implemented, and operated to comply with appropriate technical and operational standards.	Soft	Independent audit and review of 1. The inventory of standards to check for completeness and appropriateness 2. Compliance with standards on the inventory

Business Attribute	*Attribute Explanation*	*Metric Type*	*Suggested Measurement Approach*
Traceable	The development and implementation of system components should be documented so as to provide complete two-way traceability. That is, every implemented component should be justifiable by tracing back to the business requirements that led to its inclusion in the system; and it should be possible to review every business requirement and demonstrate which of the implemented system components are there to meet this requirement.	Soft	Independent expert review of documented traceability matrices and trees
Upgradeable	The system should be capable of being upgraded with ease to incorporate new releases of hardware and software.	Soft	Independent audit and review against Security Architecture Capability Maturity Model[2] of technical architecture (conceptual, logical, and physical)
Business Strategy Attributes	**This group of attributes describes the needs for fitting into an overall business strategy.**		
Brand-enhancing	The system should help to establish, build, and support the brand of the products or services based upon this system.	Soft	Market surveys
Business-enabled	Enabling the business and fulfilling business objectives should be the primary driver for the system design.	Soft	Business management focus group
Competent	The system should protect the reputation of the organization as being competent in its industry sector.	Soft	Independent audit, focus groups, or satisfaction surveys

Business Attribute	Attribute Explanation	Metric Type	Suggested Measurement Approach
Confident	The system should behave in such a way as to safeguard confidence placed in the organization by customers, suppliers, shareholders, regulators, financiers, the marketplace, and the general public.	Soft	Independent audit, focus groups, or satisfaction surveys
Credible	The system should behave in such a way as to safeguard the credibility of the organization.	Soft	Independent audit, focus groups, or satisfaction surveys
Culture-sensitive	The system should be designed, built, and operated with due care and attention to cultural issues relating to those who will experience the system in any way. These issues include such matters as religion, gender, race, nationality, language, dress code, social customs, ethics, politics, and the environment. The objective should be to avoid or minimize offence or distress caused to others.	Soft	Independent audit and review of 1. The inventory of requirements in this area to check for completeness and appropriateness 2. Compliance of system functionality with this set of requirements
Enabling time-to-market	The system architecture and design should allow new business initiatives to be delivered to the market with minimum delay.	Soft	Business management focus group
Governable	The system should enable the owners and executive managers of the organization to control the business and to discharge their responsibilities for governance.	Soft	Senior management focus group Independent audit and review against Security Architecture Capability Maturity Model[2] for governance

Business Attribute	Attribute Explanation	Metric Type	Suggested Measurement Approach
Providing good stewardship and custody	Protecting other parties with whom we do business from abuse or loss of business or personal information of value to those parties through inadequate stewardship on our part.	Soft	Independent audit, focus groups, or satisfaction surveys
Providing investment reuse	As much as possible the system should be designed to reuse previous investments and to ensure that new investments are reusable in the future.	Soft	Independent audit and review against Security Architecture Capability Maturity Model[2] of technical architecture (conceptual, logical, physical, and component)
Providing return on investment	The system should provide a return of value to the business to justify the investment made in creating and operating the system.	Hard	Financial returns and ROI indices selected in consultation with the chief financial officer
		Soft	Qualitative value propositions tested by opinion surveys at senior management and boardroom level
Reputable	The system should behave in such a way as to safeguard the business reputation of the organization.	Soft	Independent audit, focus groups, or satisfaction surveys
		Hard	Correlation of the stock value of the organization versus publicity of system event history

Endnotes

1. A "red team review" is an objective appraisal by an independent team of experts who have been briefed to think either like the user or like an opponent/attacker, whichever is appropriate to the objectives of the review.
2. The type Architectural Capability Maturity Model referred to is based upon the ideas of Capability Maturity Models.
3. MTBF: mean time between failures.
4. MTTR: mean time to repair.

Appendix F: Capability Maturity Model

Level 1—Initial

At maturity level 1, processes are usually ad hoc and the organization usually does not provide a stable environment. Success in these organizations depends on the competence and heroics of the people in the organization and not on the use of proven processes. In spite of this ad hoc, chaotic environment, maturity level 1 organizations often produce products and services that work; however, they frequently exceed the budget and schedule of their projects. Maturity level 1 organizations are characterized by a tendency to over commit, abandon processes in the time of crisis, and not be able to repeat their past successes again. Level 1 software project success depends on having quality people.

Level 2—Repeatable

At maturity level 2, software development successes are repeatable. The processes may not repeat for all the projects in the organization. The organization may use some basis to track cost and schedule. Process discipline helps ensure that existing practices are retained during times of stress. When these practices are in place, projects are performed and managed according to their documented plans.

Project status and the delivery of services are visible to management at defined points (for example, at major milestones and at the completion of major tasks).

Basic project management processes are established to track cost, schedule, and functionality. The minimum process discipline is in place to repeat earlier successes on projects with similar applications and scope. There is still a significant risk of exceeding cost and time estimate.

Level 3—Defined

The organization's set of standard processes, which is the basis for level 3, is established and improved over time. These standard processes are used to establish consistency across the organization. Projects establish their defined processes by the organization's set of standard processes according to tailoring guidelines. The organization's management establishes process objectives based on the organization's set of standard processes and ensures that these objectives are appropriately addressed.

A critical distinction between level 2 and level 3 is the scope of standards, process descriptions, and procedures. At level 2, the standards, process descriptions, and procedures may be quite different in each specific instance of the process (for example, on a particular project). At level 3, the standards, process descriptions, and procedures for a project are tailored from the organization's set of standard processes to suit a particular project or organizational unit.

Level 4—Managed

Using precise measurements, management can effectively control the software development effort. In particular, management can identify ways to adjust and adapt the process to particular projects without measurable losses of quality or deviations from specifications. At this level organizations set a quantitative quality goal for both software process and software maintenance. Subprocesses are selected that significantly contribute to overall process performance. These selected subprocesses are controlled using statistical and other quantitative techniques.

A critical distinction between maturity level 3 and maturity level 4 is the predictability of process performance. At maturity level 4, the performance of processes is controlled using statistical and other quantitative techniques, and is quantitatively predictable. At maturity level 3, processes are only qualitatively predictable.

Level 5—Optimizing

Maturity level 5 focuses on continually improving process performance through both incremental and innovative technological improvements. Quantitative process-improvement objectives for the organization are established, continually revised to reflect changing business objectives, and used as criteria in managing process improvement. The effects of deployed process improvements are measured and evaluated against the quantitative process-improvement objectives. Both the defined processes and the organization's set of standard processes are targets of measurable improvement activities.

Process improvements to address common causes of process variation and measurably improve the organization's processes are identified, evaluated, and deployed.

Optimizing processes that are nimble, adaptable, and innovative depends on the participation of an empowered workforce aligned with the business values and objectives of the organization. The organization's ability to rapidly respond to changes and opportunities is enhanced by finding ways to accelerate and share learning.

A critical distinction between maturity level 4 and maturity level 5 is the type of process variation addressed. At maturity level 4, processes are concerned with addressing special causes of process variation and providing statistical predictability of the results. Though processes may produce predictable results, the results may be insufficient to achieve the established objectives. At maturity level 5, processes are concerned with addressing common causes of process variation and changing the process (that is, shifting the mean of the process performance) to improve process performance (while maintaining statistical probability) to achieve the established quantitative process-improvement objectives.

Appendix G: Probabilistic Risk Assessment

Dr. Michael Stamatelatos

NASA Office of Safety and Mission Assurance

G.1 What Is Probabilistic Risk Assessment?

Probabilistic risk assessment (PRA) has emerged as an increasingly popular analysis tool especially during the last decade. PRA is a systematic and comprehensive methodology to evaluate risks associated with every life-cycle aspect of a complex engineered technological entity (e.g., facility, spacecraft, power plant) from concept definition, through design, construction, and operation, and up to removal from service.

Risk is defined as a feasible detrimental outcome of an activity or action (e.g., launch or operation of a spacecraft) subject to hazard(s). In a PRA, risk is characterized by two quantities: (1) the *magnitude* (or *severity*) of the adverse *consequence*(s) that can potentially result from the given activity or action, and (2) the *likelihood* of occurrence of the given adverse consequence(s). If the measure of consequence severity is the number of people that can be potentially injured or killed, risk assessment becomes a powerful analytic tool to assess safety performance.

If the severity of the consequence(s) and their likelihood of occurrence are both expressed qualitatively (e.g., through words like *high*, *medium*, or *low*), the risk assessment is called a *qualitative risk assessment*. In a *quantitative risk assessment* or a *probabilistic risk assessment*, consequences are expressed numerically (e.g., the number of people potentially hurt or killed) and their likelihoods of occurrence are expressed as *probabilities* or *frequencies* (i.e., the number of occurrences or the probability of occurrence per unit time).

Probabilistic risk assessment usually answers three basic questions:

1. What can go wrong with the studied technological entity, or what are the *initiators* or *initiating events* (undesirable starting events) that lead to adverse consequence(s)?
2. What and how severe are the potential detriments or the adverse *consequences* that the technological entity may be eventually subjected to as a result of the occurrence of the initiator?
3. How likely to occur are these undesirable consequences, or what are their *probabilities* or *frequencies*?

The answer to the first question requires technical knowledge of the possible causes leading to detrimental outcomes of a given activity or action. In order to focus on the most important initiators while screening out the unimportant ones, logic tools such as master logic diagrams (MLDs) or failure modes and effects analyses (FMEA) have been successfully used. The answers to the second and third questions are obtained by developing and quantifying *accident* (or mishap) *scenarios*, which are chains of events that link the initiator to the end-point detrimental consequences.

The answer to the second question is obtained from *deterministic* analyses (e.g., thermal, fluid, structural, and other engineering analyses) that describe the phenomena that could occur along the path of the accident scenario when the initiator and the other subsequent events (through the detrimental consequences) take place. The methods used for these deterministic evaluations depend on the specifics of the technology involved.

The answer to the third question is obtained by using Boolean logic methods for model development and by probabilistic or statistical methods for the quantification portion of the model analysis. Boolean logic tools include *inductive* logic methods such as *event tree analysis* (ETA) and *event sequence diagrams* (ESDs) analysis and *deductive* methods such as *fault tree analysis* (FTA). In cases when the probability of an event is well known from past experience, statistical *actuarial* data can be used if the uncertainty in these data are acceptably low. For rare events (e.g., system failures) for which there is no past failure experience at all or the data are very sparse, probabilistic failure models are developed with deductive logic tools such as fault trees, or inductive logic tools such as *reliability block diagrams* (RBDs) and FMEAs.

The final result of a PRA is given in the form of a *risk curve* and the associated uncertainties. The risk curve is generally the plot of the frequency of exceeding a consequence value (the ordinate) as a function of the consequence values (the abscissa). If the risk assessment is qualitative, the result can be represented as a two-dimensional matrix showing probability categories versus consequence categories.

In addition to the above model development and quantification, PRA studies require special but often very important analysis tools such as *human reliability analysis* (HRA) and dependent-failure or *common-cause analysis* (CCF). HRA deals with methods for modeling human error whereas CCF deals with methods for evaluating the effect of intersystem and intercomponent dependencies, which tend to cause significant increases in overall system or facility risk. PRA studies can be performed for *internal initiating events* as well as for *external initiating events*. Internal initiating events are here defined to be hardware or system failures or operator errors in situations arising from the normal mode of operation of the facility. External initiating events are those encountered outside the domain of the normal operation of a facility. Initiating events associated with the occurrence of natural phenomena (e.g., earthquakes, lightning, tornadoes, fires, and floods) are typical examples of external initiators.

G.2 What Are the Benefits of PRA?

Early forms of PRA had their origin in the aerospace industry before and during the Apollo space program. Later on, other industries (e.g., nuclear power industry, chemical industry), U.S. government laboratories and U.S. government agencies expanded PRA methods to higher levels of sophistication in order to assess safety compliance and performance. In recent years, government regulatory agencies, such as the Nuclear Regulatory Commission and the Environmental Protection Agency, have begun to use *risk-based* or *risk-informed regulation* as a basis for enhancing safety without applying undue conservatism. The use of PRA is expected to grow both in the government and in the private sectors.

Early on, industry began using PRA reluctantly, at the request of some regulatory agencies, to assess safety concerns. For example, the NRC required that each nuclear power plant in the United States perform an *independent plant evaluation* (IPE) to identify and quantify plant vulnerabilities to hardware failures and human faults in design and operation. Although no method was specified for performing such an evaluation, the NRC requirements for the analysis could be met only by applying PRA methods.

After completing the compulsory PRA efforts, however, performing organizations usually discovered benefits beyond mere compliance with regulation. These have included new insights into and an in-depth understanding of

- Design flaws and cost-effective ways to eliminate them in design prior to construction and operation
- Normal and abnormal operation of complex systems and facilities even for the most experienced design and operating personnel
- Design flaws and hardware-related, operator-related, and institutional reasons impacting safety and optimal performance at operating facilities and cost-effective ways to implement upgrades
- Approaches to reduce operation and maintenance costs while meeting or exceeding safety requirements
- Technical bases to request and receive exemptions from unnecessarily conservative regulatory requirements

PRA studies have been successfully performed for complex technological systems at all phases of the life cycle from concept definition and predesign through safe removal from operation. The amount of probabilistic failure information that is available as input to the quantification process of PRA models dictates the accuracy of the results and their uncertainties. Thus, at the concept definition and predesign levels of a first-of-a-kind system, the necessary specific failure information is sparse or simply does not exist. For these cases, data can be adapted or *specialized* (by mathematical techniques) from generic or similar sources and the results of the PRA are more useful to perform *relative* risk comparisons and risk ranking rather than to perform *absolute* (or *bottom line*) risk evaluations. Nevertheless, even for these types of applications, performing a PRA has proven to be an extremely valuable tool to improve concepts and designs cost-effectively.

Probabilistic risk assessment (PRA) (or probabilistic safety assessment/analysis) is a systematic and comprehensive methodology to evaluate risks associated with a complex engineered technological entity (such as airliners and nuclear power plants).

Risk in a PRA is defined as a feasible detrimental outcome of an activity or action. In a PRA, risk is characterized by two quantities:

1. The magnitude (severity) of the possible adverse consequence(s)
2. The likelihood (probability) of occurrence of each consequence

Consequences are expressed numerically (e.g., the number of people potentially hurt or killed) and their likelihoods of occurrence are expressed as probabilities or frequencies (i.e., the number of occurrences or the probability of occurrence per unit time). The total risk is the sum of the products of the consequences multiplied by their probabilities. The spectrum of risks across classes of events are also of concern, and are usually controlled in licensing processes. (It would be of concern if rare but high consequence events were found to dominate the overall risk.)

Probabilistic risk assessment usually answers three basic questions:

1. What can go wrong with the studied technological entity, or what are the initiators or initiating events (undesirable starting events) that lead to adverse consequence(s)?
2. What and how severe are the potential detriments or the adverse consequences that the technological entity may be eventually subjected to as a result of the occurrence of the initiator?
3. How likely to occur are these undesirable consequences, or what are their probabilities or frequencies?

Two common methods of answering these questions are event tree analysis and fault tree analysis—for explanations of these, see safety engineering.

In addition to the above methods, PRA studies require special but often very important analysis tools such as *human reliability analysis* (HRA) and common-cause-failure analysis (CCF). HRA deals with methods for modeling *human error,* whereas CCF deals with methods for evaluating the effect of intersystem and intra-system dependencies that tend to cause simultaneous failures and thus significant increases in overall risk.

PRA studies have been successfully performed for complex technological systems at all phases of the life cycle from concept definition and predesign through safe removal from operation. For example, the Nuclear Regulatory Commission required that each nuclear power plant in the United States perform an individual plant examination (IPE) to identify and quantify plant vulnerabilities to hardware failures and human faults in design and operation. Although no method was specified for performing such an evaluation, the NRC requirements for the analysis could be met only by applying PRA methods.

Index

A

Absolute/relative metrics, 16–17
Absolute risk evaluations, 208
Acceptable interruption window (AIW), 157
Acceptable risk, 123, 125, 126
   and information security risk
     management, 112
   over time, 128
Accounting method, 27
Accuracy, 74
Actionable information, 7, 24, 74, 81
Address resolution protocol (ARP), 157
Adhocracy culture, 177, 179
Admin violations, 23
Advanced encryption standard (AES), 157
Aircraft analogy, 75–77
Alliance for Enterprise Security Risk
   Management (AESRM), 157
Ambiguity, lack of, 74
American Institute of Certified Public
   Accountants (AICPA), 157
American Standard Code for Information
   Exchange (ASCII), 157
Annual loss expectancy (ALE), 30–31, 31,
   37–38, 38, 157
Annual rate of occurrence (ARO), 30, 37
Application programming interface (API), 157
Application service provider (ASP), 157
Application-specific integrated
   circuit (ASIC), 157
Asset classification, 139
Asset criticality, and information security risk
   management, 109–110
Asset importance, 129
Asset loss impact, 130
Asset sensitivity, and information security risk
   management, 110

Asset value, 37
   and cost of protection, 129
Assurance functions, 8–10
Assurance process integration, 132–134
Assurance providers, 7, 8
Asynchronous transfer mode (ATM), 157
Attributes, 35
   of good metrics, 73–74
Australian Standard/New Zealand Standard
   (AS/NZS), 157
Australian Standard Threat and Risk
   Assessment. *See* Threat and Risk Assessment
   (TRA)
Awareness metrics, 138, 146

B

Balanced scorecard (BSC), 44–46, 79
Bandwidth utilization, 23
Bank for International Settlements (BIS), 157
Banking Information Technology Standards
   (BITS), 157
Basic input/output system (BIOS), 157
Behavioral economics, 39
Bell-LaPadula (BLP), 157
Benchmarking, 15, 50, 136
Best-in-class security levels, 53
Best practices, 64, 122
   as poor substitute for adequate
     knowledge, 70
Biased assimilation, 39
Binary metrics
   for compliance, 141
   for security incident response, 151
Biometric information management and
   security (BIMS), 157

Border Gateway Protocol (BGP), 157
Breach losses, 126
    analysis of, 127
    effects on customer trust, 125
British Standard (BS), 158
Building management systems (BMS), 158
Business access assessment (BIA), 112
Business attributes, 46
Business case
    for costly or restrictive controls, 122
    financial metrics for developing, 26
    for security metrics, 4
Business Continuity Institute (BCI), 157
Business continuity management (BCM), 157
Business continuity planning (BCP), 131, 157
Business disruption, 113
Business drivers, 46
Business impact analysis (BIA), 157
Business impact assessment, 110, 127, 131, 139
Business intelligence (BI), 157
Business judgment, 28
Business practices, losses due to, 112
Business process assurance, 5, 84
Business strategy attributes, 48
    SABSA metrics, 197–199
Business virtues, 46
Bypass label process (BLP), 157

C

CA Unicenter, 3
Canadian Institute of Chartered Accountants
    (CICA), 158
Capability Maturity Model (CMM), 49–50,
    106, 158, 201
    Defined level, 202
    Initial level, 201
    Managed level, 202
    Optimizing level, 202–203
    Respectable level, 201
    security objectives, 90
Carelessness, 8
Carnegie Mellon University (CMU), 158
Case studies
    compliance metrics, 144–145
    Slammer worm, 144–145
    strategic alignment, 124–125
Center for Internet Security (CIS), 158
Centers of influence, 42
Central processing unit (CPU), 158

Certificate authority (CA), 158
Certificate revocation list (CRL), 158
Certification practice statement (CPS), 158
Change management processes, 140
Chief compliance officer (CCO), 158
Chief executive officer (CEO), 158
Chief financial officer (CFO), 158
Chief information officer (CIO), 158
    failures in information security, xv
Chief information security officer (CISO), 158
Chief legal counsel (CLC), 158
Chief operating officer (COO), 158
Chief privacy officer (CPO), 158
Chief security officer (CSO), 159
Clan culture, 176, 179
Clark-Wilson (CW), 159
ClearPoint Metrics, 3
Clients, losses due to, 112
CobiT, 86, 106
    acquire and implement objectives, 86, 88
    control objectives, 86, 88–89
    deliver and support objectives, 86, 88–89
    monitor and evaluate objectives, 86, 89
    plan and organize objectives, 86, 88
Committee of Sponsoring Organizations
    of the Treadway Commission
    (COSO), 158
Common-cause failure analysis (CCFA), 206,
    208–209
Common object request broker architecture
    (CORBA), 158
Common vulnerabilities and
    exposures (CVE), 159
Commonly accepted security practices and
    recommendations (CASPR), 158
Communication
    and level of integration, 134
    during security incidents, 151
Compact disc (CD), 158
Compact disc read-only memory
    (CD-ROM), 158
Competing values framework, 40–42, 175
    adhocracy organization in, 177
    clan organization in, 176
    competing values map, 175
    core assumptions and statements, 41–42
    cultural dimensions, 175
    hierarchist worldview, 176
    horizontal and in/out dimensions, 175
    market organization in, 176
    vertical stability/flexibility dimensions, 175
Competing values map, 175

Compliance audits, 141
Compliance dashboards, 3
Compliance metrics, 138–139, 140, 143
  criticality and sensitivity, 139–140
  metrics reliability, 146
  personnel competence, 145–146
  procedure functionality, efficiency,
    appropriateness, 147
  proficiency and awareness, 146
  resource adequacy, 146
  risk exposure, 140
  state of compliance, 140–145
Compromise, probability of, 111
Computational engine, in FAIR approach, 57
Computer-based training (CBT), 158
Computer emergency response team
  (CERT), 158
Computer incident response team (CIRT), 158
Computer-integrated manufacturing
  (CIM), 158
Computer security incident response team
  (CSIRT), 158
Computer Security Resources Center (CSRC),
  U.S.A., 159
Conformance to standards, 15
Consequences, 67, 206
  correlating metrics to, 64–65
Context
  in governance decisions, 101
  importance in ranking metrics, 98
*Contingency Planning Guide for Information
  Technology,* 131
Continuity of operations plan
  (COOP), 131, 158
Control effectiveness/reliability, 127, 131
Control objectives for information and related
  technology (CobiT), 158
Control self-assessment (CSA), 158
Convergence, of physical, IT, and information
  security, 133
Corporate culture, 39
Cost-benefit analysis, 36, 128
  of security attributes, 35
  and VAR method, 57
Cost effectiveness, 75, 97, 105
  and best practices approach, 71
  of existing controls, 134
Cost-effectiveness analysis (CEA), 35–36
Credit fraud, 67, 110
Critical success factor (CSF), 158
Criticality, 96, 97
  for compliance metrics, 139–140

determining, 139–140
and information security risk management,
  109–110
Cultural metrics, 39
Cultural theory, 39–40
Cultural worldviews, 171
  egalitarians, 171–172
  fatalists, 171–172
  hierarchists, 171
  individualists, 172
Current state, 91
Customer relationship management (CRM), 158
Customer trust, metrics on, 124–125
Cybercrime, xv

D

Data, *vs.* information, 145
Data communications equipment (CDE), 159
Data Encryption Standard (DES), 159
Data integration, challenges, 4
Data-oriented system development (DOSD), 159
Database management system (DBMS), 159
Decision support, 80, 119, 137
  incident management metrics for, 150–153
  information security program development
    metrics for, 115
  information security risk management for,
    108–109
  kinds of information needed for, 93
  metrics for security management, 120–122
  program development management metrics
    for, 116
  as ultimate metrics rationale, 73, 93
Degree of risk, 96, 97
Delivery management, 113
Demilitarized zone (DMZ), 159
Denial of service (DoS), 159
Desired state, 91, 115
  defining characteristics, 85
Development metrics, information security
  program, 115
Digital command language (DCL), 159
Digital linear tape (DLT), 159
Direct/indirect metrics, 17
Direct monitoring, 99
  expense of, 141
Disaster recovery (DR), 159
Disaster Recovery Institute International
  (DRII), 159

Disaster recovery planning (DRP), 131
Discounted cash flow (DFC), 29
Discretionary access controls (DAC), 159
Distributed computing environment
  (DCE), 159
Distributed control environment (DCE), 159
Distributed denial of service (DDoS), 159
Domain name server (DNS), 159
Domain name service secure (DNSSEC), 159
Dropped packets, 23
Dynamic Host Configuration Protocol
  (DHCP), 159

E

E-mail attachments, costs of infections
  from, 124
Effectiveness metrics, xiv, 17, 77–81, 134, 168
  and competing values framework, 40–42
  features in normal circumstances, 168–169
  operational limitation metrics, 170
  risk metrics, 170
  strength assessment metrics, 168
  technical target of assessment (TTOA), 168
  weakness assessment metrics, 169
Egalitarianism, 39–40, 171–172
Electronic backup, security breaches due to, 70
Electronic data interchange (EDI), 159
Electronic funds transfer (EFT), 159
Employment practices, losses due to, 112
Encryption, 8
Enhanced Interior Gateway Routing Protocol
  (EIGRP), 159
Enterprise resource planning (ERP)
  system, 115
Environmental safety, 7
Equal error rate (EER), 159
European Union (EU), 159
Event sequence diagrams (ESD), 206
Event tree analysis (ETA), 61, 206, 208
Execution management, 113
Expectations, monitoring and managing, 135
Exposure factor, 37
Extensible Business Reporting Language
  (XBRL), 163
Extensible Markup Language (XML), 163
External fraud, 112
External Gateway Routing Protocol
  (EGRP), 159
External threats, 5

F

Factor analysis of information risk
  (FAIR), 57–58
Failed logon attempts, 23
Failure Modes Effects Analysis
  (FMEA), 36, 206
Failure Modes Effects and Criticality Analysis
  (FMECA), 36
False-acceptance rate (FAR), 159
False credentials, 110
Fatalism, 39–40, 172–173
Fault tree analysis (FTA), 36–37, 206, 208
  in PRA, 61
Feasibility study goal indicators, 116
Features metrics
  abnormal circumstances, 169
  normal circumstances, 168–169
Federal Energy Regulatory Commission
  (FERC), U.S.A., 159
Federal Financial Institution Examination
  Council (FFIEC), 159
Federal Information Processing Standards
  (FIPS), 159
Federal Information Security Management Act
  (FISMA), 159
Feedback mechanisms, 5
File size changes, 23
Financial impact, 127
Financial metrics, 25–26, 124
  annual loss expectancy (ALE), 37–38
  cost-benefit analysis, 36
  cost-effectiveness analysis (CEA),
    35–36
  fault tree analysis, 36–37
  internal rate of return (IRR),
    28–30
  net present value (NPV), 29
  return on investment (ROI), 26–30
  return on security investment (ROSI),
    30–35
  ROI calculation, 27–29
  security attribute evaluation method
    (SAEM), 35
  single loss expectancy (SLE), 37–38
  value at risk (VAR), 37
Financial Security Authority (FSA), 160
Firewall logs, limitations, 73
Flexibility, *vs.* change, 41
Foreign Corrupt Practices Act (FCPA), 159
Fraud prevention, 10
Functional correlation approach, 54

G

Gap analysis, 91, 104
Generalized audit software (GAS), 160
Generally accepted information security
  principles (GAISP), 160
Generally accepted security system principles
  (GASSP), 160
Good metrics attributes, 73–74, 76
  accuracy, 74
  actionability, 74
  effective metrics, 77–81
  lack of ambiguity, 74
  manageability, 74
  meaningfulness, 74
  measurement categories, 75–77
  metrics objectives, 74
  timeliness, 74
Governance, xvi–xvii, 5, 83–84
  and current state, 91
  defined, 83
  failure of internal, 112
  four requirements of, 103
  information security strategy for, 91–92
  outcomes, 84–85
  and resource allocation, 69
  results of implementation, 5, 6
  security objectives for, 85–90
Governance metrics, 101
  and appropriate risk management, 104–105
  ensuring achievement of objectives, 104
  operational decisions, 105–106
  responsible use of resources, 105
  security governance management decisions,
    103–105
  and strategic direction, 103–104
  strategic security governance decisions,
    101–103, 102–103
Governance Metrics International (GMI), 160
Gramm-Leach-Bliley Act (GLBA), 160
Guidance, failure of metrics to provide, 65

H

Hacked systems, 70
Health Insurance Portability and
  Accountability Act (HIPAA), 160
Heating, ventilation, and air conditioning
  (HVAC), 160
HERMES, 92

Hierarchist worldview, 39–40, 171, 176, 179
  in competing values framework, 176
Hierarchy input-process-output (HIPO), 160
High-definition/High-density digital video
  disc (HD-DVD), 160
High-impact losses, 128
Homogeneity, aggregated risk from, 135
Host IDS (HIDS), 150
Hubs of influence, 43
Human error, modeling, 209
Human intelligence, role in compliance,
  142–143
Human relations model, 42
Human reliability analysis (HRA), 206, 208
Human resources (HR), 160
Hybrid metrics, 43
  balanced scorecard, 44–46
  SABSA business attributes approach,
    46–48
  systemic security management, 43
Hypertext markup language (HTML), 160
Hypertext Transfer Protocol (HTTP), 160

I

IBM Tivoli, 3
Identification and authentication (I&A), 160
Identification (ID), 160
Identity theft, internal risks for, 6
Impact management, 131
Impacts, 67, 126
  acceptable levels, 112
  correlation of metrics to, 65
  nature and magnitude, 110
Impersonation attacks, 110
Implementation strategy, for governance, 84
Incident detection metrics, 131
Incident management and response, 149–150
  chain of authority, 153
  decision support metrics, 150–153
  immediate actions, 152
  incident classification, 151
  incident response teams, 153
  multiple events/impacts, 152
  notifications, 153
  progression to disaster, 153
  response effectiveness, 152–153
  severity levels, 151–152
Incident management capability, 111
Incident management team (IMT), 160

Incident response plan (IRP), 161
Incident response team (IRT), 153, 161
Inconvenience, cost of, 124
Incremental limitations, costs of, 124
Independent plant evaluation (IPE), 207
Indicators, 38
Individualism worldview, 39–40, 172
Industrial espionage, 8
Industry sector metrics, 124
Informal organization, 43
Information
    as data with meaning, 7
    rolling up for conciseness, 101
    vs. data and knowledge, 7, 145
Information and communication technologies
    (ICT), 160
Information assets, loss of, xiv–xv
Information assurance (IA), xvii, 16
    metrics classification, 17–18
Information crimes, xv
Information processing facility (IPF), 160
Information recipients, 81, 101
Information security, 7–8
    decision support for, 108–109
    failure of, xiii
    lack of useful metrics, 107
    management requirements for risk,
        109–112
Information Security and Control Association
    (ISACA), 5, 83
Information Security Forum (ISF), 161
Information security governance. *See*
    Governance
Information security management, 137
Information security management metrics,
    119–120
    operational decision support metrics,
        137–147
    security management decision support
        metrics, 120–122
    security management decisions, 122–137
Information security manager, sample job
    description, 94–96
Information security officer (ISO), 161
Information security program development
    metrics, 115
    program development management
        metrics, 116–117
    program development operational
        metrics, 117
Information security risk management,
    107–108

and acceptable risk/impact levels, 112
and asset criticality, 109–110
and asset sensitivity, 110
decisions, 108–109
and management requirements, 109–112
and nature and magnitude of impacts, 110
operational risk metrics, 112–114
and probability of compromise, 111
and strategic initiatives/plans, 111
and threats, 111
and vulnerabilities, 110–111
Information security strategy, 91–92
Information System Security Association
    (ISSA), 161
Information systems (IS), 161
Information technology (IT), 161
Initial program load (IPL), 160
Initiating events, 206
Input/output (I/O), 160
Institute of Internal Auditors (IIA), 160
Intangible assets, 7
Integration Definition for Information
    Modeling (IDEFIX), 160
Integration testing, 116, 117
Intellectual property rights (IPRs), 160
Internal fraud, 112
Internal initiating events, 207
Internal process model, 41
Internal rate of return (IRR), 27, 29–30, 38
Internal Revenue Service (IRS), 161
Internal risks, 6
International Development Corp. (IDC), 160
International Eletrotechnical Commission
    (IEC), 160
International Federation of Accountants
    (IFA), 160
International Organization for Standardization
    (ISO), 161
International Project Management Association
    (IPMA), 160
International Shareholders Services (ISS), 161
International System Security Engineering
    Association (ISSEA), 161
Internet control message protocol (ICMP), 160
Internet engineering task force (IETF), 160
Internet Protocol (IP), 160
Internet Protocol Security (IPSec), 160
Internet service provider (ISP), 161
Intervening obstacles, 75
Intrusion detection, 98
Intrusion detection system (IDS), 160
Intrusion prevention system (IPS), 160

Intrusion successes, 23
ISO 9000, 49
ISO 10006, 92
ISO 27001, 89, 106
IT Governance Global Status
   Report, 5, 6
IT Governance Institute (ITGI), 7, 161
IT management, 137
IT metrics, 8
IT security, 8

J

Job control language (JCL), 161
Job descriptions
   information security manager, 94–96
   role in metrics development, 93

K

Key goal indicators (KGIs), 38, 116,
   122, 161
Key performance indicators (KPIs), 38, 116,
   122, 155, 161
Key success factors (KSFs), 38
Kilo lines of code (KLOC), 161
Knowledge
   as actionable information, 7
   best practices as poor substitute for, 70
   as factor in productivity, xv

L

Layer 2 Tunneling Protocol (L2TP), 161
Layered security, 108
Leading indicators, 155
Legal attributes, 48
   SABSA metrics, 192–194
Link control protocol (LCP), 161
Local area network (LAN), 161
Log analysis, 142–143
Logging granularity, insufficiency of, 73
Loss duration, 130
Loss events, categories, 112–113
Loss sensitivity, 130
Lost laptops, 70

M

Maintenance metrics, 117
Malicious insiders, 70
Malware, 23
Man-in-the-Middle (MitM), 161
Manageability attribute, 74
Management attributes, 48
   SABSA metrics, 183–185
Management information system (MIS), 161
Management metrics, 10
   differentiating from governance and
      program development metrics,
      120–121
Management readiness metrics, 167
Managerial effectiveness, 42
Mandatory access control (MAC), 161
Market culture, 176, 179
Master logic diagrams (MLDs), 206
Maturity gaps, 91
Maturity levels, 15, 49–50
Maximum tolerable outage (MTO), 161
Meaningfulness, 74, 81
Measurement categories, 75–77
Mergers and acquisition (M&A), 161
Metric accuracy, 127, 131
Metrics, xvii
   accuracy of, 131
   actionable, 81
   activities requiring, 96–97
   defined, 1
   meaningfulness, 81
   operational information security-related,
      112–114
   ranking, 98
   rationale for, 80–81
   reliability, 146
   for risk management, 126–127
   for strategic security governance decisions,
      102–103
   subject of, 79–80
   vs. monitoring and measures, 98–99
Metrics Center, 2
Metrics classifications, 165
   effectiveness metrics, 168–170
   operational metrics, 166–168
   program development metrics, 165
   support metrics, 166
Metrics development
   and activities requirring metrics, 96–97
   criticality and sensitivity in, 97
   and degree of risk, 97

new approach to, 93–94
options and cost-effectiveness, 97
and potential impact, 97
ranking metrics and monitoring
    requirements, 98
and risk over time, 97
sample job description for, 94–96
Metrics developments, 53
    factor analysis of information risk (FAIR),
        57–58
    probabilistic risk assessment (PRA), 58–61
    risk factor analysis, 58
    statistical modeling, 54
    systemic security management, 55–56
    value-at-risk analysis, 56–57
Metrics imperative, 67–68
    and managing without metrics, 70–71
    and resource allocation, 69–70
    ROSI study, 68–69
Metrics implementation, 5
    results of, 5
Metrics testing, 146
Modeling methods, 15
Monitoring, 98–99
    cost of direct, 99
    vs. metrics, 18
Monitoring requirements, ranking, 98
Multidimensional scorecards, 15
Multinational organizations, complexities in
    understanding, 102–103
Multipurpose Internet mail extensions
    (MIME), 161

N

National Fire Protection Association
    (NFPA), 161
National Foundation of Standards and
    Technology (NIS), 162
Navigation, 75, 120
Net present value (NPV), 27, 29, 38
Network address translation (NAT), 161
Network basic input/output systems
    (NetBIOS), 161
Network Control Protocol (NCP), 161
Network file system (NFS), 161
Network IDS (NIDS), 150
Network interface card (NIC), 161
Network intrusion detection system
    (NIDS), 161

Network security, outsourcing, 143
Network vulnerability scanners, limitations of
    usefulness, 77
Nondisclosure agreement (NDA), 161
Nontechnical security failures, predictors for, 64

O

Objective/subjective metrics, 16
Objectives, 4–6, 83, 123
    Capability Maturity Model, 90
    CobiT, 86
    defining for governance, 85–90
    ensuring achievement of, 104
    of good metrics, 74
    ISO 27001, 89
    process-driven, 22
    SABSA, 86
Occupant emergency plan (OEP), 162
OCTAVE, 51
Office of the Comptroller of the Currency
    (OCC), 162
Online Certificate Status Protocol
    (OCSP), 162
Open shortest path first (OSPF), 162
Open systems interconnection (OSI), 162
Open systems model, 41
Operating system (OS), 162
Operational attributes, 48
    SABSA metrics, 185–186
Operational decision support metrics, 137
    compliance metrics, 138–147
    IT and information security
        management, 137
Operational decisions, 105–106
Operational efficiency, security restrictions
    on, 124
Operational environment, 167–168
Operational information, 76
Operational limitation metrics, 170
Operational maturity, 38
Operational metrics, 17, 166
    management readiness metrics, 167
    operational environment metrics, 167–168
    operational practice metrics, 167
    operational readiness metrics, 166–167
    for program development, 117
    technical readiness metrics, 167
Operational performance, 10
Operational practice metrics, 167

Operational readiness, 166–167
Operational risk
    functional correlation approach, 54
    metrics for information security, 112–114
    sequential correlations and, 55
Operational risk management (ORM), 112
Operational security management, 4
Operationally critical threat, asset,
  and vulnerability evaluation
  (OCTAVE), 51, 162
Optational health/malfunctions, 75
Organization Culture Assessment Instrument
  (OCAI), 179–180
Organization for Economic Cooperation and
  Development (OECD), 162
Organizational culture (OC), 39
    assessment instrument, 179–180
    and organizational structure, 42–43
Organizational effectiveness, 42
Organizational focus, 40–41
Organizational performance, 3
Organizational preservation, xix
Organizational risk, 109
Organizational risk tolerance, 127–129
Organizational strategy, in systemic
  management model, 55–56
Organizational structure, 42–43
Original equipment manufacturer (OEM), 162
Outcomes, 15, 121–122
    dearth of data about, 63
    evaluating measures against, 146
    of governance and management, 5, 84–85
    for information security, 121–122, 123
Outsourcers, as sources of security breaches, 70
Oversight functions, 121

P

Paper records, security breaches of, 70
Payback method, 26–27
Penetration testing, 110, 111
People, process, and policy (PPP), 162
People issues, in security, 14
Perceptual metrics, 135
Performance measurement, 5, 15, 22–25, 85,
  136–137
    limitations at tactical and strategic
      levels, 122
Permanent virtual circuit (PVC), 162
Personal area network (PAN), 162

Personal computer/microcomputer (PC), 162
Personally identifiable information (PII), 110
Personnel compliance, 121, 145–146
Personnel support metrics, 166
Personnel utilization rates, 136
Phishing, 64
Physical asset damage, 112
Physical security metrics, 25
Physical vulnerabilities, 111
Plan-do-check-act (PDCA), 162
PlexLogic, 2
Point-of-sale (POS), 162
Point-to-Point Protocol over Ethernet
  (PPPoE), 162
Policy management metrics, 165
Potential impact, 96, 97, 142
Predictive metrics, 13, 155
    need for, 63
Present value methods, 30
PRINCE, 92
Probabilistic risk assessment (PRA), 58–61,
  60, 205
    benefits, 207–209
    defined, 205–207
Probabilities metrics, 15
Problem inertia, 64
Procedural compliance, 138, 139, 141
Procedural controls, 147
Procedural metrics, 138, 147
Process management, 113
Process maturity metrics, 165
Process metrics, 14, 15
Process quality, 38
Processor utilization, 23
Product losses, 112
Product safety, 7
Proficiency metrics, 146
Profitability, ROI and, 26
Program development metrics, 17, 165
    information security, 115
    management related, 116–117
    policy management metrics, 165
    process maturity metrics, 165
Program effectiveness, 119
Program management, 76
Project management body of knowledge
  (PMBOK), 162
Proof of concept, 116, 117
Proportionality, 129
Public key infrastructure (PKI), 162
Public switched telephone network
  (PSTN), 162

Q

Qualitative metrics, 16, 38
  competing values framework, 40–42
  cultural metrics, 39
  organizational structure, 42–43
  risk management through cultural theory,
    39–40
Qualitative risk assessment, 205
Quality and acceptance testing (UAT), 117
Quality assurance (QA), 8, 15, 162
Quality metrics, 48–49
  benchmarking, 50
  ISO 9000, 49
  maturity level, 49–50
  OCTAVE, 51
  standards, 50–51
Quantitative metrics, 16, 21–22
  discussion, 25
  performance metrics, 22–25
Quantitative risk assessment, 205

R

Rational goal model, 41
Real-time metrics, 13
Recovery point objective (RPO), 162
Recovery time, 112
Recovery time objectives (RTOs),
  128, 139, 162
Red teams, 110
Redundant array of inexpensive disks
  (RAID), 162
Regional Computer Emergency Response
  Team (RCERT), 162
Regulations
  risk-informed, 207
  role in awareness, 6
Regulatory attributes, 48
  SABSA metrics, 192–194
Relative asset valuation, 130
Relative risk comparisons, 208
Relevance, 63–64
  and correlating metrics to
    consequences, 64–65
  and problem inertia, 64
Reliability block diagrams (RBD), 206
Remaining storage capacity, 23
Remedial processes, costs of, 124
Resource adequacy, 146

Resource allocation, 116
  responsible, 83, 105
  and security breaches, 69–70
Resource constraints, 91
Resource dependency analysis, 110
Resource management, 5, 85, 136
Resource support metrics, 166
Resource utilization, 136
Resource valuation, 127, 129–130
Response effectiveness metrics, 131
Response time metrics, 131
Retail metrics, 124
Return on investment (ROI), 5, 26, 38, 135, 162
  calculating for security metrics, 4
  internal rate of return (IRR) method, 29–30
  more complex security method, 32, 35
  NPV method, 29
  payback method, 26–27
  ROI calculation, 27–29
  in security, 68–69
Return on security investment (ROSI), 27, 30,
  31, 38, 129, 135
  ALE method, 30–31
  new model, 31–32
  SLE method, 30–31
  study on security measures, 68–69
Reverse Address Resolution Protocol
  (RARP), 162
Risk
  acceptable, 103, 112
  defined, 126, 205
  degree of, 97
  in PRA, 208
  underestimation of, 67
  undermanagement of, 126
Risk assessment, 103, 127, 140
  comprehensive, 130
Risk assessment guide, 59
Risk exposure, 31, 140
Risk factor analysis, 58, 60
Risk-informed regulation, 207
Risk likelihood, 205
Risk limits, acceptable, 2
Risk magnitude, 205
Risk management, 5, 83, 84, 104, 125–126
  effectiveness of, 121
  for information security, 107–108, 108–109
  lack of integration in, 107
  metrics for, 126–127
  through cultural theory, 39–40
  vs. operational and strategic security
    management, 4

Risk management attributes, 48
  SABSA metrics, 186–191
Risk metrics, 170
Risk never to exceed (RNE), 2
Risk over time, 97
Risk Reward Theorem/Tradeoff (RRT), 162
Risk tolerance, 126, 127
Risks, interdependence of, 9
Rivest, Shamir, and Adleman (RSA), 162

S

SABSA attributes, 47, 87
SABSA business attribute metrics, 181
  business strategy attributes, 197–199
  legal and regulatory attributes, 192–194
  management attributes, 183–185
  operational attributes, 185–186
  risk management attributes, 186–191
  technical strategy attributes, 194–197
  user attributes, 181–183
SABSA business attributes approach, 46–48
Safeguard savings to cost ratio, 68
Safety
  assurance of, 1, 7
  challenges for metrics, 2
  and security, xviii
Scope of loss, 130
Scope of responsibilities, 93
  information security manager, 94–96
SecurCompass, 2
Secure electronic transfer/transactions
  (SET), 163
Secure Hypertext Transfer Protocol
  (HTTPS), 160, 162
Secure multipurpose Internet mail extensions
  (S-MIME), 163
Secure shell (SSH), 163
Secure sockets layer (SSL), 163
Securities and Exchange Commission
  (SEC), 163
Security
  as assurance of safety, 1, 7
  as complex system, 14
  defined, xviii, 1
  defining objectives for, 1
  as dynamic activity, 56
  lack of key indicators, 13
  as process *vs.* event, 64
  statistically predictive consequences, 53

Security activities, as hindrances to
  organizational activities, 123
Security attribute evaluation method
  (SAEM), 35
Security audits, limitations, 3
Security dashboards, 2, 3
Security expenditures
  and cyber-related losses, 22
  justifying cost of, 69
  per employee by industry sector, 54
Security failures, corporate reluctance to
  report, 63
Security incidents
  chain of authority, 153
  classification, 151
  defined, 151
  determining, 150–151
  domino effects, 152
  due to lack of integration, 133
  immediate actions, 152
  multiple, 152
  notifications, 153
  personnel mobilization, 153
  progression to disaster, 153
  response effectiveness, 152–153
  severity levels, 151–152
  tracking number of, 65
  triage for, 152
  vs. other events, 151
Security information management (SIM), 163
Security management, 13
  failures of, xiii
  use of business judgment, 28
Security management decision support
  metrics, 120–122
Security management decisions, 122–123
  assurance process integration, 132–134
  and business impact assessment, 131
  and comprehensive risk assessment, 130
  and control effectiveness/reliability, 131
  and metrics accuracy, 131
  and organizational risk tolerance, 127–129
  performance measurement, 136–137
  resource management, 136
  and resource valuation, 129–130
  risk management, 125–131
  strategic alignment, 123–125
  value delivery, 134–135
Security metrics, 13–14
  classification, 15–17, 17–18
  correlating to consequences, 64–65
  current state, 21

failure to provide assurance of safety, 10
financial, 25–38
fundamental characteristics, 16–17
hybrid approaches, 43–48
and objectives, 4–6
overview, 1–4
predictive goals, 2
qualitative, 38–43
quantitative, 21–25
and security program effectiveness, 14
stakeholders, 10
taxonomy of, 16
types of, 15–17
vs. security monitoring, 18
Security Parameter Index (SPI), 163
Security program effectiveness, 14
Security steering group (SSG), 163
Security strategies, 105
Security yardsticks, 64
SecurityMetrics.org, 2
Selective recall, 39
Self-insurance, cost of, 128
Semantics of Business Vocabulary and
Business Rules (SBVR), 143
Sensitivity, 96, 97
for compliance metrics, 139–140
determining, 139–140
and information security risk
management, 110
Sequential correlations, 55
Server patches, 78, 79
Service delivery objective (SDO), 163
Service level agreement (SLA), 163
Sherwood Applied Business Security
Architecture (SABSA), 14,
46–48, 162
objectives, 86
SIMS, 142–143, 150
Simulation model, in FAIR approach, 58
Simultaneous peripheral operations online
(SPOOL), 163
Single loss expectancy (SLE), 30–31, 37–38, 38
Single point of contact (SPOC), 163
Single sign-on (SSO), 163
Six Sigma, 48–49
Skills assessment testing, 151
Slammer worm case study, 144–145
SMART attributes, 74
Social engineering, 8, 110
Sociomaps, 42–43
Soft-metrics, 38
Software engineering, building security into, 69

Software process improvement and capability
determination (SPICE), 163
Sofware Engineering Institute (SEI), 163
Solution architecture and design goals, 116, 117
SOX solution dashboards, 3
Specific, measurable, achievable, relevant,
time-bound (SMART), 74, 163
Stability, *vs.* control, 41
Stakeholders, 10
Standard operating procedure (SOP), 163
Standardization metrics, 135
Standards, as baseline for metrics, 50–51
Static/dynamic metrics, 16
Statistical analysis, 15
Statistical modeling, 54–55
STORM sociomaps, 42
Strategic alignment, 5, 84
case study, 124–125
in context of information security, 123–125
Strategic business outcomes, 121
Strategic decisions, 101–103
Strategic direction, 83, 102, 103–104
Strategic initiatives/plans, and information
security risk management, 111
Strategic objectives, 119
Strategic security management, 4
Strategy-forcused organizations, 46
Strength assessment metrics, 168
Structured Query Language (SQL), 163
Supervisory control and data acquisition
(SCDA), 162
Support metrics, 17, 166
personnel-related, 166
resource-related, 166
System development life cycle (SLC) methods,
116, 163
System logs, limitations, 73
System management facility (SMF), 163
Systemic security management, 43, 55–56
Systems auditability and control (SAC), 162
Systems failures, 113

T

Tactical metrics, 119, 120
Tail-gating, 110
Taxonomy
in FAIR approach, 57
of security metrics, 16
of security ROI parameters, 32–33

Technical metrics, 14, 67
  compliance measures for, 142
  dominance of, 21–22
  lack of economic benefit, 22
  lack of information in, 137
  meaningfulness in, 81
  performance-related, 24
  vs. management metrics, 10
  vs. strategic and management metrics, 120
Technical readiness metrics, 167
Technical strategy attributes, 48
  SABSA metrics, 194–197
Technical target of assessment (TTOA)
  metrics, 168
Tensions, 56
  in systemic security management model, 55
Threat and Risk Assessment (TRA), 31
  with calculated annual cost of incidents
treated, 34
untreated, 33
Threat index, 35
Threats, and information security risk
  management, 111
Tiger teams, 110
Time value, 28, 29
Timeliness, of metrics, 74
TJX, 67
Total cost of ownership (TCO), 163
Total quality management (TQM), 128
Transmission Control Protocol/Internet
  Protocol (TCP/IP), 163
Transmission Control Protocol (TCP), 163
Transmission Control Protocol/User Datagram
  Protocol (TCP/UDP), 163
Transport layer security (TLS), 163
Trends metrics, 15
Triage, 152
Tripwire, 1

U

Unauthorized Web access, 23
Uncertainty
  degree of acceptable, 102

  due to inadequate metrics, 122
  and layered security, 108
Underestimation of risk, 67
Undermanagement of risk, 126
Uninterruptible power supply (UPS), 163
Universal resource locator (URL), 163
Universal serial bus (USB), 163
User attributes, 48
  SABSA metrics, 181–183
User Datagram Protocol (UDP), 163

V

Value at risk (VAR), 37, 38, 55, 56–57, 107
Value delivery, 5, 85, 134–135
Value methods, 15
Virtual private network (VPN), 163
Viruses detected, 23
Voice-over-IP (VoIP), 163
Vulnerabilities
  and information security risk management,
    110–111
  metrics for, 103
Vulnerability scans, 25, 107
  lack of correlation to probability of
    attack, 65
  limited usefulness, 78
  nonusefulness of, 75

W

Ways of life, 39, 40
Weakness assessment metrics, 169
Wide area network (WAN), 163
WIND, 42–43
Workplace safety, losses related to, 112

Z

Zero defects, 8